SPOUSAL PROPERTY RIGHTS UNDER THE ONTARIO FAMILY LAW ACT

SPOUSAL PROPERTY RIGHTS UNDER THE ONTARIO FAMILY LAW ACT

Professor Julien D. Payne, Q.C., LL.D.
of the Ontario Bar and Faculty of Law,
University of Ottawa, Canada

Butterworths
TORONTO AND VANCOUVER

Printed and bound in Canada

The Butterworth Group of Companies

Canada:
Butterworths, Toronto and Vancouver
United Kingdom:
Butterworth & Co. (Publishers) Ltd., London and Edinburgh
Australia:
Butterworths Pty Ltd., Sydney, Melbourne, Brisbane, Adelaide and Perth
New Zealand:
Butterworths (New Zealand) Ltd., Wellington and Auckland
Singapore:
Butterworth & Co. (Asia) Pte. Ltd., Singapore
South Africa:
Butterworth Publishers (SA) (Pty) Ltd., Durban and Pretoria
United States:
Butterworth Legal Publishers, Boston, Seattle, Austin and St. Paul
D & S Publishers, Clearwater

Canadian Cataloguing in Publication Data

Payne, Julien D., 1934-
   Spousal property rights under the Ontario Family Law Act

Companion volume to: Payne, Julien D., 1934-
Payne's divorce and family law digest.
Bibliography: p.
ISBN 0-409-80936-5

1. Marital property — Ontario. 2. Equitable
distribution of marital property — Ontario.
3. Domestic relations — Law and legislation —
Ontario. 4. Ontario. Family Law Act, 1986.
I. Title.

KE0222.P39 1987   346.71304   C87-094713-3

Sponsoring Editors: Derek Lundy/Lebby Hines
Executive Editor (P. & A.): Lebby Hines
Managing Editor: Linda Kee
Supervisory Editor: Marie Graham
Editor/Cover Design: Catherine Haskell
Production: Jill Thomson
Typesetting and Assembly: The Alger Press Limited.

PREFACE

In less than twenty years, Family Law has undergone revolutionary changes witnessed by no other field of law. The pristine glory of Family Law of the nineteen-fifties and nineteen-sixties is but a fading memory. Before the enactment of the *Divorce Act*, S.C. 1967-1968, c. 24, the principles of Family Law were simple and clearly defined. To all intents and purposes, adultery was the sole ground for divorce. Spousal support was regulated by provincial statutes and was only available to wives whose husbands had committed a designated matrimonial offence, such as adultery, cruelty or desertion. The guilty husband was legally obligated to support his dependent wife for her lifetime. Spousal property rights were firmly embedded in established principles of property law, which determined title to property by reference to the intention of the spouses. The essential criteria for determining spousal intention rested upon the title deed, if any, and upon who purchased the property. In the ordinary course of events, he who paid, owned.

[handwritten margin note: Murdoch maj said no evidence of intention. Laskin said constructive trust on unjust enrichment principle]

The valuable contributions of a homemaking wife to the economic and social well-being of the family were ignored for the purposes of any property entitlement, except where a direct financial contribution had been made by that spouse to the acquisition of property in her husband's name.

The "divorce lawyer" of the nineteen-fifties and early sixties bore little or no resemblance to the "family law practitioner" of the nineteen-eighties. In 1960, divorce lawyers were scorned by their legal brethren, many of whom were proud to assert that "they didn't take divorce cases". Today, the responsible family law practitioner is no longer perceived as running a divorce mill where the sole grounds for relief are adultery or perjury. Family Law practice has come of age. The price paid for this maturation is the inherent complexity of present-day Family Law.

Fundamental changes in the grounds for divorce were introduced by the *Divorce Act*, S.C. 1967-68, c. 24, and were re-constituted in the *Divorce Act, 1985*, S.C. 1986, c. 4. These changes, which reflected a movement away from exclusive reliance on the "matrimonial offence" concept, have created few practical problems for the family law practitioner or the courts. The legal complexities of marriage breakdown or divorce have little to do with the grounds for or the bars to divorce. Complexity and confusion arises, however, with respect to the consequences of marriage breakdown or divorce. Spousal support rights and obligations now engender novel arguments respecting the objectives of such orders. Joint custody is emerging as a possible alternative to the traditional order that granted sole custody to one parent and reasonable access rights to the other. But in no sphere of Family Law is the law so complex as in the context of property entitlement on marriage breakdown or divorce.

v

Part I of the *Family Law Act, 1986*, S.O. 1986, c. 4, has established unique criteria for the determination of spousal property entitlements on marriage breakdown or death. The fundamental concept underlying Part I of the *Family Law Act, 1986* is one of marriage as an equal economic partnership. Although this concept is readily comprehensible, the statutory provisions implementing it are complex and will undoubtedly generate litigation. The innovative character of Part I of the *Family Law Act, 1986* offers little comfort to the lawyer who seeks to negotiate a fair and reasonable property settlement. A few insights may be gained by examining the jurisprudence that interpreted and applied Part I of the *Family Law Reform Act*, R.S.O. 1980, c. 152. But Part I of the *Family Law Act, 1986* is radically different from its predecessor. Consequently, reliance upon previous judicial authority is fraught with risk. Reference to other provincial property sharing regimes may also be of assistance in interpreting and applying the provisions of Part I of the Act. Dangers also abound here, however, by reason of differences of approach in the provincial statutory sharing regimes.

Many pitfalls thus face the author who seeks to analyse Part I of the *Family Law Act, 1986*. As stated in the preface to *Payne's Commentaries on the Divorce Act, 1985* (Richard De Boo, 1986): "There is no substitute for the benefit of hindsight. Furthermore, omniscience has never been defined as a prerogative of authors, lawyers, or judges. Whether the opinions of the author are shared by his readership is not of fundamental importance, if his opinions serve as a launching pad for analysis and reflection."

Fewer pitfalls arise with respect to an analysis of Parts II (MATRIMONIAL HOME) and Part IV (DOMESTIC CONTRACTS) of the *Family Law Act, 1986* because these are substantially based on Part III (MATRIMONIAL HOME) and Part IV (DOMESTIC CONTRACTS) of the *Family Law Reform Act*, R.S.O. 1980, c. 152. Accordingly, much greater reliance can be placed on the jurisprudence that has previously emerged. It should not be assumed, however, that there have been no important legislative changes respecting the matrimonial home and domestic contracts. Several significant changes have been introduced by the *Family Law Act, 1986*. Accordingly, judicial decisions interpreting and applying the *Family Law Reform Act*, R.S.O. 1980, c. 152, must be carefully scrutinized to ascertain whether the language of the sections in question has been altered or supplemented by the current statutory provisions.

Subject to the aforementioned caveats, this text may provide some useful insight into the prospective operation of Parts I, II and IV of the *Family Law Act, 1986*.

This book constitutes a companion volume to the looseleaf service, *Payne's Divorce and Family Law Digest* (Toronto: De Boo, 1986-) (formerly entitled *Payne's Digest on Divorce in Canada*). While the *Digest* examines judicial decisions in detail, this text is intended to provide an overall commentary on property rights arising pursuant to the *Family Law Act, 1986*.

An overview of the contents of this text is available to the reader who examines the Table of Contents and the relevant sections of the *Family Law Act, 1986* as amended, which are reproduced herein. The basic approach of the author has been to cite and examine the relevant statutory provisions in their numerical sequence under designated subheadings.

Some guidance is provided to the legal practitioner with respect to the drafting of interim and permanent separation agreements. In this context, Mr. Glen Kealey, a Family Law practitioner in the City of Ottawa, was responsible for the preparation of materials.

Hopefully, the combination of commentary and draft agreements will prove of value to the busy legal practitioner. However, they must be perceived as untested and do not purport to release any legal advisor from assuming a personal responsibility for protecting the interests of his or her client.

> Professor Julien D. Payne, Q.C., LL.D.,
> of the Ontario Bar and Faculty of Law,
> University of Ottawa.

August 10, 1987

ACKNOWLEDGEMENTS

The author wishes to acknowledge the significant contribution of Mr. Glen Kealey, a family law practitioner in the City of Ottawa, who assumed the responsibility for drafting the separation agreements that appear in this text.

Special thanks are also due to Mona Carkner and Mary Headley for their typing of various drafts and the final manuscript under extreme pressures of time.

The author extends his sincerest appreciation for the time-consuming efforts of his wife, Marilyn, who assumed exclusive responsibility for proofreading the diverse manuscripts and typescripts that ultimately resulted in the present text and who also prepared the Table of Contents and the Table of Cases. The author consequently denies any responsibility for any errors of form or substance in light of this delegation of authority to his wife. The aforementioned denial of responsibility by the author constitutes an unsolicited retaliation to his wife's persistent refusal to execute a domestic contract and last will and testament whereby all of his/her/their property shall be his and his alone now and unto eternity.

Julien D. Payne, Q.C., LL.D.

NOTICE

This publication is designed to provide information and opinions with respect to the subject matter covered. It is sold on the understanding that the author, the publisher and the copyright holder are not engaged in rendering legal or other professional advice and cannot be held in any way legally responsible for reliance placed thereupon by any person, including any member of the legal profession.

TABLE OF CONTENTS

FAMILY LAW ACT
PART IV — DOMESTIC CONTRACTS

PRECEDENTS

APPENDICES

TABLE OF CASES

PART I

FAMILY PROPERTY

1.0 INTRODUCTION

In 1978, the Province of Ontario enacted the *Family Law Reform Act*, S.O. 1978, c. 2, to ameliorate the hardship and injustice arising under the doctrine of separation of property, whereby each spouse retained his or her own property on the breakdown or dissolution of marriage. This doctrine produced totally unfair results in the so-called traditional nuclear family where the husband was a breadwinner and the wife was a homemaker: see *Murdoch v. Murdoch*, [1975] 1 S.C.R. 423, [1974] 1 W.W.R. 361, 41 D.L.R. (3d) 367, 13 R.F.L. 185.

Section 4 of the *Family Law Reform Act*, S.O. 1978, c. 2, subsequently R.S.O. 1980, c. 152, addressed some of the problems arising from *Murdoch v. Murdoch, supra,* by empowering the court to order a division of "family assets" and, in exceptional circumstances, a division of non-family assets on marriage breakdown, regardless of which spouse was the owner of the assets: see *Leatherdale v. Leatherdale*, [1982] 2 S.C.R. 743, 142 D.L.R. (3d) 193, 45 N.R. 40, 30 R.F.L. (2d) 255. Generally speaking, however, a non-owning spouse would be granted an equal share of the family assets, which included the matrimonial home and other assets ordinarily used or enjoyed by the family, but no interest in business assets would be granted to the non-owning spouse.

Part I of the *Family Law Act, 1986* eliminates the former distinction between "family assets" and "non-family assets" and essentially provides for an equalization of the *value* of assets accumulated by either spouse during the marriage in the event of a subsequent marriage breakdown: see *Re Henry and Cymbalisty* (1986), 55 O.R. (2d) 51, at 55 (Unified Fam. Ct.).

2.0 OBJECTIVES OF FAMILY LAW ACT

The objectives sought under the *Family Law Act, 1986* are defined in vague terms by the preamble, which reads as follows:

Preamble

Whereas it is desirable to encourage and strengthen the role of the family; and whereas for that purpose it is necessary to recognize the equal position of spouses as individuals within marriage and to recognize marriage as a form of partnership; and whereas in support of such recognition it is necessary to provide in law for the orderly and equitable settlement of the affairs of the spouses upon the breakdown of the partnership, and to provide for other mutual obligations in family relationships, including the equitable sharing by parents of responsibility for their children;

Therefore, Her Majesty, by and with the advice and consent of the Legislative Assembly of the Province of Ontario, enacts as follows:

In general terms, the fundamental objective of Part I of the Act, entitled "FAMILY PROPERTY", is to ensure that on marriage breakdown or death each spouse shall receive a fair share, which will usually be an equal share, of the value of assets accumulated during the course of matrimonial cohabitation. Thus, subsection 5(7) of the *Family Law Act, 1986* provides as follows:

Purpose

5.—(7) The purpose of this section is to recognize that child care, household management and financial provision are the joint responsibilities of the spouses and that inherent in the marital relationship there is equal contribution, whether financial or otherwise, by the spouses to the assumption of these responsibilities, entitling each spouse to the equalization of the net family properties, subject only to the equitable considerations set out in subsection (6).

3.0 DEFINITION OF "SPOUSE"

Definitions

1.—(1) In this Act,

"spouse"

"spouse" means either of a man and woman who,
  (a) are married to each other, or
  (b) have together entered into a marriage that is voidable or void, in good faith on the part of the person asserting a right under this Act.

Polygamous marriages

(2) In the definition of "spouse", a reference to marriage includes a marriage that is actually or potentially polygamous, if it was celebrated in a jurisdiction whose system of law recognizes it as valid.

For the purpose of Part I of the *Family Law Act, 1986,* subsection 1(1) specifically defines "spouse" as meaning a man and woman who are married to each other or who have entered into a void or voidable marriage, provided that in either of the latter circumstances, the person asserting a right under the Act acted in good faith. "Homosexual marriages" and "common law relationships" thus fall outside the ambit of Part I of the *Family Law Act, 1986.* Any claim to property entitlement arising from a homosexual or lesbian relationship or a "common law relationship" can only be pursued, therefore, on the basis of the common law or principles of equity. Thus, in *Anderson v. Luoma* (1986), 50 R.F.L. (2d) 127 (B.C.S.C.), a woman living in a lesbian relationship was denied any right to property division under the *Family Relations Act,* S.B.C. 1979, c. 121, but was held entitled to a 20 per cent interest in certain property pursuant to the application of the doctrine of constructive trust. In reaching this conclusion, the court followed *Pettkus v. Becker,* [1980] 2 S.C.R. 834, 117 D.L.R. (3d) 257, 34 N.R. 384, 8 E.T.R. 143, 19 R.F.L. (2d) 165, wherein the doctrine of constructive trust, based on the principle of unjust enrichment, was applied to confer an equal beneficial interest in property on the "common law wife" who had actively assisted her cohabitant in a bee-keeping and honey-making business. In *Anderson v. Luoma, supra,* an alternative claim based on contractual rights was dismissed on the ground that no contract was established by the evidence. Whether any such contract would be void at common law as contrary to public policy is uncertain in light of changing public and judicial perceptions and, more specifically, section 15 of the *Canadian Charter of Rights and Freedoms.* In *Chrispen v. Topham* (1986), 48 Sask. R. 106, 28 D.L.R. (4th) 754, 3 R.F.L. (3d) 149 (Q.B.), a cohabitation agreement was held to be valid and enforceable in Saskatchewan, being no longer perceived as illegal or contrary to public policy. No uncertainty arises in Ontario with respect to the validity of domestic contracts negotiated between "common law spouses" of the opposite sex. Pursuant to the express provisions of section 53 of the *Family Law Act, 1986,* a man and woman who are cohabiting or intend to do so, may enter into a cohabitation agreement to regulate their rights and obligations during cohabitation, or on the cessation of cohabitation or on the death of either party, with respect to (a) the ownership or division of property and (b) support. In the absence of any contractual claim or interest acquired by way of resulting or constructive trust, however,

3

"common law spouses" receive no protection such as that accorded to "spouses" under Part I of the *Family Law Act, 1986*: see *Pettkus v. Becker, supra; Sorochan v. Sorochan*, [1985] 5 W.W.R. 289, 29 D.L.R. (4th) 1, 2 R.F.L. (3d) 225 (S.C.C.). This contrasts with the provisions of Part III of the Act which establish (support) rights and obligations between unmarried cohabitants, provided that the conditions set out in the extended definition of "spouse" under section 29 of the Act are satisfied. In order to satisfy the conditions under s. 29, an applicant for support must establish that the parties have cohabited continuously for not less than three years or that they have cohabited "in a relationship of some permanence" and are the natural or adoptive parents of a child. Section 29 of the Act does not require that the requisite period or degree of cohabitation immediately precede the application for support under the Act. Pursuant to subsection 50(1) and subject to subsection 2(8), however, the (support) application must be brought not later than two years from the date of separation. In the context of a support application, clauses s. 34(1)(c) and (d) of the *Family Law Act, 1986* empower the court to make an interim or final order for the transfer of property to or the vesting of property in a dependant, whether absolutely, for life, or for a term of years, or for interim or permanent possession of the matrimonial home. The rights of the owner may thus be qualified by a court in the exercise of its support jurisdiction. Although exclusive possession of the matrimonial home has on isolated occasions been granted to a "common law spouse" under the *Family Law Reform Act*, R.S.O. 1980, c. 152, no order for a transfer of property to or for the vesting of property in a dependent "common law spouse" has yet been made.

4.0 JURISDICTION

4.1 Definition of "court"

Definitions

1.—(1) In this Act,

"court"

"court" means the Provincial Court (Family Division), the Unified Family Court, the District Court or the Supreme Court;

. . .

Definitions

4.—(1) In this Part,

"court"

"court" means a court as defined in subsection 1(1), but does not include the Provincial Court (Family Division);

Although the provinces may enact legislation relating to "Property and Civil Rights in the Province" pursuant to the authority conferred by subsection 92(13) of the *Constitution Act, 1867*, section 96 precludes the provincial legislatures from conferring such jurisdiction on any court other than the "Superior, District and County Courts": *Reference re Section 6 of the Family Relations Act*, S.B.C. 1978, c. 20, [1982] 1 S.C.R. 62, 36 B.C.L.R. 1, [1982] 3 W.W.R. 1, 131 D.L.R. (3d) 257, 40 N.R. 206, 26 R.F.L. (2d) 113. Accordingly, subsection 4(1) of the *Family Law Act, 1986*, when read in conjunction with subsection 1(1), defines court to mean the Unified Family Court (in the judicial district of Hamilton-Wentworth), the District Court or the Supreme Court, and expressly excludes the Provincial Court (Family Division) from assuming any authority over the division of property values on marriage breakdown or death.

4.2 Indian lands

The *Family Law Act, 1986* confers no jurisdiction on a court to interfere with interests in land on an Indian reserve, but the court is not precluded from making a monetary judgment for the purpose of effectuating a division of the net family properties: *Sandy v. Sandy* (1979), 27 O.R. (2d) 248, 107 D.L.R. (3d) 659, 13 R.F.L. (2d) 81 (C.A.); see also *Derrickson v. Derrickson et al.*, [1986] 3 W.W.R. 193, 50 R.F.L. (2d) 337 (S.C.C.) and *Paul v. Paul et al.*, [1986] 3 W.W.R. 210, 50 R.F.L. (2d) 355 (S.C.C.).

4.3 Conflict of Laws

Conflict of laws

15. The property rights of spouses arising out of the marital relationship are governed by the internal law of the place where both spouses had their last common habitual residence or, if there is no place where the spouses had a common habitual residence, by the law of Ontario.

4.4 Domestic contracts

Act subject to contracts

2.—(10) A domestic contract dealing with a matter that is also dealt with in this Act prevails unless this Act provides otherwise.

Subsection 2(10) of the *Family Law Act, 1986* substantially re-enacts the provisions of subsection 2(9) of the *Family Law Reform Act*, R.S.O. 1980, c. 152: see *infra*, 7.0 EQUALIZATION OF NET FAMILY PROPERTIES, subheading 7.13.6 "Property excluded by domestic contract" and *infra*, PART IV — DOMESTIC CONTRACTS.

5.0 APPLICATIONS RESPECTING OWNERSHIP AND POSSESSION OF PROPERTY

5.1 Ownership of property

Determination of questions of title between spouses

[handwritten: not invoked by TH.]

[handwritten: "procedural" in character]

10.—(1) A person may apply to the court for the determination of a question between that person and his or her spouse or former spouse as to the ownership or right to possession of particular property, other than a question arising out of an equalization of net family properties under section 5, and the court may,

[handwritten: s.10 claim may be brought at any time]

[handwritten: s.5 only allowed if "trigg event"]

   (a) declare the ownership or right to possession;
   (b) if the property has been disposed of, order payment in compensation for the interest of either party;
   (c) order that the property be partitioned or sold for the purpose of realizing the interests in it; and
   (d) order that either or both spouses give security, including a charge on property, for the performance of an obligation imposed by the order,

and may make ancillary orders or give ancillary directions.

[handwritten: s.10 "determines" ownership of property between spouses other than question relating to equalization under s.5.]

Section 10 of the *Family Law Act, 1986* empowers a spouse or former spouse to apply to the court for the determination of any question relating to the possession or ownership of property that is independent of a question arising out of an equalization of net family properties under section 5 of the Act. Like section 7, but unlike section 8, of the *Family Law Reform Act*, R.S.O. 1980, c. 152, section 10 is procedural in character: *McLaren v. McLaren* (1979), 24 O.R. (2d) 481, 8 R.F.L. (2d) 201 (C.A.). It offers no direct guidelines to the court concerning the principles to be applied in determining questions of title and possession. The parties to such an application are presumably entitled to invoke established principles of the common law and equity, including the doctrines of resulting and constructive trust. The right to assert the existence of a resulting or constructive trust in the context of an application under section 10 of the *Family Law Act, 1986* is not precluded by an equalization entitlement under section 5 of the Act and may, indeed, be a prerequisite to calculating the net family property of each spouse for the purposes of any equalization claim. A wife may accordingly assert a beneficial interest in property held in the husband's name where the value of that property has significantly increased between the date of the spousal separation and the date of trial: *Rawluk v. Rawluk* (1986), 55 O.R. (2d) 704, 29 D.L.R. (4th) 754, 3 R.F.L. (3d) 113 (S.C.); *Seed v. Seed* (1986), 5 R.F.L. (3d) 120 (Ont. S.C.); see also *Rose v. Rose and Megow*, unreported, February 6, 1987 (Ont. S.C.) and *Crawford v. Crawford* (1987), 6 R.F.L. (3d) 308 (Ont. S.C.); see *contra*, *Benke v. Benke* (1986), 4 R.F.L. (3d) 58 (Ont. Dist. Ct.).

[margin handwritten note: J. McLeod says a "reverse" "const-trust" can be imposed if value drops share loss as well as gain. Proff doesn't like it.]

In view of the fact that the limitation periods referred to in subsection 7(2) of the Act are expressly restricted to applications for property value entitlement under section 5, an application under section 10 of the Act presumably falls subject to the general provisions of the *Limitations Act*, R.S.O. 1980, c. 240. This difference in treatment could present problems where an application under section 10 of the Act is brought after the limitation period under subsection 7(2) has expired and the respondent seeks to bring a counter-application for equalization of the net family properties in accordance with section 5 of the Act. In this circumstance, the court might well invoke subsection 2(8) of the Act in order to permit the adjudication of the respective claims notwithstanding the expiry of the limitation period arising under subsection 7(2) of the Act.

The *Family Law Act, 1986* is silent on the question whether the disposition of an application under section 10 precludes any subsequent assertion of rights under section 5 of the Act. Under the *Family Law Reform Act*, R.S.O. 1980, c. 152, the jurisdiction of the court to order property division was not precluded by a previous order determining ownership. Indeed, section 4 of the *Family Law Reform Act* expressly applied "notwithstanding any order made under section 7". In the absence of any similar provision in Part I of the *Family Law Act, 1986*, the issue of any possible estoppel will no doubt be resolved in due course by judicial pronouncements. In principle, however, a judicial determination of a question of title under section 10 of the *Family Law Act, 1986* is not inconsistent with a subsequent equalization order made under the authority of section 5 of the Act.

[margin handwritten note: Use s. 10 for questions of title.]

Subsection 10(1) of the *Family Law Act, 1986* which substantially re-enacts section 7 of the *Family Law Reform Act*, cannot be invoked by third parties: *Chalmers v. Copfer* (1978), 7 R.F.L. (2d) 393 (Ont. Co. Ct.). Where an application is brought by a spouse or former spouse, however, a third party may be added in accordance with the Ontario Rules of Civil Procedure: see *Bray v. Bray* (1979), 9 C.P.C. 241 (Ont. S.C.). Third party creditors may assert their rights at common law, in equity or under statute, including the federal *Bankruptcy Act*, R.S.C. 1970, c. B-3, and provincial statutes relating to fraudulent conveyances and preferences. Execution creditors may accordingly attach the interest of a debtor spouse in a matrimonial home held under joint tenancy: see *Maroukis v. Maroukis*, [1984] 2 S.C.R. 137, 12 D.L.R. (4th) 321, 54 N.R. 268, 41 R.F.L. (2d) 113.

The assertion of ownership rights under subsection 10(1) of the *Family Law Act, 1986* is not conditioned on marriage breakdown. Such an application may be pursued even though the spouses are still cohabiting in a viable marriage.

An application under subsection 10(1) may also be made or continued against the estate of a deceased spouse: *Family Law Act, 1986,* subsection 10(2); compare subsection 5(2) of the Act, whereby an application for an equalization of net family properties can only be brought by a surviving spouse whose net family property is less than that of the deceased spouse.

5.2 Presumptions

Section 14 of the *Family Law Act, 1986* re-enacts the provisions of subsection 11(1) of the *Family Law Reform Act,* R.S.O. 1980, c. 152, which in turn re-enacted clause 1(3)(d) of the *Family Law Reform Act,* S.O. 1975, c. 41.

At common law, when a husband purchased property in the name of his wife or transferred property to her, he was presumed to have made a gift of the property to her. Where, however, the wife purchased property in her husband's name or transferred property to him, he would be presumed to hold the property in trust for his wife as the beneficial owner. The abolition of the presumption of advancement as between spouses effectuated by clause 1(3)(d) of the *Family Law Reform Act,* S.O. 1975, c. 41, and continued under section 14 of the *Family Law Act, 1986,* establishes equality between the sexes in that where either spouse purchases property in the name of the other or transfers property to the other spouse, the purchase or transfer gives rise to a presumption of resulting trust, whereby the transferee holds the property in trust for the benefit of the transferor. The presumption of advancement arising with respect to the parent who purchases property in the name of a child or who transfers property to a child remains unaffected by the statutory abrogation of the presumption of advancement as between spouses.

Section 14 of the *Family Law Act, 1986* is confined in its application to questions of ownership. It has no direct application to claims for an equalization of net family properties under section 5 of the Act.

The presumption arising under section 14 is a *prima facie* presumption and not a conclusive presumption. It may be rebutted by cogent evidence that a gift was intended: see *Meszaros v. Meszaros* (1978), 22 O.R. (2d) 695 (S.C.).

Pursuant to subsection 16(2) of the *Family Law Act, 1986*, it is immaterial whether the circumstances giving rise to the presumption occurred before or after the coming into force of the Act: compare, however, *McLaren v. McLaren* (1979), 24 O.R. (2d) 481, 8 R.F.L. (2d) 301 (C.A.).

The presumption of resulting trust has no application where property is held in the name of the spouses as joint tenants, and money on deposit in the name of both spouses is deemed to be held under joint tenancy. In either of these two circumstances, the beneficial interests of the spouses are governed by established principles of property law: compare *Ling v. Ling* (1980), 29 O.R. (2d) 717, 17 R.F.L. (2d) 62, at 66-67 (C.A.).

See *infra*, 7.0 EQUALIZATION OF NET FAMILY PROPERTIES, subheading 7.2 "Significance of ownership to equalization scheme".

6.0 TRIGGERING EVENTS FOR EQUALIZATION OF NET FAMILY PROPERTIES

6.1 General observations

Equalization of net family properties

5.—(1) When a divorce is granted or a marriage is declared a nullity, or when the spouses are separated and there is no reasonable prospect that they will resume cohabitation, the spouse whose net family property is the lesser of the two net family properties is entitled to one-half the difference between them.

Idem

(2) When a spouse dies, if the net family property of the deceased spouse exceeds the net family property of the surviving spouse, the surviving spouse is entitled to one-half the difference between them.

Improvident depletion of spouse's net family property

(3) When spouses are cohabiting, if there is a serious danger that one spouse may improvidently deplete his or her net family property, the other spouse may on an application under section 7 have the difference between the net family properties divided as if the spouses were separated and there were no reasonable prospect that they would resume cohabitation.

. . .

Core idea is that "net family property" should be divided equally between spouses on breakdown of marriage

The *Family Law Act, 1986* essentially preserves the doctrine of separation of property during matrimonial cohabitation. Subject to the provisions of section 21 of the Act, which ordinarily require spousal consent before the matrimonial home is disposed of or encumbered, each spouse has the freedom to acquire or dispose of property during matrimonial cohabitation: see *Menage v. Hedges,* unreported, June 8, 1987 (Ont. Unified Fam. Ct.).

The doctrine of separation of property may cease to apply, however, in the event of marriage breakdown or death. Pursuant to subsections 5(1), (2) and (3) of the *Family Law Act, 1986,* a system of deferred property sharing is activated by the occurrence of any of the following "triggering events:"

s. 4(1)

s. 5(1) (2) (3)

"triggering" events

- (i) when a divorce is granted;
- (ii) when a marriage is declared a nullity;
- (iii) when the spouses are separated without any reasonable prospect of resuming cohabitation;
- (iv) when a spouse dies, if the net family property of the deceased spouse exceeds that of the surviving spouse;
- (v) when, during cohabitation, there is a serious danger that one spouse may improvidently deplete his or her net family property.

s. 7 is "procedural" section for s. 5

In this last situation, the language of subsection 5(3) of the *Family Law Act, 1986* makes it abundantly clear that a spouse's right to the equalization of the net family properties is conditioned on an application being brought under section 7 of the Act. When death constitutes the triggering event under subsection 5(2) of the Act, the surviving spouse is put to an election to take under the will or intestacy "or to receive the entitlement under section 5": see *infra,* 9.0 ENTITLEMENT ON DEATH, subheading 9.3 "Election by surviving spouse". It is uncertain, however, whether the equalization of net family properties is automatically effectuated by the occurrence of any of the triggering events defined in subsection 5(1) of the Act, in the absence of a claim based on subsection 5(6) of the Act, which empowers the court to make an order that deviates from the equalization formula where its application would be unconscionable having regard to one or more of the specific factors enumerated in clauses (a) to (h): compare *Maroukis v. Maroukis,* [1984] 2 S.C.R. 137, 12 D.L.R. (4th) 321, 54 N.R. 268, 41 R.F.L. (2d) 113 and *G.E. Cox Ltd. v. Canadian Imperial Bank of Commerce* (1986), 23 D.L.R. (4th) 613 (N.B.C.A.). The difference in language between the relevant statutory provisions applied in the aforementioned decisions and that of subsection 5(1) of the *Family Law Act, 1986* may warrant the conclusion that the equalization of net family properties applies immediately upon the occurrence of one of the designated triggering events, but is subject to re-apportionment at the instance of a spouse upon application to the court under subsection 7(1) where the circumstances fall within the ambit of subsection 5(6) of the *Family Law Act, 1986*. The interpretation to be accorded to subsection 5(1) may be of critical importance with respect to the competing rights of spouses and third party creditors. Assume, for example, that spouses separate on June 24, 1987, at a time when the husband is $20,000 in debt and his wife has assets of $40,000. Are the husband's creditor's entitled to recover $20,000 from the husband as his immediate share of the net family properties, bearing in mind that in applying the statutory equalization formula, the husband's net position is fixed at zero as of the valuation date? Or could the husband elect to go through bankruptcy proceedings after waiving his right to claim an equalization payment, perhaps in consideration for the wife's release of any claim for future support? The answer to these questions would appear to depend upon the interpretation to be accorded to subsection 5(1). In the above scenario, would the husband's conduct contravene bankruptcy or fraudulent preference statutes? The decision of the Alberta Court of Appeal in *Sembaliuk et al. v. Sembaliuk and two other actions*, 58 A.R. 189, 35 Alta. L.R. (2d) 193, [1985] 2 W.W.R. 385, 15 D.L.R. (4th) 303, 43 R.F.L. (2d) 425, might suggest a negative response to this question.

If the right to an equalization of net family properties crystallizes only with a judgment of the court (see *Maroukis v. Maroukis, supra*), an application for such relief will frequently be joined under the Ontario Rules of Civil Procedure with a petition for divorce or nullity. This had been the customary practice under the *Family Law Reform Act*, R.S.O. 1980, c. 152. Under that Act, however, the right to commence proceedings for a property division was barred once a decree absolute had been granted: *Re Gibbins and Gibbins* (1978), 22 O.R. (2d) 116, 92 D.L.R. (3d) 285, 8 R.F.L. (2d) 394 (Div. Ct.); *Re De Freitas and De Freitas* (1979), 25 O.R. (2d) 174, at 175-76, 10 R.F.L. (2d) 238 (C.A.); *McLaren v. McLaren* (1979), 24 O.R. (2d) 481, at 484, 8 R.F.L. (2d) 301 (C.A.). In contrast to the position under the *Family Law Reform Act, supra,* subsection 7(3) of the *Family Law Act, 1986,* permits an application for the sharing of property values to be commenced after a divorce or judgment of nullity, provided that the limitation period therein set out is not contravened.

6.2 Limitation periods

Subsection 7(3) of the *Family Law Act, 1986,* S.O. 1986, c. 4, provides as follows:

Limitation

7.—(3) An application based on subsections 5(1) or (2) shall not be brought after the earliest of,
   (a) two years after the day the marriage is terminated by divorce or judgment of nullity;
   (b) six years after the day the spouses separate and there is no reasonable prospect that they will resume cohabitation;
   (c) six months after the first spouse's death.

Pursuant to section 12 of the *Divorce Act, 1985*, S.C. 1986, c. 4, there are no longer dual decrees by way of a decree *nisi* and a decree absolute in divorce proceedings and the divorce judgment takes effect on the thirty-first day after the day on which the judgment was "rendered" or at such later date as all rights of appeal have been exhausted.

It appears that the court may extend a limitation period arising under section 7(3) of the *Family Law Act, 1986, supra,* pursuant to the provisions of subsection 2(8) of the Act. Subsection 2(8) provides that "[the] court may, on motion, extend a time prescribed by this Act if it is satisfied that,

   (a) there are *prima facie* grounds for relief;
   (b) relief is unavailable because of delay that has been incurred in good faith; and
   (c) no person will suffer substantial prejudice by reason of delay."

An applicant who seeks an extension of time under subsection 2(8) of the *Family Law Act, 1986* assumes the burden of establishing on a balance of probabilities that the requirements of this subsection have been complied with but the applicant is not otherwise required to prove "special circumstances" that justify such an extension: *Vivier v. Vivier* (1987), 5 R.F.L. (3d) 450 (Ont. Dist. Ct.). An allegation, whether or not substantiated, that some alternative form of relief may be available against the applicant's solicitor in negligence creates no bar to a judicial extension of the limited period. In determining whether there are *prima facie* grounds for relief within the meaning of clause 2(8)(a) of the *Family Law Act, 1986* the court will have regard to the attendant circumstances, including the retrospective effect of Part I of the Act. Where the delay following a decree absolute of divorce was incurred in good faith, the question left for decision is whether or not the applicant has established on a balance of probabilities that the respondent will not suffer substantial prejudice *by reason of the delay*. Obviously, an extension of the limitation period could ultimately involve some inherent prejudice to the respondent. The critical issue to be resolved is whether substantial prejudice results as a consequence of the delay and not by reason of any ultimate judicial disposition of the merits of the application for an equalization of the spousal net family properties: *Vivier v. Vivier, supra,* at 456-47 (Ont. Dist. Ct.); compare *Rae v. Rae*, unreported, April 13, 1987 (Ont. S.C.) (Peppiatt, Master).

6.3 Separation as a triggering event *s. 5 (1)*

Where spousal separation is relied upon as the triggering event under subsection 5(1) of the *Family Law Act, 1986,* the court must be satisfied that "there is no reasonable prospect that they will resume cohabitation". As in the context of divorce, it is submitted that spouses may be "separated" within the meaning of subsection 5(1), notwithstanding that they remain under the same roof, provided that they are living independent lives while sharing common accommodation: compare *Cooper v. Cooper* (1972), 10 R.F.L. (2d) 184 (Ont. S.C.); *Dupere v. Dupere* (1975), 9 N.B.R. (2d) 554, 1 A.P.R. 554, 19 R.F.L. 270 (S.C.); affd (1975), 10 N.B.R. (2d) 148, 4 A.P.R. 148 (C.A.). It is further submitted that the court must find that "there is no reasonable prospect that [the spouses] will resume cohabitation", where either spouse is adamantly opposed to any reconciliation: see *Challoner v. Challoner* (1973), 5 N.S.R. (2d) 432, at 434, 12 R.F.L. 311 (C.A.), citing *Payne's Digest on Divorce in Canada;* compare *Sheriff v. Sheriff* (1982), 31 R.F.L. (2d) 434, at 436 (Ont. C.A.).

6.4 Death as a triggering event

The death of a spouse constitutes a triggering event for the *prima facie* equalization of net family properties but only where the net family property of the deceased spouse exceeds the net family property of the surviving spouse: *Family Law Act, 1986*, S.O. 1986, c. 4, subsections 5(2) and (6).

The death of a spouse did not constitute a triggering event for the purpose of a court-ordered property division under section 4 of the *Family Law Reform Act*, R.S.O. 1980, c. 152: see *Palachik and Palachik v. Kiss*, [1983] 1 S.C.R. 623, 146 D.L.R. (3d) 385, 33 R.F.L. (2d) 225. Consequently, widows or widowers sometimes found themselves in a substantially inferior position to that enjoyed by separated spouses. This injustice has now been eliminated by subsection 5(2) of the *Family Law Act, 1986* which presumptively entitles a surviving spouse, but not the estate of a deceased spouse, to one-half of the difference between the net family properties of each spouse.

See *infra*, 9.0 ENTITLEMENT ON DEATH.

6.5 Improvident depletion of net family property

Although Part I of the *Family Law Act, 1986* substantially preserves the doctrine of separation of property as between the spouses until such time as the marriage is terminated or irretrievably broken down, one exception is admitted to this approach. Pursuant to subsection 5(3) of the *Family Law Act, 1986*, if there is a serious danger that one spouse may improvidently deplete is or her net family property, the other spouse, though still cohabiting, may apply under section 7 to have the net family properties divided as though the spouses were separated and had no reasonable prospect of resuming cohabitation. If an order for division is made by reason of the triggering event of apprehended improvident depletion, neither spouse can thereafter pursue any further application based on some other triggering event. This is so even if the spouses continue to cohabit after the court-ordered division, unless a domestic contract provides otherwise: *Family Law Act, 1986*, subsections 5(4) and (5). An unsuccessful application in the context of subsection 5(3) of the Act would not, however, preclude subsequent reliance on the alternative triggering events defined in subsection 5(1) or (2) of the Act.

A serious danger that a spouse may improvidently deplete his or her net family property could be attributable to factors beyond the control of the spouse responsible for its management. Physical or mental disability may render a spouse incompetent to manage the property and thus give rise to a reasonable apprehension of improvident depletion. Alternatively, an improvident depletion may be apprehended in consequence of prospective intentional or negligent misconduct on the part of the title-holding spouse. In circumstances involving a disability, the threatened spouse may be wiser to apply for a guardianship order respecting the estate of the disabled spouse, because a successful application made pursuant to subsection 5(3) of the *Family Law Act, 1986* bars any subsequent application by reason of the express provisions of subsection 5(4) of the Act.

6.6 Alternative triggering events

Notwithstanding the particular limitation in subsection 5(3) of the Act, it is submitted that any successful application for division by reason of one of the several alternative triggering events under subsection 5(1) or (2) will bar a subsequent application based on some other triggering event, assuming, of course, that the parties do not remarry each other: compare *Blomberg v. Blomberg* (1985), 367 N.W. 2d 643 (Minn. Ct. App.) (pension benefits earned during first marriage excluded from division on dissolution of remarriage). This interpretation appears to be consistent with the definition of "valuation date" in subsection 4(1) of the *Family Law Act, 1986* which refers to "the earliest" of the specified dates set out therein.

7.0 EQUALIZATION OF NET FAMILY PROPERTIES

7.1 General observations

Upon the occurrence of one of the triggering events specified in subsections 5(1), (2) and (3) of the *Family Law Act, 1986*, a spouse whose net family property is the lesser of the two net family properties is entitled to one-half the difference between them, subject to the court's discretionary power to re-apportion the sharing if an equalization of the net family properties would be unconscionable, having regard to the specific factors enumerated in subsection 5(6) of the Act.

The concept of "net family property" is specifically defined in subsection 4(1) of the Act, which provides as follows:

Definitions

4.—(1) In this Part,

. . .

"net family property"
"net family property" means the value of all the property, except property described in subsection (2), that a spouse owns on the valuation date, after deducting,
  (a) **the spouse's debts and other liabilities, and**
  (b) **the value of property, other than a matrimonial home, that the spouse owned on the date of the marriage, after deducting the spouse's debts and other liabilities, calculated as of the date of the marriage.**

The terms "property" and "valuation date" are also specifically defined in subsection 4(1) of the *Family Law Act, 1986*, as amended by subsection 1(1) of the *Family Law Amendment Act*, S.O. 1986, c. 35. The current definitions read as follows:

"property"
"property" means any interest, present or future, vested or contingent, in real or personal property and includes:
  (a) **property over which a spouse has, alone or in conjunction with another person, a power of appointment exercisable in favour of himself of herself,**
  (b) **property disposed of by a spouse but over which the spouse has, alone or in conjunction with another person, a power to revoke the disposition or a power to consume or dispose of the property, and**

15

(c) **in the case of a spouse's rights under a pension plan that have vested, the spouse's interest in the plan including contributions made by other persons.**

"valuation date" means the earliest of the following dates:
1. **The date the spouses separate and there is no reasonable prospect that they will resume cohabitation.**
2. **The date a divorce is granted.**
3. **The date the marriage is declared a nullity.**
4. **The date one of the spouses commences an application based on subsection 5(3) (improvident depletion) that is subsequently granted.**
5. **The date before the date on which one of the spouses dies leaving the other spouse surviving.**

In calculating value as of a given date, the calculation shall be made as of the close of business on that date: *Family Law Act, 1986*, subsection 4(4).

Pursuant to subsection 4(2) of the *Family Law Act, 1986*, as amended by subsection 1(2) of the *Family Law Amendment Act,* S.O. 1986, c. 35, the value of the following property that either spouse owns on the valuation date is excluded from the net family property:

onus on claimant to prove an "exclusion" under s. 4(2)

1. Property, other than a matrimonial home, that was acquired by gift or inheritance from a third person after the date of the marriage.
2. Income from property referred to in paragraph 1, if the donor or testator has expressly stated that it is to be excluded from the spouse's net family property.
3. Damages or a right to damages for personal injuries, nervous shock, mental distress or loss of guidance, care and companionship, or the part of a settlement that represents those damages.
4. Proceeds or a right to proceeds of a life insurance policy as defined in the *Insurance Act* [R.S.O. 1980, c. 218] that are payable on the death of the life insured.
5. Property, other than a matrimonial home, into which property referred to in paragraphs 1 to 4 can be traced.
6. Property that the spouses have agreed by a domestic contract is not to be included in the spouse's net family property.

The onus of proving a "deduction" under the definition of "net family property" in subsection 4(1) of the Act and of proving an "exclusion" under subsection 4(2) of the *Family Law Act, 1986*, as amended by S.O. 1986, c. 35, falls on the person claiming the deduction or exclusion: *Family Law Act, 1986*, subsection 4(3): see *Oliva v. Oliva* (1986), 2 R.F.L.

(3d) 188, at 199 (Ont. S.C.); *Kukolj v. Kukolj* (1986), 3 R.F.L. (3d) 359 (Ont. Unified Fam. Ct.); *Ganz v. Ganz and Ganz*, unreported, June 4, 1986 (Ont. S.C.); *Dewar v. Dewar* (1986), 1 A.C.W.S. (3d) 329 (Ont. Dist. Ct.); *Humphreys v. Humphreys* (1987), 7 R.F.L. (3d) 113 (Ont. S.C.); *Menage v. Hedges*, unreported, June 8, 1987 (Ont. Unified Fam. Ct.). Future spouses should, therefore, prepare an inventory of their assets at the date of their marriage and maintain on-going records respecting these assets and any other assets that fall within the ambit of subsection 4(2) of the *Family Law Act, 1986.*

The *Family Law Act, 1986* provides for the equalization of net family properties but does not necessarily involve the equalization of spousal debts or liabilities, although this may result in certain circumstances. Thus, subsection 4(5) of the Act provides as follows:

Net family property not to be less than zero

4.—(5) If a spouse's net family property as calculated under subsections (1), (2) and (4) is less than zero, it shall be deemed to be equal to zero.

The overall significance of the aforementioned statutory provisions may be summarized in the following steps:

1. Each spouse shall value his or her property, other than property excluded under subsection 4(2) of the Act, as of the date of the triggering event. — 2. subtract debts and liabilities.

2. Each spouse shall calculate his or her debts and liabilities, apparently as of the date of the "triggering event."

3. Each spouse shall calculate the value of property, other than a matrimonial home, owned by that spouse on the date of the marriage and deduct from this value all debts and liabilities existing at the date of the marriage. The express exclusion of a matrimonial home from these calculations presumably refers to pre-marital assets that are subsequently invested in a matrimonial home: compare *Kukolj v. Kukolj* (1986), 3 R.F.L. (3d) 359 (Ont. Unified Fam. Ct.); *Harris v. Harris* (1986), 39 A.C.W.S. (2d) 68 (Ont. Dist. Ct.). But the status of a matrimonial home is not immutable and a residence that was formerly occupied by the spouses but is no longer so occupied prior to the cessation of matrimonial cohabitation may entitle the owner spouse to a deduction of its pre-marital value under subsection 4(1) of the *Family Law Act, 1986: Folga v. Folga* (1986), 2 R.F.L. (3d) 358 (Ont. S.C.).

4. The net family property of each spouse is then determined by subtracting the amounts calculated under paragraphs 2 and 3,

supra, from the amount calculated under paragraph 1, *supra*. A spouse's net family property will be treated as having a zero value if the above calculations result in a deficit.

s.5 ⟶   5. When the net family prpoerty of each spouse has been calculated, the spouse whose net family property is the lesser of the two is *prima facie* entitled to one-half of the difference between them.

    6. 5(6) unequal division "pr'd on appeal
                              10 steps.

In *Oliva v. Oliva* (1986), 2 R.F.L. (3d) 188, at 190-91 (Ont. S.C.), McDermid L.J.S.C. enumerated the following ten steps to be followed for the purpose of determining an equalization claim under Part I of the *Family Law Act*:

1. List and determine the value of all the property owned by each spouse on the valuation date — in this case the date of separation.

2. List and determine the amount of each spouse's debts and other liabilities as of the valuation date.

3. Deduct the total obtained in para. 2 from the total obtained in para. 1 for each spouse.

4. List and determine the value of all the property, other than an interest in a matrimonial home, owned by each spouse on the date of the marriage.

5. List and determine the amount of each spouse's debts and other liabilities calculated as of the date of the marriage.

6. Deduct the total obtained in para. 5 from the total obtained in para. 4 for each spouse.

7. Deduct the total obtained in para. 6 from the total obtained in para. 3 for each spouse.

8. From the total obtained in para. 7 deduct the value of the exclusions, if any, to which each spouse is entitled under s. 4(2) of the Act.

9. Determine the amount which is 50 per cent of the difference between the higher and lower values obtained for each spouse in para. 8.

10. Having regard to the factors contained in s. 5(6), decide whether the amount of the equalization payment is "unconscionable" and, if so, determine the proper amount which should be paid.

7.2 Significance of ownership to equalization scheme

nfp   Sections 4 and 5 of the *Family Law Act, 1986* presuppose that the net family property of each spouse is distinct and separate. A determination of the net family property of each spouse may raise preliminary questions as to the ownership of particular assets. For example, where property, such as a bank account, is held in the joint names of the spouses, the beneficial interest(s) in the property may or may not be reflected by the legal title. The presumption of joint beneficial interests arising under section 14 of the *Family Law Act, 1986* is provisional and

18

1. 1st ask who own what - Rawluk can use "const-trust" to determine
   - can use s. 10 title, ownership section
2. Valuation on v-date - triggering date s. 7.1 Lim periods for trigg events
3. Use 5 step or 10 step Olivia formula □ max on 15/89 [7]

Family Property

not conclusive. It may be rebutted by cogent evidence pointing to a
contrary intention. Even where property is held in the name of only one
spouse, the doctrines of "resulting" and "constructive trusts" may impact on
the beneficial ownership of such property. It remains to be seen how the
courts will resolve these problems. Strictly speaking, a determination of
the beneficial ownership rights of each spouse should be a condition
precedent to any equalization of the net family properties of the spouses:
see *Rawluk v. Rawluk* (1986), 55 O.R. (2d) 704, 29 D.L.R. (4th) 754, 3
R.F.L. (3d) 113 (S.C.); *Seed v. Seed* (1986), 5 R.F.L. (3d) 120 (Ont. S.C.);
see also *Rose v. Rose and Megow*, unreported, February 6, 1987 (Ont. S.C.)
and *Crawford v. Crawford* (1987), 6 R.F.L. (3d) 308 (Ont. S.C.); compare
Benke v. Benke (1986), 4 R.F.L. (3d) 58 (Ont. Dist. Ct.), *supra*, 5.0
APPLICATIONS RESPECTING OWNERSHIP AND POSSESSION
OF PROPERTY, subheading 5.1 "Ownership of property". The need
for such a determination becomes more apparent if one spouse has debts
exceeding his or her assets at the "valuation date." Consider, for example,
the following circumstances. A husband and wife have a joint bank
account at the time of separation with a value of $100,000. The spouses
have no other assets and the husband owes his creditors $100,000. If the
joint bank account were purely one of convenience and all deposits had
been made by the husband, his net family property would be valued at
zero and there would be nothing to divide between the spouses. If,
however, the circumstances revaled that the wife owned the account of
convenience, she being the sole depositor, her net family property would
be valued at $100,000 and her husband's at zero. The husband would
accordingly be entitled to a presumptive equalization right of $50,000. If
the joint bank account were beneficially owned in equal shares by both
spouses, the husband's net family property would be zero and the wife's
$50,000. The husband would accordingly be entitled to pursue an
equalization claim in the amount of $25,000.

Assets acquired by either or both spouses for their children or
property purchased by any child from money provided by the parent(s)
may constitute a gift and thus be excluded from any calculation of the
spousal net family properties for the purposes of an equalization claim
under Part I of the *Family Law Act, 1986*: see *Kukolj v. Kukolj* (1986), 3
R.F.L. (3d) 359 (Ont. Unified Fam. Ct.); and *Humphreys v. Humphreys*
(1987), 7 R.F.L. (3d) 113 (Ont. S.C.); compare *Marsham v. Marsham*
(1987), 7 R.F.L. (3d) 1 (Ont. S.C.).

7.3 Definition of "property"

The definition of "property" in subsection 4(1) of the Act appears to
be comprehensive. It presumably includes choses in action, leasehold
interests, life tenancies (see *Martin v. Martin* (1986), 2 R.F.L. (3d) 14

19

(Ont. Dist. Ct.)), contingent interests under wills or trusts (compare *Brinkos v. Brinkos, infra*), pensions, deferred profit sharing plans, severance pay entitlements (*Marsham v. Marsham, supra*) option rights, partnership interests, business or professional goodwill and licences (*Re Corless and Corless* (1987), 58 O.R. (2d) 19, 34 D.L.R. (4th) 594, 5 R.F.L. (3d) 256 (Unified Fam. Ct.) but compare *Menage v. Hedges, supra*)) and accounts receivable (*Re Corless and Corless, supra*; compare *Re Armstrong and Armstrong* (1986), 39 A.C.W.S. (2d) 162 (Ont. Dist. Ct.)). Property acquired by either spouse after the triggering event that identifies the "valuation date" under subsection 4(1) of the *Family Law Act, 1986* is excluded from the "net family property" but may be subject to equal division under subsection 10(1) of the Act, where it is held under joint tenancy: *Martin v. Martin, supra*.

A spouse's right to future income from a trust established during the marriage has been held to fall outside the definition of "property" in subsection 4(1) of the *Family Law Act, 1986: Brinkos v. Brinkos* (1986), 4 R.F.L. (3d) 381 (Ont. S.C.).

7.4 Pensions

Subsection 1(1) of the *Family Law Amendment Act*, S.O. 1986, c. 35, which supersedes clause (c) of the definition of "property" in subsection 4(1) of the *Family Law Act, 1986*, provides that "property" includes:

(c) in the case of a spouse's rights under a pension plan that have vested, the spouse's interest in the plan including contributions made by other persons.

It is submitted that clause (c) does not imply that the valuation of a vested pension plan is invariably to be determined by reference to the contributions of the employee and employer, plus interest: see *Ryan v. Ryan*, unreported, July 23, 1986 (Ont. Dist. Ct.); *Re Armstrong and Armstrong* (1986), 39 A.C.W.S. (2d) 162 (Ont. Dist. Ct.); compare *Kukolj v. Kukolj* (1986), 3 R.F.L. (3d) 359 (Ont. Unified Fam. Ct.), applying clause (c) of the definition of "property" in subsection 4(1) of the *Family Law Act, 1986*. Although this method of valuation may be appropriate for a defined contributions pension plan, its validity is questionable when applied to a defined benefits pension plan. It is generally conceded that expert actuarial evidence is required in order to attribute a capitalized value to a defined benefits plan: compare *Marsham v. Marsham, supra*. As to relevant factors to be considered, see *Tataryn v. Tataryn*, 30 Sask. R. 282, [1984] 3 W.W.R. 97, 6 D.L.R. (4th) 77, 38 R.F.L. (2d) 272 (C.A.); *Messier v. Messier* (1986), 5 R.F.L. (3d) 251 (Ont. Dist. Ct.); *Humphreys v. Humphreys* (1987), 7 R.F.L. (3d) 113 (Ont. S.C.). Such capitalization of the value of a defined benefits plan has been avoided in several provinces by the use of a so-called "if and when" 20 order. This form of order was endorsed by the British Columbia Court of Appeal in *Rutherford v. Rutherford,* [1980] 2 W.W.R. 330, affd in part [1981] 6 W.W.R. 485, 23 R.F.L. (2d) 337 (B.C.C.A.) and by the Manitoba Court of Appeal in *George v. George,* 23 Man. R. (2d) 89, [1983] 5 W.W.R. 606, 149 D.L.R. (3d) 486, 35 R.F.L. (2d) 225; compare *Wilson v. Wilson* (1986), 2 R.F.L. (3d) 86 (Alta. C.A.); see generally, Jean McBean, "The Treatment of Pensions under the Alberta Matrimonial Property Act: Some Unresolved Issues", *Payne's Divorce and Family Law Digest,* Essays tab., E-25 and Julien D. Payne, "Selected Annotations of Cases on the Division and Valuation of Pensions in Matrimonial Causes", *ibid.,* E-43. In the *Rutherford* and *George* cases, the courts endorsed the following formula to be applied where an "if and when order" is deemed appropriate to the division of pension benefits:

$$\frac{1}{2} \times \frac{\text{total number of months or years of matrimonial cohabitation during which pension contributions made}}{\text{total number of months or years during which pension contributions made}} \times \text{actual pension received}$$

[handwritten annotations in margin: "Rutherford — (H) declared to be a 'trustee' of wife's share."; beside fraction "3 / 20"; below "1/2 ×" "3.5"; "'if & when' avoids need for actuarial valuation"]

In Alberta, a variation of this formula has been applied whereby the court looks to the total number of months or years during which the parties were married rather than to the period of matrimonial cohabitation: see *Wilson v. Wilson, supra;* Jean McBean, *loc. cit.*

[handwritten margin: "Rutherford 2 steps — 1) 'if & when' 2) impose 'trust'"]

The *Rutherford* and *George* formula was applied in *Porter v. Porter* (1986), 1 R.F.L. (3d) 12 (Ont. Dist. Ct.) (Kerr D.C.J.); see also *Harris v. Harris* (1986), 39 A.C.W.S. (2d) 68 (Ont. Dist. Ct.), wherein the husband's employment pension was divided on an "if and when" basis in the absence of actuarial evidence of the amount required to purchase an annuity to provide the wife with a fair share of the pension but the Canada Pension Plan was left undisturbed because it provides its own mechanism for division; compare *Re Armstrong and Armstrong, supra.* In *Nelson v. Nelson,* unreported, July 17, 1986 (Ont. S.C.), Doyle L.J.S.C. diverted from the *Rutherford* and *George* formula by determining the value of the husband's defined benefits plan on the basis of his average annual salary for the best six years prior to the separation, because that date constituted the "valuation date" under the *Family Law Act, 1986* and the wife was not entitled to benefit from her husband's contributions and increased pension benefits arising after separation.

[handwritten margin: "Masham says can't use an 'if and when' in Ontario we share values"; "You value pension first, then you can use 'if + when'"]

It is seriously open to question, however, whether an "if and when" order for the sharing of pension benefits upon maturity is consistent with the express statutory provisions of the *Family Law Act, 1986.* The definition of "net family property" in subsection 4(1) of the *Family Law Act, 1986* specifically requires a valuation of all includable property as of

[handwritten margin: "Masham says must value pension in Ontario."]

21

Marsham said "if and when" not good in Ontario

Marsham says must value the pension in Ontario

then use "if + when" on payment as a (trust) is imposed

10 year rule not violated.

the date of the triggering event: *Marsham v. Marsham,* unreported May 5, 1987 (Ont. S.C.). Furthermore, clause 9(1)(c) of the Act precludes the deferral of an equalization payment beyond a maximum period of ten years and may thereby undermine the potential for an "if and when" order: see *infra,* 11.0 POWERS OF COURT, subheadings 11.4 "Deferred or instalment payments" and 11.5 "Transfers of property; partition and sale".

In *McCutcheon v. McCutcheon* (1986), 2 R.F.L. (3d) 327 (Ont. Dist. Ct.), pension refund benefits payable by reason of the husband's voluntary termination of his employment were included in his "net family property". An order for the distribution of property *in specie* was coupled with an order for child support that was secured against the husband's right to the pension refund. The husband's former employers were directed to pay the refund to the wife for her to invest in order to provide for child support payments. It is doubtful, however, whether a court has any jurisdiction to impose obligations on a third party, such as a spouse's employer, who is not a party to the cause.

A surviving spouse's benefits under a pension plan should not be included in the net family property of the spouse with the pension plan because that spouse has personally no interest therein: *Marsham v. Marsham, supra.* Whether or not an actuarial valuation of such benefits will be attributed in determining the net family property of the surviving spouse will depend upon the probability of the spouses still being married to each other at the time of the pensioner's death. If the court finds it highly probable that the spouses will be divorced before the pensioner's death, no amount will be attributed to the surviving spouse's net family property: *Humphreys v. Humphreys,* unreported, April 24, 1987 (Ont.S.C.).

It is submitted that periodic pension benefits already being received are not to be included in the calculation of the pensioner's net family property. Such benefits constitute income in the hands of the recipient that is relevant to any application for spousal support: see *Kopecky v. Kopecky; Kopecky v. Kopecky* (1983), 24 Alta. L.R. (2d) 79 (Q.B.) and *Clarke v. Clarke* (1986), 72 N.S.R. (2d) 387, 173 A.P.R. 387, 29 D.L.R. (4th) 492, 1 R.F.L. (3d) 29 (C.A.).

7.5 University degrees; professional licences; goodwill

7.5.1 Other jurisdictions

The definition of "property" in subsection 4(1) of the *Family Law Act, 1986* is sufficiently broad to include an interest in a business or professional partnership. In valuing a professional practice, "goodwill" is a factor to be considered: *Criton v. Criton* (1986), 50 R.F.L. (2d) 44 (Sask. C.A.). It has been held inappropriate, however, to value the goodwill of a professional practice by capitalizing excess earnings, where the spouse is a sole practitioner and there is no continuum of returning patients (*Nassar v. Nassar and Weiller*, [1984] 6 W.W.R. 634 (Man. Q.B.)) or where the practice has no value on the open market: *Smith v. Mackie* (1986), 48 R.F.L. (2d) 232, 246 (B.C.S.C.). It has also been held that an anaesthetist employed by a hospital has no "practice" that constitutes divisible property and that his future income should not be regarded as a divisible asset: *Barley v. Barley* (1984), 43 R.F.L. (2d) 100 (B.C.S.C.). Similarly, a husband's medical degree with its consequential enhanced earning capacity acquired during marriage has been excluded from division under the *Family Relations Act*, R.S.B.C. 1979, c. 121: *Jirik v. Jirik* (1983), 37 R.F.L. (2d) 385 (B.C.S.C.). An interest in a law practice has, however, been characterized as a divisible family asset and it is immaterial that the claimant spouse is not qualified to practise law, because the statutory entitlement is to a monetary judgment: *Underhill v. Underhill* (1983), 34 R.F.L. (2d) 419, at 431-32 (B.C.C.A.), disapproving *Piters v. Piters*, 20 B.C.L.R. 393, [1981] 1 W.W.R. 285, 19 R.F.L. (2d) 217 (S.C.) and *Ladner v. Ladner* (1980), 20 R.F.L. (2d) 243 (B.C.S.C.); compare *Jackh v. Jackh*, 22 B.C.L.R. 182, [1981] 1 W.W.R. 481, 113 D.L.R. (3d) 267, 18 R.F.L. (2d) 310 (S.C.).

In the context of spousal property rights, the valuation of a professional degree or licence by reference to the increased earning capacity thereby generated has generally been rejected in Canadian and United States jurisdictions: see cases cited, *supra*; see also *Whitehead (Burrell) v. Burrell* (1983), 35 R.F.L. (2d) 440 (B.C.S.C.); *In re Marriage of Graham* (1978), 574 P. 2d 75 (Colo. Sup. Ct.); *Inman v. Inman* (1982), 8 Fam. Law Reptr. 2329 (Ky. Ct. App.); *Archer v. Archer* (1985), 493 A. 2d 1074 (Md. Ct. App.); *Stevens v. Stevens* (1986), 492 N.E. 2d 131 (Ohio Sup. Ct.); but see *contra Woodsworth v. Woodsworth* (1983), 337 N.W. 2d 332 (Mich. Ct. App.) and *O'Brien v. O'Brien* (1986), 498 N.Y.S. 2d 743 (N.Y. Ct. App.). In *Woodsworth v. Woodsworth, supra*, it was suggested that the husband's law degree could be valued by reference to the differential between the income earning potential flowing from the degree and the probable income of the husband without this qualification. And in *O'Brien v. O'Brien, supra*, the wife was granted $188,000, which represented a 40 per cent interest in her husband's medical licence. Expert evidence of the value of the licence was based on a comparison of the average income of a college graduate and that of a general surgeon until the age of 65 years, with consideration being given to income taxes, an inflation rate of ten per cent and a real interest rate of three per cent. However, as pointed out in *Archer v. Archer, supra*, these two decisions reflect a minority opinion in the United States and "the issue of whether a professional degree is a marital property asset has generated a split of opinion among Michigan's intermediate appellate courts" (*ibid.*, at 1080).

23

7.5.2 *Ontario*

In *Re Corless and Corless* (1987), 58 O.R. (2d) 19, 34 D.L.R. (4th) 594, 5 R.F.L. (3d) 256 (Unified Fam. Ct.), a husband's interest in a law partnership was valued for the purpose of an equalization claim under section 5 of the *Family Law Act, 1986*, on the basis of the amount that would have been payable to him on a voluntary withdrawal from the partnership, with due consideration being given to his interest in the capital account and the value of hours worked but not billed on the "valuation date", subject to a discount for such factors as administrative costs, the cost of financing and collecting outstanding accounts and prospective income tax liabilities. The husband's law degree and right to practise law were characterized as "property" within the meaning of subsection 4(1) of the *Family Law Act, 1986*, but a "nil value" was attributed to them because they were personal in nature and incapable of being transferred or exchanged. Steinberg U.F.C.J. concluded that "value" in the context of an equalization claim signifies "exchange value" and that the court could not adopt a "value in use" approach that would attribute a value to the right to practise law on the basis of income earning projections.

In *Menage v. Hedges*, unreported, June 8, 1987 (Ont. Unified Fam. Ct.), Fleury, U.F.C.J. partially disagreed with *Re Corless and Corless, supra*, by concluding that a medical degree or a licence to practice medicine is not "property" within the meaning of subsection 4(1) of *the Family Law Act, 1986*, although certain aspects of a professional practice, including assets, accounts receivable and transferable goodwill, may constitute quantifiable assets and personal property for the purposes of Part I of the Act. Fleury, U.F.C.J. held that future enhanced earning potential, as distinct from assets already acquired from the realization of an existing potential, does not constitute "property" for the purposes of an equalization of spousal net family properties under the *Family Law Act, 1986*. Otherwise, all future income streams of separated spouses, whether from employment or professional practice, would have to be included in the computation of net family property, and this was not contemplated by the Legislature and would "call for a re-writing of the *Family Law Act, 1986*".

If one spouse has made direct or indirect contributions to the other spouse's acquisition of a professional degree or licence, as, for example, by paying the requisite fees or by assuming a primary or exclusive responsibility for household expenses during the educational or training program, the contributing spouse might be in a position to claim an interest in the value of the degree or licence by invoking resulting or constructive trust doctrines in the context of an application under section 10 of the *Family Law Act, 1986*. It is doubtful, however, whether such a claim would justify the recovery of a monetary judgment in excess of the value of the financial contributions made, together with prejudgment interest: compare *Sullivan v. Sullivan* (1984), 34 Cal. 3d 762, 691 P. 2d 1020, 209 Cal. Reptr. 354.

The present earning capacity generated by a professional degree or licence is, of course, a relevant consideration in the determination of the right to and quantum of spousal support: see *Whitehead (Burrell) v. Burrell, supra*, subheading 7.5.1 "Other jurisdictions". This may be of increasing importance in light of the provisions of subsection 15(7) of the *Divorce Act, 1985*, S.C. 1986, c. 4, whereby an order for spousal support "should . . . recognize the economic advantages and disadvantages to the spouses arising from the marriage or its breakdown". Subsection 33(8) of the *Family Law Act, 1986*, similarly provides that an order for spousal support "should recognize the spouse's contribution to the relationship and the economic consequences of the relationship for the spouse": see Bruce Ziff, "Recent Developments in Canadian Law: Marriage and Divorce" (1986), 18 Ottawa L. Rev. 121, at 156.

In the context of spousal support, the relevance of future income potential generated by a professional degree or licence was addressed by Killeen D.C.J. in *Keast v. Keast* (1986), 1 R.F.L. (3d) 401 (Ont. Dist. Ct.). The trial judge held that an order for spousal support under the *Family Law Act, 1986*, is not confined to providing for the basic needs of a dependent spouse. A wife, who has made physical, psychological and financial sacrifices and contributions to the realization of her husband's career as a doctor, may be entitled to quasi-restitutionary or compensatory support in addition to periodic support that accommodates her basic needs. Applying these criteria on the basis of clauses 33(9)(b) and (j) of the *Family Law Act, 1986*, Killeen D.C.J. ordered the husband to pay lifelong periodic support of $600 per month to the wife. Supplementary compensatory support was granted to the wife for her contribution to the husband's career potential, the amount being fixed at $1,000 per month, with payments to be made for a ten year period commencing in 1990. The quantum of compensatory support was determined having regard to expert evidence indicating the differential between the husband's prospective lifetime income as a doctor and the income that he would have earned in his former profession as a teacher. The decision in *Keast v. Keast, supra*, was distinguished in *Re Corless and Corless, supra*, in the context of the wife's application for support. Steinberg U.F.C.J. concluded that the wife's assumption of homemaking responsibilities and deferral of her career development pending her husband's acquisition of professional qualifications did not constitute "a contribution . . . to the realization of the [husband's] career potential" within the meaning of clause 33(9)(j) of the *Family Law Act, 1986* because she had played no role in the husband's decision to enter the legal profession nor in his practice and she had not financed his education or entertained his clients. The deferral of her career plans was, nevertheless, deemed relevant to her application for spousal support by reason of subclause 33(9)(l)(ii) of the *Family Law Act, 1986*, which requires the court to have regard to "the effect on the spouse's earning capacity of the responsibilities assumed during cohabitation". Finding that the wife's earning potential had been affected by her assumption of family responsibilities and that her entrepreneurial skills had not yielded a substantial return but would so do in the foreseeable future, periodic spousal support was ordered for a fixed term of 24 months to bridge the gap until the wife could be expected to achieve economic independence.

And in *Magee v. Magee* (1987), 6 R.F.L. (3d) 453 (Ont. Unified Fam. Ct.), Goodearle U.F.C.J. concluded that subsection 5(6) of the *Family Law Act, 1986*, should not be applied to justify deviation from the norm of equalization of the spousal net family properties on the basis of the wife's substantial contributions to her husband's professional development. Rather, those contributions should be taken into consideration in the context of her spousal support claim pursuant to s. 33(8) and clause 33(9)(j) of the *Family Law Act, 1986*, which provide a broader basis for judicial intervention in exceptional circumstances. In light of the attendant circumstances, Goodearle U.F.C.J. granted an order for lump sum support in addition to gradated periodic support over a period of five years.

7.6 Value

The notion of "value" is central to the application of Part I of the *Family Law Act, 1986*. There is, however, no definition of "value" in the Act. Where practicable, it is probable that the courts will apply the concept of fair market value, which has been applied in the context of the *Income Tax Act*, R.S.C. 1952, c. 148 to mean "the highest price available estimated in terms of money which a willing seller may obtain for the property in an open and unrestricted market from a willing, knowledgeable purchaser acting at arms length": *Re Mann Estate*, [1972] 5 W.W.R. 23, at 27 (B.C.S.C.) (Tucker J.); see also *Henderson Estate v. M.N.R.; Bank of New York v. M.N.R.* (1973), 27 D.T.C. 5471, at 5476 (Fed. Ct.) (Catternach J.), affd (1975), 29 D.T.C. 5332 (Fed. C.A.). In *Dibbley v. Dibbley and Liddle* (1986), 5 R.F.L. (3d) 381, at 391 (Ont. S.C.), *infra*, subheading "Valuation of business; private companies", Rosenberg J. concluded that fair market value for the purposes of the *Family Law Act, 1986* signifies "the price that a willing buyer would pay to a willing seller after reasonable exposure to the market" and no account should be taken of selling costs or of income tax liabilities where no sale of the property is envisaged: compare *Crawford v. Crawford* (1987), 6 R.F.L. (3d) 308 (Ont. S.C.), *infra*, subheading 7.9 "Income tax and other prospective liabilities". In *Postma v. Postma* (1987), 6 R.F.L. (3d) 50 (Ont. S.C.), Carter L.J.S.C. applied a fair market valuation to a chicken farm, notwithstanding that the value to the owner would be significantly higher by reason of a non-transferable chicken quota, in the event that the husband could secure the financing to purchase his wife's joint interest in the chicken farm.

Fair market value is not to be confused with "book value". In *Silverstein v. Silverstein* (1978), 20 O.R. (2d) 185, 87 D.L.R. (3d) 116, 1 R.F.L. (2d) 239, at 241-42 (S.C.), Galligan J. observed:

> I think that at the very beginning of cases under the *Family Law Reform Act* the profession should realize the necessity of giving full, complete and up-to-date information in the statements required by those sections. In the statement of property filed by the husband in this case, the value of certain property is put in at its book value which is the depreciated cost value according to the books maintained by the companies in which he is interested. That value is useless and in my opinion is not a particular of property that complies with the intention of the legislature when it enacted s. 5. Form 10 — which is the document required by R. 775c — requires the party filing a statement of property to take one's oath to the "Estimated Value" of the property. That means its estimated current market value, not what it cost years ago, less its accumulated depreciation. The statement of property filed by the husband gives no indication of what the property is actually worth to him at this time.

fmv

Where the determination of a fair market value is impractical, as in the case of pension benefits, the objectives of the *Family Law Act, 1986* necessitate the court determining a "fair value" in light of the attendant circumstances: see *Marsham v. Marsham* (1987), 7 R.F.L. (3d) 1 (Ont. S.C.) and *Menage v. Hedges*, unreported, June 8, 1987 (Ont. Unified Fam. Ct.). In the words of one commentator:

> Fair value is not a static concept; it is a fluid one which adapts to the circumstances. It is not necessarily any one of intrinsic value, rateable value, value to owner, or fair market value. It might be a combination of them. . . . The same property might have to be valued at the date of the marriage or at the date it was received as a gift and then again at the date of separation or the day before the date of death. By using the broad and fluid interpretation of fair value, as a basis of valuation, there is nothing inconsistent in having the same property valued on a different basis on each date, i.e. (i) on a liquidation basis at the date of marriage and then on a going concern basis at the day before the date of death; or (ii) there may be goodwill included in a valuation at the date of marriage and at the date of separation but on the day before the date of death, it might not exist. . . . It is fallacious to say that the quantification of fair value should be the same no matter what the nature or occasion of the transaction is, who the parties to the transaction are, or how the transaction is being financed. Fairness is a relative concept. A fair value is one which is just and equitable, not necessarily one which conforms to predetermined norms.

Stephen R. Cole, C.A., "Family Law Valuation Concepts", Canadian Bar Association — Ontario and Law Society of Upper Canada, *The New Family Law Act and the New Divorce Act*, January 24 and 25, 1986, at 14-14a.

And in *Rawluk v. Rawluk* (1986), 55 O.R. (2d) 704, at 709, 29 D.L.R. (4th) 754, 3 R.F.L. (3d) 113 (S.C.), Walsh J. stated:

> While the Act speaks of value, it contains no definition of that term nor, indeed, guidelines of any kind to assist in the determination of its meaning other than the provision contained in s. 4(4) that when value is required to be calculated as of a given date, it shall be calculated as of close of business on that date. Absent any statutory direction, "value" must then be determined on the peculiar facts and circumstances as they are found and developed on the evidence in each individual case. While this approach does not lead to uniformity and predictability of result, it does recognize the individuality inherent in each marriage and case and permit the flexibility so often necessary to ensure an equitable result.

In *Re Armstrong and Armstrong* (1986), 39 A.C.W.S. (2d) 162 (Ont. Dist. Ct.), it was concluded that the value of future entitlements such as prospective severance payments or future annuity payments from a deferred benefit pension plan would normally be their present value replacement costs. And in *Humphreys v. Humphreys* (1987), 7 R.F.L. (3d) 113 (Ont. S.C.), Galligan J. concluded that the actuarial capitalized valuation of the husband's pension rights should be premised on the "termination method", which calculates the value as if the husband's employment terminated on the "valuation date", rather than the "retirement method", which involves speculative assumptions concerning the date of retirement and prospective increases in salary. See also *Nelson v. Nelson*, unreported, July 17, 1987 (Ont. S.C.) (Doyle L.J.S.C.), *supra*, subheading 7.4 "Pensions".

As to the educational degrees and professional licences, see *supra*, subheading 7.5 "University degrees; professional licences; goodwill".

7.7 Valuation of business; private companies

If difference in "experts" opinions split the difference

In the words of Cameron J. in *Hart v. Hart (No. 3)* (1986), 60 Nfld. & P.E.I.R. 287, 181 A.P.R. 287, at 288 (Nfld. Unified Fam. Ct.):

> Generally there are four basic approaches to valuation of a business:
> 1. Market price (in the case of public company);
> 2. Assets approach;
> 3. Earnings or investment value approach; and
> 4. A combination of the above. (See *Re Domglas Inc.; Domglas Inc. v. Jurislowsky, Fraser & Co. Ltd. et al.* (1980), 3 B.L.R. 135, at 191-192 affd [1982] C.A. 377, 22 B.L.R. 121, 138 D.L.R. (3d) 521 (Que. C.A.)).
>
> Market price has no application in this case.
> The assets approach is generally used where the hypothetical purchaser is really looking to the company's underlying assets and not to the shares per se. This method may also be appropriate where the business being valued is a going concern, but not earning an adequate return on its invested capital. A determination of a liquidation value is an asset approach.

. . .

The earnings or investment value approach is appropriate when the business is earning a reasonable return on its capital. In this approach the hypothetical purchaser wishes to acquire the future earnings of the business.

. . .

In the combined approach, as the name implies, the appraiser uses the different approaches referred to above and weights the resulting values in light of particular factors to determine a final valuation. (See *Re Domglas Inc.*, *supra*, 13 B.L.R. 185, at 201).

In the context of an application under the *Family Law Act, 1986*, Carter L.J.S.C. has concluded that the valuation of shares in a private corporation is to be determined by reference to the business as a going concern. Factors to be considered include (i) the nature and history of the enterprise; (ii) the economic outlook; (iii) the book value and financial condition; (iv) the earning capacity; (v) the dividend paying capacity; (vi) the goodwill or other intangible values; (vii) the size of the block to the valued; and (viii) the market price of stock of similar corporations. The valuation of the stock of a closely held corporation presents a unique factual situation that is not within the ambit of any exact science and the reasonableness of any valuation thus depends upon the judgment and experience of the appraiser and the completeness of the information relied upon to support the opinions presented: *Indig v. Indig*, unreported, August 15, 1986 (Ont. S.C.), considering *Diligenti v. RWMD Operations Kelowna Ltd. et al. (No. 2)* (1977), 4 B.C.L.R. 134, at 137 (S.C.) and *Lavene v. Lavene* (1978), 382 A. 2d 621, at 624 (N.J. Super. Ct.).

In valuing the shares of a private company, the evidence of experts may yield to experience in light of a prior recorded sale of shares: *Sheehan v. Sheehan*, unreported, March 31, 1986 (Ont. S.C.) (Flannigan L.J.S.C.), citing *Remus v. Remus* (1987), 5 R.F.L. (3d) 304, at 309 (Ont. S.C.) (Walsh J.).

In determining the value of a business, the evidence of a person engaged in the "real world" of marketing such businesses may be preferred to that of a chartered accountant: *Sheehan v. Sheehan, supra*.

In *Dibbley v. Dibbley and Liddle* (1987), 5 R.F.L. (3d) 381 (Ont. S.C.), *supra*, subheading 7.6 "Value", the husband's partnership interest in a firm of chartered accountants was valued on the basis of his capital account, goodwill to which he would be entitled on leaving the partnership if he did not take his clients with him and the book value of assets, with a deduction being made for the valuation of his partnership interest at the date of his marriage.

7.8 Valuation date

The definitions of "net family property" and "valuation date" in subsection 4(1) of the *Family Law Act, 1986* imply that the court is unconcerned with changes in the value of property that occur between the date of the triggering event and the date of the adjudication of an equalization claim: see *Menage v. Hedges*, unreported, June 8, 1987 (Ont. Unified Fam. Ct.); see also *Benke v. Benke* (1986), 4 R.F.L. (3d) 58 (Ont. Dist. Ct.); compare *Rawluk v. Rawluk* (1986), 55 O.R. (2d) 704, 29 D.L.R. (4th) 754, 3 R.F.L. (3d) 113 (S.C.) and *Seed v. Seed* (1986), 5 R.F.L. (3d) 120 (Ont. S.C.), *supra*, 5.0 APPLICATIONS RESPECTING OWNERSHIP AND POSSESSION OF PROPERTY, subheading 5.1 "Ownership of property" and *supra*, 7.0 EQUALIZATION OF NET FAMILY PROPERTIES, subheading 7.2 "Significance of ownership to equalization scheme". Any appreciation or depreciation in value is apparently irrelevant to a determination of the value of the net family property of each spouse, regardless of whether the change in value is attributable to extrinsic economic forces or to the conduct of either spouse: *Kelly v. Kelly* (1986), 50 R.F.L. (2d) 360 (Ont. S.C.). Where the value of property appreciates or depreciates by reason of inflation or depressed market conditions, such increased or reduced value should logically be shared equally by the spouses: see *Heinrich v. Heinrich* (1985), 48 R.F.L. (2d) 449, at 450 (Sask. Q.B.); *Andris v. Andris* (1984), 40 R.F.L. (2d) 315, at 316-17 (Sask. Q.B.) and *Van Meter v. Van Meter* (1983), 25 Sask. R. 109 (Q.B.); *Medernach v. Medernach* (1985), 40 Sask. R. 269 (Q.B.). The same result should not ensue, however, where the appreciation in value is solely attributable to the skill or efforts of one spouse after the triggering event: compare *Crawford v. Crawford* (1987), 6 R.F.L. (3d) 308 (Ont. S.C.). Correspondingly, any depreciation in value arising from a mismanagement of the assets by one of the spouses after the triggering event should not operate to the prejudice of the other spouse: compare *Gutheil v. Gutheil and Clewes* (1983), 34 R.F.L. (2d) 50 (Man. Q.B.). The provisions of subsection 5(6) of the *Family Law Act, 1986*, and particularly clauses (b), (d), (f) and (h), may enable the court to achieve equity between the spouses in the aforementioned circumstances by invoking its discretion to re-apportion the entitlements of each spouse on the basis that an equalization of the net family properties as of the date of the triggering event would be unconscionable. This course of action was rejected, however, in *Kelly v. Kelly* (1986), 50 R.F.L. (2d) 360 (Ont. S.C.), wherein Potts J. observed (at p. 366):

> [I]t would not be unconscionable to leave matters as they stand.
>
> Moreover, even if I had decided that it was unconscionable, I seriously doubt that s. 5(6) has any application because valuation is determined as of the date of separation and "debts or other liabilities" mentioned in para. (*f*) and 'other circumstances' mentioned in para. (*h*) refer to debts or other liabilities and other circumstances in existence prior to, or as of, the date of separation. There are no transitional provisions in the *Family Law Act* which would apply in these circumstances.

Accordingly, there will be no adjustment for declining prices of real estate under that section.

For criticism of these conclusions, see James G. McLeod, Annotation, *ibid.*, at 360-63.

7.9 Income tax and other prospective liabilities

In calculating the "net family property" of either spouse for the purposes of an equalization claim under section 5 of the *Family Law Act, 1986*, the tax implications of a prospective property disposition may be taken into consideration: see, for example, *Kelly v. Kelly* (1986), 2 R.F.L. (3d) 1 (Ont. S.C.); *Oliva v. Oliva* (1986), 2 R.F.L. (3d) 188 (Ont. S.C.); *Harris v. Harris* (1986), 39 A.C.W.S. (2d) 68 (Ont. Dist. Ct.); *Re Armstrong and Armstrong* (1986), 39 A.C.W.S. 162 (Ont. Dist. Ct.); *Re Corless and Corless* (1987), 58 O.R. (2d) 19, 34 D.L.R. (4th) 594, 5 R.F.L. (3d) 256 (Unified Fam. Ct.); *Postma v. Postma* (1987), 6 R.F.L. (3d) 50 (Ont. S.C.) (Carter L.J.S.C.); and see generally *Payne's Divorce and Family Law Digest*, §45.5 "Matrimonial property". These may include the effect of the recent capital gains tax holiday: *Kelly v. Kelly, supra*, (calculations to be based on the husband's taking advantage of one-half of any tax losses available to him and one-half of the $500,000 capital gains exemption); compare *Ganz v. Ganz and Ganz*, unreported, June 4, 1986 (Ont. S.C.) (no deduction allowed for income tax). Consideration has also been given to prospective real estate and legal fees that might be incurred in consequence of any court-ordered equalization entitlement: *Kelly v. Kelly, supra; Oliva v. Oliva, supra; Sullivan v. Sullivan* (1986), 5 R.F.L. (3d) 28, at 35 (Ont. Unified Fam. Ct.); but see *contra, Folga v. Folga* (1986), 2 R.F.L. (3d) 358, at 363 (Ont. S.C.) (*per* Gravely L.J.S.C.).

Such prospective liabilities might be relevant to a determination of the "net family property" of each spouse as defined in subsection 4(1) of the *Family Law Act, 1986*, which specifically requires the deduction of the spouse's "debts and other liabilities". In the alternative, clause 5(6)(h) of the Act may provide a means whereby prospective income tax liabilities, real estate and legal fees, if substantial, can be taken into account by way of a re-apportionment of the provisional right to an equalization of the net family properties, if such equalization would be unconscionable under the circumstances.

In *Remus v. Remus* (1987), 5 R.F.L. (3d) 304 (Ont. S.C.), income tax liabilities that accrued prior to the "valuation date" were held to fall within the ambit of the phrase "debts and other liabilities" under clause (a) of the definition of "net family property" in subsection 4(1) of the *Family Law Act, 1986*, notwithstanding that their payment was deferred until the husband's fiscal year-end. The tax implications that could arise from the husband's future transfer or collapse of his R.R.S.P.'s was

[handwritten margin note: MacPherson case O.C.A. said if sale necessary, costs of disposition plus income tax are deductible]

31

ignored, however, as being too speculative in light of his testimony that he had no intention of disposing of them because they were intended to provide for his retirement. And in *Menage v. Hedges*, unreported, June 8, 1987 (Ont. Unified Fam. Ct.), wherein Fleury U.F.C.J. was not satisfied that there was any substantial likelihood that the husband would surrender his R.R.S.P. and thereby trigger adverse tax consequences, the possibility of sale or surrender was perceived as "far too speculative for this type of notional tax liability to be considered as a debt or liability within the meaning of the *Family Law Act, 1986*". Similarly, no account was taken of selling costs or income tax liabilities in *Dibbley v. Dibbley and Liddle* (1986), 5 R.F.L. (3d) 381 (Ont. S.C.), wherein no sale of the property was envisaged. Notional real estate commissions were also ignored in *Bakocs v. Bakocs*, unreported, August 5, 1986 (Ont. S.C.), wherein no sale was effectuated and no evidence was adduced and the court refused to take judicial notice of "going rates". In *Messier v. Messier* (1986), 5 R.F.L. (3d) 251 (Ont. Dist. Ct.), however, the capitalized value of the husband's unmatured pension was discounted by 30 per cent by reason of "income tax liabilities that will arise eventually". See also *Humphreys v. Humphreys* (1987), 7 R.F.L. (3d) 113 (Ont. S.C.), wherein a discount of 21 per cent was allowed. In *Marsham v. Marsham* (1987), 7 R.F.L. (3d) 1 (Ont. S.C.) the capitalized value of the husband's unmatured pension was discounted by a factor of 36 per cent to take account of his probable future income tax liabilities. No similar discount was permitted, however, in the valuation of the husband's severance pay entitlement as of the date of separation, because of the feasibility of his avoiding income tax by a roll-over into an R.R.S.P. And in *Nemish v. Nemish*, unreported, August 11, 1986 (Ont. S.C.) the husband, who was in the 50 per cent tax bracket, was allowed to discount his R.R.S.P.'s by a factor of 30 per cent. In the words of Sirois J. in *Crawford v. Crawford* (1987), 6 R.F.L. (3d) 308, at 312 (Ont. S.C.) who permitted a discount in the fair market value of real estate to take account of prospective legal fees, real estate commission and income tax liabilities, "each case depends on its own circumstances".

7.10 Expert evidence: "Splitting the difference"

Valuation is not an exact science and expert opinions may differ on the value of specific assets and even on the appropriate method for effectuating a valuation. For example, the valuation of a spouse's shares in an active company could be based on a future earnings approach or on a liquidation approach and the formula selected may radically affect the determination of their value: see *Nurnberger v. Nurnberger* (1983), 25 Sask. R. 241, at 246-247 (Q.B.). In assessing the value of a spouse's interest in a joint business venture, the court may allow a discount by reason of the difficulty that might be experienced in attempting to dispose of a minority holding: *Agioritis v. Agioritis* (1982), 25 R.F.L. (2d) 256 (Sask.Q.B.). Projections as to prospective tax liabilities are often speculative, and when deemed relevant to a court-ordered property entitlement, have led to diverse judicial practices: see text *supra*, and *Payne's Divorce and Family Law Digest*, §45.5 "Matrimonial property".

Where a court is faced with conflicting expert evidence respecting the value of specific assets, the court may find it appropriate to split the difference by averaging the appraisals submitted on behalf of the respective spouses: *Benke v. Benke* (1986), 4 R.F.L. (3d) 58, at 72 (Ont. Dist. Ct.); *Lawler v. Lawler* (1982), 31 R.F.L. (2d) 78 (Ont. Co. Ct.); *Dembiczak v. Dembiczak* (1986), 48 R.F.L. (2d) 113 (Sask. C.A.). This practice cannot be universally applied because it may lead to unjust and absurd results and would constitute an abrogation of the court's responsibility: *Duff v. Duff* (1983), 43 Nfld. & P.E.I.R. 151, 127 A.P.R. 151 (Nfld. C.A.), citing *Atlantic and North West Railway v. Judah* (1894), 20 R.L. 527, at 536. In the words of Mifflin C.J.N. in *Duff v. Duff, supra*, at 155:

> Contradictory evidence of value must be carefully weighed by the trial judge and, if he is unable to arrive at a fair and reasonable valuation based on all the evidence adduced so as to order one spouse to pay to the other an amount to provide for a division of the property, his only recourse is to order the property to be sold and the net proceeds divided between them.

In *Heinrich v. Heinrich* (1985), 48 R.F.L. (2d) 449, at 450 (Sask. Q.B.), where the court could not determine the value of farmland in the face of marked differences between two appraisals, McLellan J. concluded that "[t]he fairest way to divide the value of the farmland would be to distribute one parcel to the respondent, despite the request of the applicant for a cash payment". And in *Moss v. Moss* (1986), 5 R.F.L. (3d) 62 (Nfld. Unified Fam. Ct.), wherein an application was brought pursuant to s. 27 of the *Matrimonial Property Act*, S.N. 1979, c. 32, (as amended) Cameron J. was unable to determine the value of the husband's business in light of the evidence adduced and granted an order, albeit reluctantly, that the husband transfer to his wife a designated number of shares in his company.

7.11 Deduction of debts and liabilities

In undertaking the statutory calculations for the purpose of determining the "net family property" of each spouse, subsection 4(1) provides for the deduction of "the spouse's debts and other liabilities": see *Remus v. Remus, supra*, subheading "Income tax and other prospective liabilities". Deductions are also to be made of the net value of pre-marital property, other than a matrimonial home. It appears that clause (a) of the definition of "net family property" in subsection 4(1) of the *Family Law Act, 1986* envisages the deduction of debts and other liabilities existing as of the "valuation date". It is apparently immaterial whether the debts or liabilities were incurred for the benefit of the family as a whole or for the personal benefit of the spouse who incurred them. It also appears to be irrelevant whether the debts or liabilities were incurred before marriage or during the subsistence of a viable marriage. Pre-marital debts or liabilities that have remained undischarged at the valuation date are presumably deductible from the net family property of the obligated spouse. This may be somewhat incongruous in light of the fact that pre-marital assets are generally excluded from the divisible property. [But see *Family Law Act, 1986*, clauses 5(6)(a), (b) and (f); see also *Kelly v. Kelly* (1986), 50 R.F.L. (2d) 360 (Ont. S.C.), *supra*]. In *Jackson v. Jackson* (1986), 5 R.F.L. (3d) 8 (Ont. S.C.), however, wherein the husband had an outstanding pre-marital loan, the court concluded that this debt constituted a "negative deduction" and should accordingly be added to the value of his net family property. See also *Menage v. Hedges*, unreported, June 8, 1987 (Ont. Unified Fam. Ct.).

The right to deduct outstanding debts existing on the valuation date is not subject to any overriding discretion of the court under clause (a) of the definition of "net family property" in subsection 4(1) of the *Family Law Act, 1986*, although an adjustment of the *prima facie* right to an equalization of the net family properties of the spouses may, in exceptional circumstances, be effectuated under subsection 5(6) of the Act. In *Rawluk v. Rawluk* (1986), 55 O.R. (2d) 704, at 710-711, 29 D.L.R. (4th) 754, 3 R.F.L. (3d) 113 (S.C.), Walsh J. stated:

> It was submitted on behalf of the wife that it would be most unfair if the entire unpaid balance of $38,267.15 owing by the husband to Revenue Canada was permitted as a deduction from his net family property. The basis for this submission was that the evidence of the wife and the husband's accountant, Bernard Spiegel, C.A., disclosed that had the husband taken advantage of and acted upon his wife's and accountant's intervention with the Minister of National Revenue, the husband's tax liability might well have been reduced to approximately $14,000.
>
> In my view, the wording of s. 4(1)(a) is not discretionary. A spouse's debts and other liabilities can not be allowed or disallowed as a deduction from his or her net family property on the basis of fairness, equity or for any reason other than the spouse seeking their exclusion as a deduction, has failed to prove that they were, in fact, a *bona fide* debt or liability existing on the valuation date.
>
> Any equitable redress as sought here by the wife can only be accomplished through a variation of the equalization payment by resort to s. 5(6). However, the facts here fall far short of the extremely stringent conditions imposed by the Legislature before resort may be had to that section.

The words "other liabilities" in clause (a) of the definition of "net family property" in subsection 4(1) of the *Family Law Act, 1986* are

34

[handwritten: is co-signa of "uote" a liability]

inherently vague and could well include contingent liabilities such as that of the guarantor of a third party loan.° This paragraph also raises intrinsically difficult problems in the context of the relationship, if any, between spousal property entitlements and spousal or child support rights and obligations: see *Re Armstrong and Armstrong* (1986), 39 A.C.W.S. (2d) 162 (Ont. Dist. Ct.). Traditionally, most courts have viewed property and support rights as distinct. The prevalent judicial practice has been to determine property entitlements prior to any adjudication of spousal or child support claims. Whether this practice is consistent with clause (a) of the definition of "net family property" in subsection 4(1) of the *Family Law Act, 1986*, remains to be seen. Assume, for example, that a husband is under a subsisting obligation to pay periodic spousal support to his wife and child pursuant to a court order or the provisions of a separation agreement. Are these continuing obligations relevant to a determination of his net family property? Would it make any difference if support arrears had already accumulated to a total of $15,000 over the preceding 18 months? If present and pre-determined prospective support obligations fall within the ambit of "other liabilities" under clause (a) of the definition of "net family property" in subsection 4(1) of the *Family Law Act, 1986*, the traditional practice whereby the courts determined the property entitlement of a spouse before determining spousal and child support rights and obligations would be reversed. More importantly, the primary objective of Part I of the *Family Law Act, 1986* namely, the equal sharing of property acquired by either spouse during the marriage through their joint contributions to the economic and social welfare of the family, would be undermined with resulting prejudice to a financially dependent spouse or a custodial parent. It is accordingly submitted that Ontario courts should reject the reasoning in *Nurnberger v. Nurnberger* (1983), 25 Sask. R. 241, at 246-47 (Q.B.), wherein Carter J. had regard to the fact that the husband "may have to pay maintenance to his wife for some time to come and that ought to be accounted for in some way in the assessment [of the value] of the shares". Rather than determining spousal property entitlements in light of present and prospective support rights and obligations, the courts should adhere to their past practice of determining the property entitlements and then determining the needs of the spouses and their children, having regard, *inter alia*, to the division of the net family properties. Where the support rights and obligations are already in existence, a subsequent property entitlement might constitute a change of circumstances sufficient to warrant the rescission or variation of the support order. Such an interpretation may, however, fly in the face of the express provisions of clause (a) of the definition of "net family property" in subsection 4(1) of the *Family Law Act, 1986*, and a statutory amendment may be required to clarify the position.

[handwritten right margin: Proff says Courts will determine 1) Property sharing first 2) Then deal with support]

Quite apart from the issue of the relationship between spousal property entitlements and support rights and obligations, clause (a) may present problems in cases involving spousal loans. In the absence of a domestic contract, which prevails against the statutory sharing regime pursuant to subsection 2(10) of the Act, if one spouse owes a debt to the other as of the valuation date, this debt can presumably be deducted in calculating the obligor's net family property, provided that this does not reduce his or her net family property to less than zero (see *Family Law Act, 1986,* S.O. 1986, c. 4, subsection 4(5)), and will be added to the creditor spouse's net family property for the purpose of effectuating the *prima facie* right to an equalization of the net family properties of each spouse. Consider the following examples involving unsecured creditors.

(i)   A husband has assets worth $20,000 but owes $10,000 to his wife, whose net family property (including the debt owed) is worth $20,000. In these circumstances, the husband has net family property with a value of $10,000 and he would be presumptively entitled to an equalization payment of $5,000.

(ii) A husband has no assets and owes his wife $10,000. He has no other debts. The wife owns assets of $20,000, which include the $10,000 owed to her. In these circumstances, the husband is entitled to $10,000 by way of an equalization payment, which will presumably be set off by the wife against his outstanding loan.

(iii) A husband has no assets but owes his wife $10,000 and his parents $30,000. The wife has assets of $20,000, if we include the debt of $10,000 owed to her. The husband's net family property is assessed at zero pursuant to subsection 4(5) of the Act. But what is the value of the wife's net family property in light of the fact that she is unlikely to recover the entirety of the loan?

7.12 Valuation of pre-marital property

In calculating the value of divisible property, the definition of "net family property" in subsection 4(1) of the *Family Law Act, 1986* requires the deduction of "(b) the value of property, other than a matrimonial home, that the spouse owned on the date of the marriage, after deducting the spouse's debts and other liabilities, calculated as of the date of the marriage": see *Dibbley v. Dibbley and Liddle* (1986), 5 R.F.L. (3d) 381 (Ont. S.C.), *supra*, subheading "Valuation of business; private companies". If pre-marital debts are still outstanding at the "valuation date", it is submitted that they should first be set-off under clause (b) against the value of pre-marital assets, other than a matrimonial home. If the pre-marital debts exceed the value of the pre-marital assets, they may then be set-off against the value of divisible property as of the date of the triggering event pursuant to clause (a) of the statutory definition of "net family property" in s. 4(1) of the Act: but see *contra, Jackson v. Jackson* (1986), 5 R.F.L. (3d) 8 (Ont. S.C.) and see *Menage v. Hedges,* unreported, June 8, 1987 (Ont. Unified Fam. Ct.) subheading 7.11 "Deduction of debts and liabilities". A spouse is clearly not entitled to deduct such debts twice in consequence of the separate provisions of clauses (a) and (b) of the statutory definition of "net family property" in subsection 4(1) of the *Family Law Act, 1986.*

In determining the value of pre-marital property, clause (b) requires that the value be "calculated as of the date of the marriage": see *Oliva v. Oliva* (1986), 2 R.F.L. (3d) 188 (Ont. S.C.). It is probable that the value of this exemption cannot be indexed to any depreciation in the purchasing power of the dollar between the date of marriage and the "valuation date" as defined in subsection 4(1) of the Act: see *Burgmaier v. Burgmaier* (1985), 47 R.F.L. (2d) 251 (Sask. Q.B.), considering *Farr v. Farr,* [1984] 1 S.C.R. 252, 35 Sask. R. 81, [1981] 4 W.W.R. 1, 52 N.R. 326, 7 D.L.R. (4th) 577, wherein the so-called "capital base" theory was rejected by reason of the express provisions of the *Matrimonial Property Act,* S.S. 1979, c. M-6.1. Consequently, any appreciation in the value of pre-marital property will be shared equally by the spouses on the valuation date, unless the court finds that this would be unconscionable having regard to subsection 5(6) of the Act, and particularly clause (h) thereof. Where the appreciation in value is attributable to extrinsic considerations, such as inflation or market conditions, subsection 5(6) of the Act presumably has no application because an equal sharing of the increased value between the spouses would not appear to be unconscionable. Conversely, where pre-marital property has depreciated in value between the date of the marriage and the "valuation date" by reason of extrinsic economic conditions, the title-holding spouse presumably remains entitled to a full deduction of the pre-marital value under clause (b) of the definition of "net family property" in subsection 4(1) of the Act, but clause 5(6)(h) of the Act might be deemed applicable in these circumstances.

Pursuant to the provisions of clause (b), *supra,* and paragraphs 4(2)1 and 4(2)5 of the *Family Law Act, 1986,* the value of a matrimonial home is included in the determination of the "net family property" of each spouse: compare *Kukolj v. Kukolj* (1986), 3 R.F.L. (3d) 359 (Ont. Unified Fam. Ct.), *supra,* 7.0 EQUALIZATION OF NET FAMILY PROPER-TIES, subheading 7.1 "General observations". It is immaterial under clause (b), *supra,* that the residence was owned by a spouse prior to the marriage, provided that the residence was occupied by the spouses as a family residence on the "valuation date" as defined in subsection 4(1) of the *Family Law Act, 1986: Folga v. Folga* (1986), 2 R.F.L. (3d) 358 (Ont. S.C.), *supra,* 7.0 EQUALIZATION OF NET FAMILY PROPERTIES, subheading 7.1 "General observations". Similarly, it is immaterial under paragraphs 4(2)1 and 4(2)5 of the Act that the matrimonial home was acquired by one of the spouses as a gift or inheritance from a third party after the date of the marriage or with the proceeds of such a gift or inheritance: *Harris v. Harris* (1986), 39 A.C.W.S. (2d) 68 (Ont. Dist. Ct.). The objective of these provisions may have been to ensure that the spouses will always share equally the value of the equity in the matrimonial home on marriage breakdown or death. This result generally ensued where marriage breakdown triggered a claim for the division of "family assets" under section 4 of the *Family Law Reform Act*, R.S.O. 1980, c. 152. In fact, no similar guarantee is assured under the *Family Law Act, 1986*. By way of illustration of the aforementioned statutory provisions, consider a husband who has $100,000 in cash at the date of his marriage and a wife who had no assets or debts or liabilities at that time. Shortly after the marriage, the husband purchases clear title to a matrimonial home in his own name for $100,000. Ten years later, the marriage breaks down and the matrimonial home is then worth $160,000. The spouses have no other assets. In this example, the husband's net family property would appear to be $160,000 and the wife's would be zero. The husband would not be entitled to deduct the value of his pre-marital property ($100,000 cash) from the value of the matrimonial home as of the valuation date (*i.e.* $160,000): see definition of "matrimonial home" in subsections 4(1) and (18)1 of the *Family Law Act, 1986* and see *Kukolj v. Kukolj, supra*. The wife would accordingly be presumptively entitled to an equalization payment of $80,000. Similarly, if the husband had purchased the matrimonial home in his own name with the $100,000 on the day before his marriage, his wife would presumptively be entitled to an equalization payment of $80,000. The same result would apparently ensue if the husband purchased the matrimonial home in his wife's name as a wedding gift on the day before or the day after their marriage. In either of these circumstances, assuming that the presumption of resulting trust under section 14 of the Act is rebutted by clear evidence of a gift, and subject to the application of subsection 5(6), particularly clauses (c) and (h), of the Act, the husband would receive no credit for the $100,000 invested in the home. This flows from the fact that clause (b) of the definition of "net family property" in subsection 4(1) of the Act only permits a *deduction* of the value of pre-marital assets, *other than a matrimonial home*, from the value of assets owned as of the valuation date or triggering event. Clause (b) does not permit a credit to be allocated where a spouse owned no assets as of the valuation date.

7.13 Excluded property

Subsections 4(2) and (3) of the *Family Law Act, 1986*, as amended by subsection 1(2) of the *Family Law Amendment Act*, S.O. 1986, c. 35, provide as follows:

Excluded property

4.—(2) **The value of the following property that a spouse owns on the valuation date does not form part of the spouse's net family property:**

1. **Property, other than a matrimonial home, that was acquired by gift or inheritance from a third person after the date of the marriage.**
2. **Income from property referred to in paragraph 1, if the donor or testator has expressly stated that it is to be excluded from the spouse's net family property.**
3. **Damages or a right to damages for personal injuries, nervous shock, mental distress or loss of guidance, care and companionship, or the part of a settlement that represents those damages.**
4. **Proceeds or a right to proceeds of a policy of life insurance, as defined in the *Insurance Act*, [R.S.O., 1980, c. 218] that are payable on the death of the life insured.**
5. **Property, other than a matrimonial home, into which property referred to in paragraphs 1 to 4 can be traced.**
6. **Property that the spouses have agreed by a domestic contract is not to be included in the spouse's net family property.**

(3) **The onus of proving a deduction under the definition of "net family property" or an exclusion under subsection (2) is on the person claiming it.**

7.13.1 *Property acquired by gift or inheritance*

The value of property, other than a matrimonial home, that is acquired by one of the spouses by way of a gift or inheritance from a third party after the marriage is excluded from the determination of that spouse's net family property: *Family Law Act, 1986*, paragraph 4(2)1.; see *Jackson v. Jackson* (1986), 5 R.F.L. (3d) 8 (Ont. S.C.) (Kent L.J.S.C.) and *Menage v. Hedges*, unreported, June 8, 1987 (Ont. Unified Fam. Ct.); see also *Rosenthal v. Rosenthal* (1986), 3 R.F.L. (3d) 126 (Ont. S.C.) (McMahon L.J.S.C.), *infra*, subheading, "7.13.5 Traceable property". Third party gifts or inheritances that are no longer owned or traceable by the recipient on the "valuation date" do not fall within the category of excluded property under paragraph 4(2)1 of the *Family Law*

Act, 1986: Rawluk v. Rawluk (1986), 55 O.R. (2d) 704, 29 D.L.R. (4th) 754, 3 R.F.L. (3d) 113 (S.C.); *Schaefer v. Schaefer* (1986), 38 A.C.W.S. (2d) 142 (Ont. S.C.); *Harris v. Harris* (1986), 39 A.C.W.S. (2d) 68 (Ont. Dist. Ct.); *Humphreys v. Humphreys,* unreported, April 24, 1987 (Ont. S.C.). It is submitted that the value of the excluded property is to be determined as of the valuation date and not as of the date of the gift: compare *Oliva v. Oliva* (1986), 2 R.F.L. (3d) 188 (Ont. S.C.).

The provisions of paragraph 4(1)1 of the Act do not encompass inter-spousal gifts: compare clause 5(6)(c) of the Act. Third party gifts or inheritances to both spouses will be included in a determination of their respective net family properties for the purpose of effectuating an equalization or apportionment under section 5; their interests therein will not be determined simply on the basis of ownership pursuant to an application under section 10 of the Act: see *Keast v. Keast* (1986), 1 R.F.L. (3d) 401, at 407 (Ont. Dist. Ct.); *Ganz v. Ganz and Ganz,* unreported, June 4, 1986 (Ont. S.C.); *Nemish v. Nemish,* unreported, August 11, 1986 (Ont. S.C.).

Paragraph 4(2)5 of the *Family Law Act, 1986* makes it abundantly clear that the exclusion under paragraph 4(2)1 has no application to third party post-marital gifts or inheritances to the extent that they have been invested in a matrimonial home: *Harris v. Harris* (1986), 39 A.C.W.S. (2d) 68 (Ont. Dist. Ct.); *Nemish v. Nemish, supra.*

7.13.2 *Interest from third party post-marital gift and inheritance*

Subject to the express contrary intention of the donor or testator, the income generated by third party post-marital gifts or inheritances is subject to inclusion in the determination of the net family property of the recipient spouse, provided that such income has not been spent on untraceable assets: see *Family Law Act, 1986,* paragraphs 4(2)2 and 4(2)5 The word "income" in paragraph 4(2)2 does not apparently include any appreciation in the capital value of the property received by gift or inheritance that is unconnected with the use of income generated by such property: compare *Oliva v. Oliva* (1986), 2 R.F.L. (3d) 188 (Ont. S.C.). If the gift or inheritance is retained *in specie,* and it is not a matrimonial home, its value will not form part of the spouse's net family property and a similar exclusion presumably applies under paragraph 4(2)5 to any substituted property, other than a matrimonial home, that is traceable to the gift or inheritance.

The right of the donor or testator to expressly stipulate that income from the gift or inheritance shall be excluded from the recipient's net family property is specifically recognized by paragraph 4(2)2 of the Act and will no doubt impact on the drafting of relevant documents or wills. In the absence of an express stipulation, the intention of the donor or testator is presumably irrelevant for the purposes of paragraph 4(2)2 of the *Family Law Act, 1986*, even though the gift or inheritance was received prior to the commencement of the Act: see *Oliva v. Oliva, supra*, at pp. 205-06.

7.13.3 Damages

Paragraph 4(2)3 of the Act could be construed to exclude from a spouse's net family property any damages awarded for injury to the person, including that portion of the award that represents compensation for a future loss of income. Logically, all payments received by way of workers' compensation benefits should be similarly excluded, although it may be technically improper to characterize such benefits as representing "damages". The exclusion of damages for lost wages and worker's compensation benefits would be consistent with the objectives of the *Family Law Act, 1986*, which is directed towards the equalization of the net family property of the spouses and not towards the equalization of their future income or its equivalent. Surely, damages awarded in an inter-spousal tort action should not be shared by the spouses under the statutory equalization formula, subject to the overriding discretion of the court under clause 5(6)(h) of the Act or subject to their possible indirect recovery by way of a spousal support order. A restrictive and contrary literal interpretation of paragraph 4(2)3 of the *Family Law Act, 1986* may receive some support, however, from the judgments of the Manitoba courts in *Dixon v. Dixon* (1981), 14 Man. R. (2d) 40, 25 R.F.L. (2d) 266 (Co. Ct.), *Hilderman v. Hilderman* (1985), 45 R.F.L. (2d) 190 (Man. Q.B.) and *Pollock v. Pollock* (1985), 37 Man. R. (2d) 161 (Q.B.). These decisions justify a distinction being drawn between damages or worker's compensation received for "physical loss" and those received for "economic loss". In *Hilderman v. Hilderman, supra*, at 192-93, Carr J. observed:

> I understand Mr. Hilderman (in his own way) to be relying on the provisions of s. 8(1) of the [*Marital Property*] Act. That section provides:
> "8(1) This Act does not apply to the proceeds of any damage award or settlement or insurance claim made in favour of a spouse for personal injury, or disability, except to the extent that the proceeds are compensation for loss to both spouses."
> Mrs. Hilderman argues that the moneys received do not constitute a "damage award or settlement or insurance claim" and are therefore not excluded from the application of the Act.
> I am inclined to the view that the proceeds do fall within the section and I reach that conclusion because of the nature of the particular settlement in this case. Mr. Hilderman testified that his settlement, unlike some, was not compensation for lost wages. A claim under the Workers Compensation Act, C.C.S.M., c. W200, can be for lost wages. Such was the case with the award that was considered in *Dixon v. Dixon*

(1981), 25 R.F.L. (2d) 266, 14 Man. R. (2d) 40 (Co. Ct.). There, Ferg Co. Ct. J. (as he then was) held that the husband's workers' compensation award was not excluded from sharing because it represented lost wages. The learned trial judge held, at p. 43:

damages for "economic" loss must be included in net family property

"loss of income" component

"To come within this section [section 8(1)], the monies would have to be classified as a damage award, a settlement or an insurance claim, for personal injury or disability, but I am satisfied the monies are not in one of those classes. Workers' Compensation is paid to partially replace lost wages due to injury on the job. It is not, as argued, insurance, nor is it damages, nor is it a settlement. If the legislature had intended to exclude workers compensation payments from shareability between spouses, then it could have, and indeed should have, so specified. It did not do so. Philosophically or equitably, this makes sense since compensation is paid to replace lost wages, and would in the ordinary course go into the family pot to pay for ordinary living expenses."

If Mr. Hilderman's evidence is accepted — and it was not seriously challenged in this regard — his award is of a different kind than the award contemplated by Ferg Co. Ct. J. in the *Dixon* case, *supra*. In fact, the award to Mr. Hilderman had nothing at all to do with lost wages nor can I accept that it relates to future earnings. Rather, it was an award under s. 32(1) of the Workers Compensation Act, which section provides as follows:

"32(1) Where permanent partial disability results from the injury, the board shall allow compensation in periodical payments during the lifetime of the workman sufficient, in the opinion of the board, to compensate for the physical loss occasioned by the disability, but not exceeding seventy-five per cent of his average earnings."

This is one of the few sections in the Act that speaks to the question of for what the compensation is paid. Most sections simply deal with how a loss is to be quantified. Section 32(1) speaks of "physical loss" and an award of this kind is, in my view, akin to a personal injury claim. Mr. Hilderman brought home the nature of the award when, to paraphrase his evidence he stated: If she wants to share the award, let her share the disability.

I am therefore prepared to conclude that the workers' compensation award in this case is the kind of award contemplated by the provisions of s. 8(1) of the [*Marital Property*] Act [C.C.S.M., c. F-20]. . . .

Compare *Webb v. Webb* (1985), 70 B.C.L.R. 15, 49 R.F.L. (2d) 279 (S.C.); *Williams v. Follack et al.* (1986), 2 B.C.L.R. (2d) 298, 27 D.L.R. (4th) 299 (S.C.); *Smith v. Smith* (1986), 1 R.F.L. (3d) 219 (B.C.S.C.) and *Young v. Young* (1986), 5 R.F.L. (3d) 337 (B.C.S.C.) (McKinnon L.J.S.C.).

● It is submitted that the following opinion of Montgomery J. in *de Champlain v. de Champlain*, though made in the context of an application to restrain the husband's dissipation of damages awarded to his disabled spouse, thus exemplifying the maxim "better safe than sorry", is to be preferred to the approach adopted by the Manitoba courts. In *de Champlain v. de Champlain* (1986), 2 R.F.L. (3d) 22, at 23 (Ont. S.C.) Montgomery J. stated:

This act is remedial in nature. It should therefore be broadly interpreted. In my opinion, "damages" in s. 4(2)3 includes both special and general damages; it includes past and future loss of income, future care cost, general damages for pain,

Champlain v. C [handwritten margin note]
Ontario + approach [handwritten margin note]

suffering and loss of amenities of life. It encompasses all heads of damages that might be awarded by a court and those heads of damages for which settlement is negotiated in personal injury cases.

o income component (excluded) [handwritten margin note]
o damage component [handwritten margin note]

It was with considerable surprise that I heard this motion since I was the trial judge who awarded Deborah in excess of $2,000,000 in a medical malpractice action in September 1985. With the exception of Family Law Reform Act awards to the husband, child and Deborah's parents the entire award was to Deborah and constitutes damages within the meaning of s. 4(2)3 of the Act.

Manitoba [handwritten margin note]
o damage component only [handwritten margin note]

For a valuable commentary on divergent judicial opinions in the United States, see Kathy P. Holder, "In Sickness and in Health? Disability Benefits as Marital Property" (1985-86), 24 J. Fam. Law 657.

o income component (included) [handwritten margin note]

7.13.4 Life insurance policies

The provisions of paragraph 4(2)4 of the *Family Law Act, 1986* should be examined in the context of section 6, and particularly, subsections (4), (6) and (6a): see *infra*, 9.0 ENTITLEMENT ON DEATH, subheading 9.3 "Election by surviving spouse". See generally, Maurice C. Cullity, "The Family Law Act, 1986: Estates and Estate Planning", The Law Society of Upper Canada Continuing Education Program, *The New Family Law Act — For Solicitors*, March 4, 1986, especially pp. 30-32. Paragraph 4(2)4, unlike subsection 6(6), of the Act is of general application in that it is not confined to a life insurance policy "taken out on the life of the deceased spouse" and "owned by the deceased spouse".

Although the proceeds or a right to the proceeds of a life insurance policy are excluded from the net family property of either spouse, the court has the authority under subclause 34(1)(i) of the *Family Law Act, 1986*, in the context of support proceedings, to make an *inter vivos* interim or final order requiring a spouse with a life insurance policy to designate the other spouse or a child as the irrevocable beneficiary under that policy.

s. 34 1(i) [handwritten margin note]
court can order you to make spouse beneficiary in support context [handwritten margin note]

7.13.5 Traceable property

Where the value of property is excluded from the determination of a spouse's net family property under paragraphs 4(2)1 to 4 of the Act, a similar exclusion applies under paragraph 4(2)5 to any traceable substituted property: see *Schaefer v. Schaefer* (1986), 38 A.C.W.S. (2d) 142 (Ont. S.C.) wherein tracing was effectuated, notwithstanding that the property had not been segregated so as to establish a direct link to the original gifts and inheritances.

In *Rosenthal v. Rosenthal* (1986), 3 R.F.L. (3d) 126 (Ont. S.C.) (McMahon L.J.S.C.), a direct transfer of shares from the husband's employer to the husband by way of gift was excluded from the husband's "net family property" pursuant to paragraphs 4(2)1 and 4(2)5 of the *Family Law Act, 1986*. But subsequent transfers for which the employer was entitled to payment by way of demand notes were held to fall outside the ambit of the aforementioned paragraphs, notwithstanding the employer's subsequent forgiveness of the debt. This conclusion was reached on the basis that the doctrine of tracing incorporates the notion of tracing forwards but not tracing backwards. Accordingly, the subsequent forgiveness of the debt did not convert the sale into a gift. The trial judge further concluded that the husband was estopped from asserting that the transfers were sales for the purpose of avoiding gift tax but were gifts for the purpose of an equalization claim under Part I of the *Family Law Act, 1986*.

It is submitted that *Rosenthal v. Rosenthal, supra*, did not technically involve a "tracing" problem. Of more serious import, however, is the question whether inherently complex equitable tracing principles, which evolved in the context of the administration of trusts, should be applied to inter-spousal claims under Part I of the *Family Law Act, 1986*. It remains to be seen whether Ontario courts will apply traditional equitable doctrines of tracing (see generally, D.W.M. Waters, *The Law of Trusts in Canada*, 2nd ed., 1984) or whether innovative judicial doctrines will emerge, as they have in community property jurisdictions in the United States, in order to functionally address the overall objectives of Part I of the *Family Law Act, 1986* (see, for example, P. Bell, "The Evolution of the Community-Out-First Presumption: A Matter of Trust" (1983), 24 S. Tex. L.J. 191 and L. Gach, "The Mix-Hicks Mix: Tracing Troubles under California's Community Property System" (1978-79), 26 U.C.L.A. Law Rev. 1231).

7.13.6 *Property excluded by domestic contract*

Pursuant to paragraph 4(2)6 of the *Family Law Act, 1986*, spouses may exclude any property from their "net family property" by the terms of a domestic contract, as defined in section 51 of the Act. Paragraph 4(2)6 co-exists with subsection 2(10) of the Act, which provides that "[a] domestic contract dealing with a matter that is also dealt with in this Act prevails unless this Act provides otherwise": see *Puopolo v. Puopolo* (1986), 2 R.F.L. (3d) 73 (Ont. S.C.); *Gleadall v. Gleadall*, unreported, April 23, 1986 (Ont. S.C.).

Not all spousal agreements constitute "domestic contracts" as defined and regulated by Part IV of the *Family Law Act, 1986*: see, for example, *Miller v. Miller*, [1984] 2 S.C.R. 310, 41 R.F.L. (2d) 273, affg 39 O.R. (2d) 74, 139 D.L.R. (3d) 128, 29 R.F.L. (2d) 395 (C.A.); compare clause 5(6)(g) of the *Family Law Act, 1986*.

° The provisions of paragraph 4(2)6 of the *Family Law Act, 1986* being confined to "[a] domestic contract dealing with a matter *that is also dealt with in this Act*", are insufficiently broad to encompass contractual terms regulating federal pension benefits. The same may be true of subsection 2(10) of the *Family Law Act, 1986*, which provides that "[a] domestic contract *dealing with a matter that is also dealt with in this Act* prevails unless this Act provides otherwise". In *Minister of National Health and Welfare v. Preece*, Canadian Employment Benefits and Pension Guide Reports, CCH, No. 8914, where spouses had executed separation agreements which included general releases purporting to waive all present and future property claims, these covenants were upheld as incidental to the principle of contractual autonomy in the absence of any express statutory provision to the contrary. Similar consequences have ensued from a final and comprehensive judicial disposition of inter-spousal property claims: *Carricato v. Minister of National Health and Welfare*, Canadian Employment Benefits and Pension Guide Reports, CCH, No. 8935; compare *Flesch v. Minister of National Health and Welfare*, Canadian Employment Benefits and Pension Guide Reports, CCH, No. 8931. Recent amendments to the governing federal legislation necessitates, however, a review of the current legal position. Although spousal agreements executed prior to June 4, 1986, may preclude a division of Canada Pension Plan credits, agreements executed on or after June 4, 1986, are now expressly regulated by section 23 of *An Act to Amend the Canada Pension Plan and the Federal Court Act*, S.C. 1986, c. 38. Relevant provisions of this section read as follows:

23. The said Act is further amended by adding thereto, immediately after section 53.2 thereof, the following heading and sections:

Division of Unadjusted Pensionable
Earnings

. . .

Definition of "spousal agreement"
53.4 (1) In this section, "spousal agreement" means
(a) a pre-marriage agreement between spouses-to-be, which agreement is to take effect on marriage; or
(b) an agreement between spouses or former spouses, including a separation agreement, entered into
    (i) before the day of any application made under section 53.2 or 53.3, or
    (ii) for the purpose of a division under paragraph 53.3(1)(a), before the issuance of the decree absolute of divorce, judgment granting a divorce under the *Divorce Act, 1985* or judgment of nullity of the marriage as the case may be.

[Handwritten margin note:] "domestic contract" can't avoid pension sharing if pension governed by Federal Act

Spousal agreement or court order not binding on Minister

(2) Except as provided in subsection (3), where a spousal agreement was entered into or a court order was made on or after June 4, 1986, the provisions of that spousal agreement or court order are not binding on the Minister for the purposes of a division of unadjusted pensionable earnings under section 53.2 or 53.3.

Spousal agreement binding on Minister

(3) Where

(a) a spousal agreement entered into on or after June 4, 1986 contains a provision that expressly mentions this Act and indicates the intention of the spouses or former spouses that there be no division of unadjusted pensionable earnings under section 53.2 or 53.3,

(b) that provision of the spousal agreement is expressly permitted under the provincial law that governs the spousal agreement, and

(c) that provision of the spousal agreement has not been invalidated by a court order,

the Minister shall not make a division under section 53.2 or 53.3.

Clauses 53.4(3)(a) and (c), *supra*, are self-explanatory. General release clauses in an otherwise valid spousal contract, which make no specific reference to the Canada Pension Plan legislation, will no longer be binding on the Minister for the purpose of ousting the spousal right to a division of credits under the Canada Pension Plan (see s. 53.4(2) and 53.4(3)(a), *supra*), if the spousal agreement was made on or after June 4, 1986. Clause 53.4(3)(b) raises interpretational problems insofar as the *Family Law Act, 1986* makes no specific reference to the impact of contracting out on any federal statutory rights, or indeed on any provincial statutory rights arising other than by way of the *Family Law Act, 1986*. Arguably, clause 53.4(3)(b) necessitates an express reference to the Canada Pension Plan legislation to be included in the *Family Law Act, 1986* in order for any contracting out of the division of credits to be effective. Certainly, subsections 4(2) and (6) and subsection 2(10) of the *Family Law Act, 1986* are insufficiently broad at the present time to encompass the Canada Pension Plan, by reason of their express confinement to "a matter that is also dealt with in this Act". Different considerations may apply to other federal statutory pension schemes: see, for example, the *Pension Benefits Standards Act*, S.C. 1986, c. 40, section 25, which now permits an inter-spousal assignment of benefits for plan members but provides for the general application of "provincial property law".

8.0 UNEQUAL DIVISION OF NET FAMILY PROPERTIES

8.1 Judicial discretion based on unconscionability

Variation of share *discretion*

5.—(6) The court may award a spouse an amount that is more or less than half the difference between the net family properties if the court is of the opinion that equalizing the net family properties would be unconscionable, having regard to,

    (a) a spouse's failure to disclose to the other spouse debts or other liabilities existing at the date of the marriage;

    (b) the fact that debts or other liabilities claimed in reduction of a spouse's net family property were incurred recklessly or in bad faith;

    (c) the part of a spouse's net family property that consists of gifts made by the other spouse; *inter-spousal gifts*

    (d) a spouse's intentional or reckless depletion of his or her net family property;

    (e) the fact that the amount a spouse would otherwise receive under subsection (1), (2) or (3) is disproportionately large in relation to a period of cohabitation that is less than five years;

    (f) the fact that one spouse has incurred a disproportionately larger amount of debts or other liabilities than the other spouse for the support of the family;

    (g) a written agreement between the spouses that is not a domestic contract; or

    (h) any other circumstance relating to the acquisition, disposition, preservation, maintenance or improvement of property.

Pursuant to subsection 5(6), *supra*, the court is empowered to deviate from the norm of an equalization of the net family properties of the spouses. Deviation from the norm may be ordered, however, only where equalization would be unconscionable *and* such unconscionability arises by reason of one or more of the factors specifically identified in clauses (a) to (h) of subsection 5(6): *Magee v. Magee* (1987), 6 R.F.L. (3d) 453 (Ont. Unified Fam. Ct.). In the words of Galligan J. in *Skrlj v. Skrlj* (1986), 2 R.F.L. (3d) 305, at 309 (Ont. S.C.):

s. 5(6) Unequal property sharing only if unconscionable plus link it to one of factors in s. 5(6)

> As I read the *Family Law Act, 1986*, it leaves the court with no discretion to decide spouses' affairs in accordance with a particular court's sense of fairness. Subject to a discretion if it finds "unconscionability," under s. 5(6), the courts must decide the rights of separating spouses in strict compliance with the terms of the Act, even if, in

an individual case, a judge may feel that the result does not appear fair according to that particular judge's sense of fairness. I think the legislature has clearly expressed its intent to remove judicial discretion from property disputes between separating spouses.

After reiterating these observations in his later judgment in *Humphreys v. Humphreys* (1987), 7 R.F.L. (3d) 113 (Ont. S.C.), Galligan J. observed:

> Counsel has not brought to my attention any appellate court decision, nor any decision of a court of concurrent jurisdiction which suggests that 'Palm Tree Justice' is back.

The use of the term "unconscionable" implies that the court should not interfere with the right to an equalization of the net family properties in the absence of compelling circumstances that shock the conscience of the court: see *Kelly v. Kelly* (1986), 50 R.F.L. (2d) 360 (Ont. S.C.). The onus of proving unconscionability within the meaning of subsection 5(6) of the *Family Law Act, 1986*, falls on the party asserting it and the term "unconscionable" will be given a strict, not a liberal, interpretation: *Crane v. Crane* (1986), 3 R.F.L. (3d) 428 (Ont. S.C.) (Mossop L.J.S.C.). The term "unconscionable" signifies a threshold whereby an unequal re-apportionment of the difference in value between the "net family property" of each spouse may be ordered, where to do otherwise would be "patently unfair" or "inordinately inequitable": *Sullivan v. Sullivan* (1986), 5 R.F.L. (3d) 28 (Ont. Unified Fam. Ct.); compare *Scott v. Scott* (1987), 6 R.F.L. (3d) 422 (Ont. Dist. Ct.). Subsection 5(6) of the *Family Law Act, 1986* "was intended to resolve patently unconscionable situations and only within the carefully stipulated criteria set forth in clauses (*a*) to (*h*) therein. The use of the word 'unconscionable' . . . expressly precludes resort to this [subsection] unless the imbalance to be addressed is shockingly unfair and one that simply cannot be left as it is.": *Magee v. Magee* (1987), 6 R.F.L. (3d) 453 (Ont. Unified Fam. Ct.) (per Goodearle U.F.C.J.); and see *supra*, 7.0 EQUALIZATION OF NET FAMILY PROPERTIES, subheading 7.5 "University degrees; professional licences; goodwill". In determining whether an equalization of the net family properties of the spouses would be unconscionable, the court may be entitled to look at the total effect and results of any dispositions made in the current or corollary actions: see *Kelly v. Kelly, supra*, referring to *Mance v. Mance* (1980), 22 R.F.L. (2d) 445 (Ont. Co. Ct.) and *Woods v. Woods* (1975), 22 R.F.L. 370 (Ont. S.C.). An equalization of the differential in value of the spousal net family properties may be deemed "unconscionable" by reason of a spouse's neglect of his or her responsibilities for the economic and social welfare of the family or the wholly disproportionate contribution of one spouse to child care, household management and financial provision as compared to that of the other spouse: *McCutcheon v. McCutcheon* (1986),

2 R.F.L. (3d) 327 (Ont. Dist. Ct.); *Sullivan v. Sullivan, supra; Moniz v. Moniz*, unreported, September 11, 1986 (Ont. S.C.); compare *Crane v. Crane, supra*.

The language of subsection 5(6) of the *Family Law Act, 1986* appears to be sufficiently broad to permit the court to award a spouse all or any part of the other spouse's net family property.

8.1.1 *Undisclosed pre-marital debts or liabilities*

Pursuant to the definition of "net family property" in clause 4(1)(b) of the *Family Law Act, 1986*, pre-marital debts or other liabilities that are still outstanding on the "valuation date" are deducted from the value of the divisible property of the obligated spouse: see text *supra*, subheading 7.12 "Valuation of pre-marital property". Where such debts or other liabilities were not disclosed to the other spouse prior to their marriage, injustice could obviously result from an equalization of their net family properties. Clause 5(6)(a) of the *Family Law Act, 1986* provides a means whereby such injustice may be averted by a court order for an unequal apportionment of the difference between the net family property of each spouse. Such apportionment must satisfy, however, the general criterion of unconscionability set out in subsection 5(6).

[handwritten margin note: failure to disclose pre-marital debts and liabilities may lead unequal division of property.]

8.1.2 *Debts or other liabilities incurred recklessly or in bad faith*

The right to deduct spousal debts and other liabilities from the net family property of the obligated spouse is expressly recognized by the definition of "net family property" in subsection 4(1) of the *Family Law Act, 1986*. To off-set the unconscionability that could result from an equalization of the net family property of each spouse, where the debts or other liabilities were incurred recklessly or in bad faith, clause 5(6)(b) empowers the court to order an unequal apportionment between the spouses of their respective net family properties. Clause 5(6)(b) can only be invoked where the debts or other liabilities of the obligated spouse were incurred either recklessly or in bad faith. The negligent mismanagement of business affairs falls outside the ambit of clause 5(6)(b), although it might conceivably be brought in through the back door by reliance on clause (h) of subsection 5(6): see *Dibbley v. Dibbley and Liddle* (1987), 5 R.F.L. (3d) 381, at 396 (Ont. S.C.); compare *Scott v. Scott* (1987), 6 R.F.L. (3d) 422 (Ont. Dist. Ct.).

[handwritten margin note: Negligent not enough but try 6(h) "... any other circumstance]

8.1.3 *Inter-spousal gifts*

Inter-spousal gifts form part of a spouse's net family property. Only gifts from third parties are excluded from a spouse's net family property under paragraph 4(2)1. of the *Family Law Act, 1986*: see text *supra*, subheading 7.13 "Excluded property". Pursuant to clause 5(6)(c) of the Act, the court may order an unequal apportionment of the difference between the net family property of each spouse, if unconscionable results would ensue from an equalization of their net family properties, having regard to the nature or value of any inter-spousal gifts. In *Bregman v. Bregman*, unreported, December 18, 1986 (Ont. S.C.), Walsh J. concluded that clause 5(6)(c) of the *Family Law Act, 1986* could be invoked where the wife purchased the matrimonial home out of funds received on the death of her first husband with no contribution from her present husband, whose own substantial assets could have been made available to assist in the purchase.

qut vestraining s. 12 order

8.1.4 Depletion of net family property

Pursuant to clause 5(6)(d) of the *Family Law Act, 1986*, the court may deviate from the norm of equalization of the net family properties of each spouse, where this would produce unconscionable results by reason of a spouse's intentional or reckless depletion of his or her net family property. Unlike subsection 5(3) of the Act, clause 5(6)(d) is confined in its application to circumstances where the improvident depletion of a spouse's net family property is intentional or reckless. Carelessness in the management of property would thus appear to be insufficient to warrant the application of clause 5(6)(d). What is required is wilful conduct that is intended to defeat or prejudice the rights of the other spouse in his or her pursuit of an equalization claim or reckless conduct whereby the culpable spouse is indifferent as to its effect on the other spouse's statutory rights. Compare *Family Law Act, 1986*, clause 5(6)(h), *infra*, subheading "8.1.8 Any circumstance relating to the acquisition, disposition or management of property"; see also *supra*, subheading "8.1.2 Debts or other liabilities incurred recklessly or in bad faith"; and see *Dibbley v. Dibbley and Liddle, supra*.

Must be intentional depletion Otherwise try - s. 5(6) h

8.1.5 Duration of cohabitation

Pursuant to clause 5(6)(e) of the *Family Law Act, 1986*, the court may order an unequal apportionment of the difference between the net family property of each spouse, where equalization would produce unconscionable results by yielding a disproportionately large allocation to a spouse having regard to the circumstance that cohabitation continued for less than five years. The provisions of clause 5(6)(e) cannot apparently be invoked where the period of cohabitation has exceeded five years. Whether "cohabitation" within the meaning of clause 5(6)(e) refers only to "matrimonial cohabitation" or includes any period of "pre-marital cohabitation will require elucidation. The exclusion of pre-marital cohabitation from the calculation of the designated five-year period would be consistent with the definition of "spouse" in subsection 1(1) of the *Family Law Act, 1986*, whereby unmarried cohabitants are excluded from any section 5 entitlement, but would fly in the face of the definition of "cohabit" in subsection 1(1) of the Act.

8.1.6 *Debts and other liabilities incurred for support of family*

An unequal judicial apportionment of the difference between the value of the spousal net family properties may be ordered pursuant to clause 5(6)(f) of the *Family Law Act, 1986*, if equalization would be unconscionable having regard to "the fact that one spouse has incurred a disproportionately larger amount of debts or other liabilities than the other spouse for the support of the family". Clause 5(6)(f) is presumably confined to debts or other liabilities that are still outstanding. It is not, however, expressly restricted to third party debts or liabilities: compare *Hammermeister v. Hammermeister* (1980), 5 Sask. R. 137, 19 R.F.L. (3d) 301 *sub nom. Spicer v. Hammermeister* (Q.B.). The language of clause 5(6)(f) is, therefore, sufficiently broad to take account of existing consensual or court-ordered family support rights and obligations. An order for unequal apportionment might seem appropriate where family dependants have a continuing need for periodic support and an equalization of the difference between the net family property of each spouse would be insufficient to accommodate that need and would in addition undermine the future ability of a spouse to pay support to his or her dependants. But in *Kelly v. Kelly* (1986), 50 R.F.L. (2d) 360, at 366 (Ont. S.C.), Potts J. was of the opinion that "debts or other liabilities" under clause 5(6)(f) and "other circumstances" under clause 5(6)(h) of the *Family Law Act, 1986* refer to debts or other liabilities and other circumstances in existence prior to, or as of, the date of separation. Even if one prefers the opinion of Professor James G. McLeod (Annotation to *Kelly v. Kelly, supra*, at 361) that such a restrictive interpretation of clauses 5(6)(f) and (h) is not "required in light of the language of the Act" and that the court may take account of circumstances arising between the date of separation and the date of adjudication, the words "has incurred" in clause 5(6)(f) imply that court-ordered future support payments are to be ignored in determining whether an equalization of the net family property of each spouse would be unconscionable: see text *supra*, subheading 7.11 "Deduction of debts and liabilities". Perhaps, the balancing of property and support entitlements in these circumstances could be achieved by an order deferring the property entitlement under the authority conferred on the court by clause 9(1)(c) of the *Family Law*

Act, 1986. Any equalization or balancing payment must, however, be wholly discharged within the designated statutory period of ten years.

8.1.7 Written agreement

Pursuant to clause 5(6)(g) of the *Family Law Act, 1986*, an unequal judicial apportionment of the difference between the net family property of each spouse may be ordered, where equalization would be unconscionable in light of a written agreement between the spouses that does not constitute a domestic contract. An improperly constituted "domestic contract" that fails to comply with the formal requirements of section 55 of the *Family Law Act, 1986* may presumably satisfy the requirements of clause 5(6)(g) of the Act: compare *Burton v. Burton* (1981), 24 R.F.L. (2d) 238 (Ont. C.A.). Indeed the words "written agreement" are sufficiently broad to encompass any mutual arrangements that have been reduced to writing by the spouses, regardless of whether these arrangements constitute a legally binding contract under established principles of the Law of Contracts.

8.1.8 Any other circumstance relating to the acquisition, disposition or management of property

An unequal judicial apportionment of the difference between the net family property of each spouse may be ordered under clause 5(6)(h) of the *Family Law Act, 1986*, where equalization would be unconscionable having regard to "any other circumstance relating to the acquisition, disposition, preservation, maintenance or improvement of property". Clause 5(6)(h) should be read in light of subsection 5(7) of the Act, which provides as follows:

> **Purpose**
> **5.—(7) The purpose of this section is to recognize that child care, household management and financial provision are the joint responsibilities of the spouses and that inherent in the marital relationship there is equal contribution, whether financial or otherwise, by the spouses to the assumption of these responsibilities, entitling each spouse to the equalization of the net family properties, subject only to the equitable considerations set out in subsection (6).**

↳ s. 5(6) unequal division if "unconscionable

The language of clause 5(6)(h) and subsection 5(7) of the *Family Law Act, 1986* is modelled on the language of clause 4(4)(f) and subsection 4(5) of the *Family Law Reform Act*, R.S.O. 1980, c. 152. It accordingly appears that clause 5(6)(h) of the *Family Law Act, 1986* cannot be invoked to justify an unequal apportionment of the difference between the net family property of each spouse merely by reason of a traditional division of functions between spouses whereby one spouse discharges the responsibilities of homemaker and the other spouse those of the breadwinner. Thus in *Young v. Young* (1981), 32 O.R. (2d) 19, 120 D.L.R. (3d) 662, 21 R.F.L. (2d) 388, at 392-393 (C.A.), Wilson J.A. observed:

> I do not think the legislature intended in s. 4(5) of the [Family Law Reform] Act to prescribe the type of lifestyle a couple must adopt in order to qualify for equality of division of family assets under s. 4(1). It cannot have been intended that, where the wife occupies the traditional role of homemaker and mother and the husband that of bread-winner, the prima facie rule of equality must necessarily be overset. Indeed, the intention of the legislature as expressed in s. 4(5) seems to me to be quite otherwise. Three things are mentioned in the subsection as constituting joint responsibilities of the spouses — child care, household management and financial provision. It is further stated that joint contribution towards these responsibilities is "inherent in the marital relationship" and entitles each spouse to an equal division of family assets. I do not think this means that each spouse need contribute equally to the discharge of each of these responsibilities and that every husband who puts more into his career than he does into his family is in peril of inequality. Conversely, I do not think the wife is exposed to unequal division because she elects to be a full-time homemaker and contributes little to the financial provision for the family. The subsection was not, in my view, intended as an invitation to counsel and the courts to go into the niceties of the evidence as to the performance of the respective spouses in each of these three areas. I think rather that the subsection was intended to express the legislative rationale for the prima facie equal division under subs. (1), namely, that marriage is a mutual affair and that each party is expected to pull his or her weight in discharging the totality of the responsibilities.

An unequal apportionment of the difference between the family net property of each spouse may, nevertheless, be justified where a spouse, without just cause, fails to discharge his or her marital responsibilities as defined in subsection 5(7) of the *Family Law Act, 1986*: compare *Robinson v. Robinson* (1982), 28 R.F.L. (2d) 342, at 346-347 (Sask. Q.B.); *Bray v. Bray* (1979), 16 R.F.L. (2d) 78 (Ont. Co. Ct.); *Grime v. Grime* (1980), 16 R.F.L. (2d) 365 (Ont. S.C.); and see *McCutcheon v. McCutcheon, Sullivan v. Sullivan* and *Moniz v. Moniz, supra,* subheading 8.1 "Judicial discretion based on unconscionability".

In *Kelly v. Kelly* (1986), 50 R.F.L. (2d) 360 (Ont. S.C.), wherein the husband's property depreciated in value between the date of separation and the date of adjudication, the court held the wife entitled to an equal share of its value as of the date of separation. The existence of a preservation order that precluded the husband from disposing of the property was held to be of no consequence in the absence of any evidence indicating the husband's desire to sell the property. Potts J. concluded that it would not be unconscionable if no adjustment were made to take account of the depreciation in value of the property. Potts J. further observed (at p. 366):

53

Moreover, even if I had decided that it was unconscionable, I seriously doubt that s. 5(6) has any application because valuation is determined as of the date of separation and "debts or other liabilities" mentioned in para. (*f*) and "other circumstances" mentioned in para. (*h*) refer to debts or other liabilities and other circumstances in existence prior to, or as of, the date of separation. There are no transitional provisions in the Family Law Act which would apply in these circumstances.

For criticism of these observations, see James G. McLeod, Annotation to *Kelly v. Kelly, supra*, at 361; see text, *supra*.

9.0 ENTITLEMENT ON DEATH

9.1 Relevant statutory provisions

Subsection 5(2) and section 6 of the *Family Law Act, 1986*, as amended by S.O. 1986, c. 35, s. 2, (by repealing and substituting subsec. 6(6), by adding new subsec. 6(6a) and by repealing cl. 6(8)(b)) provide as follows:

Equalization of net family properties
5.—(2) when a spouse dies, if the net family property of the deceased spouse exceeds the net family property of the surviving spouse, the surviving spouse is entitled to one-half the difference between them.

Election: spouse's will
6.—(1) When a spouse dies leaving a will, the surviving spouse shall elect to take under the will or to receive the entitlement under section 5.

Idem: spouse's intestacy
(2) When a spouse dies intestate, the surviving spouse shall elect to receive the entitlement under Part II of the *Succession Law Reform Act* [R.S.O. 1980, c. 488], or to receive the entitlement under section 5.

Idem: spouse's partial intestacy
(3) When a spouse dies testate as to some property and intestate as to other property, the surviving spouse shall elect to take under the will and to receive the entitlement under Part II of the *Succession Law Reform Act*, or to receive the entitlement under section 5.

Property outside estate
(4) A surviving spouse who elects to take under the will or to receive the entitlement under Part II of the *Succession Law Reform Act*, or both in the case of a partial intestacy, shall also receive the

other property to which he or she is entitled because of the first spouse's death.

Gifts by will

(5) The surviving spouse shall receive the gifts made to him or her in the deceased spouse's will in addition to the entitlement under section 5 if the will expressly provides for that result.

Insurance, etc.

(6) Where a surviving spouse,

(a) is the beneficiary,

(i) of a policy of life insurance, as defined in the *Insurance Act*, [R.S.O. 1980, c. 218], that was taken out on the life of the deceased spouse and owned by the deceased spouse or was taken out on the lives of a group of which he or she was a member, or

(ii) of a lump sum payment provided under a pension or similar plan on the death of the deceased spouse; and

(b) elects or has elected to receive the entitlement under section 5,

the payment under the policy or plan shall be credited against the surviving spouse's entitlement under section 5, unless a written designation by the deceased spouse provides that the surviving spouse shall receive payment under the policy or plan in addition to the entitlement under section 5.

Idem

(6a) If a surviving spouse,

(a) elects or has elected to receive the entitlement under section 5; and

(b) receives payment under a life insurance policy or a lump sum payment provided under a pension or similar plan that is in excess of the entitlement under section 5,

and there is no written designation by the deceased spouse described in subsection (6), the deceased spouse's personal representative may recover the excess amount from the surviving spouse.

Effect of election to receive entitlement under section 5

(7) When a surviving spouse elects to receive the entitlement under section 5, the gifts made to him or her in the deceased spouse's will are revoked and the will shall be interpreted as if the surviving spouse had died before the other, unless the will

expressly provides that the gifts are in addition to the entitlement under section 5.

Idem

(8) When a surviving spouse elects to receive the entitlement under section 5, the spouse shall be deemed to have disclaimed

  (a) the entitlement under Part II of the *Succession Law Reform Act.*

Manner of making election

(9) The surviving spouse's election shall be in the form prescribed by the regulations made under this Act and shall be filed in the office of the Surrogate Clerk for Ontario within six months after the first spouse's death.

Deemed election

(10) If the surviving spouse does not file the election within that time, he or she shall be deemed to have elected to take under the will or to receive the entitlement under the *Succession Law Reform Act,* or both, as the case may be, unless the court, on application, orders otherwise.

Priority of spouse's entitlement

(11) The spouse's entitlement under section 5 has priority over,

  (a) the gifts made in the deceased spouse's will, if any, subject to subsection (12);

  (b) a person's right to a share of the estate under Part II (Intestate Succession) of the *Succession Law Reform Act;*

  (c) an order made against the estate under Part V (Support of Dependants) of the *Succession Law Reform Act,* except an order in favour of a child of the deceased spouse.

Exception

(12) The spouse's entitlement under section 5 does not have priority over a gift by will made in accordance with a contract that the deceased spouse entered into in good faith and for valuable consideration, except to the extent that the value of the gift, in the court's opinion, exceeds the consideration.

Distribution within six months of death restricted

(13) No distribution shall be made in the administration of a deceased spouse's estate within six months of the spouse's death, unless,

    (a) the surviving spouse gives written consent to the distribution; or

    (b) the court authorizes the distribution.

Idem, notice of application

(14) No distribution shall be made in the administration of a deceased spouse's [estate] after the personal representative has received notice of an application under this Part, unless,

    (a) the applicant gives written consent to the distribution; or

    (b) the court authorizes the distribution.

Extension of limitation period

(15) If the court extends the time for a spouse's application based on subsection 5(2), any property of the deceased spouse that is distributed before the date of the order and without notice of the application shall not be brought into the calculation of the deceased spouse's net family property.

Exception

(16) Subsections (13) and (14) do not prohibit reasonable advances to dependants of the deceased spouse for their support.

Definition

(17) In subsection (16), "dependant" has the same meaning as in Part V of the *Succession Law Reform Act*.

Liability of personal representative

(18) If the personal representative makes a distribution that contravenes subsection (13) or (14), the court makes an order against the estate under this Part and the undistributed portion of the estate is not sufficient to satisfy the order, the personal representative is personally liable to the applicant for the amount that was distributed or the amount that is required to satisfy the order, whichever is less.

Order suspending administration

(19) On motion by the surviving spouse, the court may make an order suspending the administration of the deceased spouse's estate for the time and to the extent that the court decides.

Pursuant to section 3 of the *Family Law Amendment Act*, S.O. 1986, c. 35:

3. Subsections 6(6) and (6a) of the said Act, as set out in subsection 2(1) of this Act, apply with respect to deaths that occurred before or occur after the coming into force of this Act.

9.2 Death as a triggering event

As stated previously, the death of a spouse constitutes a triggering event for the *prima facie* equalization of the net family property of each spouse but only where the net family property of the deceased spouse exceeds that of the surviving spouse: see *supra*, 6.0 TRIGGERING EVENTS, subheading 6.4 "Death as a triggering event". The presumptive right to an equalization of the net family property of each spouse on death is expressly confined to the surviving spouse and cannot be sought by the personal representative of a deceased spouse.

[handwritten margin note: "Death is a triggering event "for property sharing only if deceased spouse nfp exceeds surviving spouse. s. 5(2)"]

9.3 Election by surviving spouse

The right of a surviving spouse to pursue an equalization claim under section 5 of the *Family Law Act, 1986* is subject to the exercise of an election under section 6 of the Act. Pursuant to subsections 6(1), (2) and (3) of the Act, a surviving spouse must make an election to assert his or her testate or intestate succession rights *or* to pursue an equalization claim under section 5 of the Act. Subsection 6(9) requires a properly executed election to be filed in the office of the Surrogate Clerk for Ontario within six months of the death: see *Re Varga Estate*, unreported, May 4, 1987 (Ont. S.C.). This is subject to any extension of time permitted by the court under subsection 2(8) of the *Family Law Act, 1986*. But where an extension of time is granted to permit an equalization claim under section 5 of the Act, any property distributed before the date of the order for an extension and without notice of the application therefor, is excluded from the calculation of the deceased spouse's net property: subsection 6(15).

Where no election has been filed within the prescribed time limit, the surviving spouse is deemed to have elected to take under the will or intestacy, unless the court, on application, orders otherwise: subsection 6(10). Such an application may be filed more than six months after the death, if the requirements of subsection 2(8) of the Act are met. What is more uncertain is whether subsection 6(10) permits the surviving spouse to pursue alternative claims under the will or intestacy and under section 5 of the Act with the election being exercised having regard to the respective outcome of these alternative claims. If this interpretation is accorded to subsection 6(10), a surviving spouse might be ill-advised to file any election, because once filed, it would appear to be final and irrevocable. In *Re Van der Wyngaard* (1987), 7 R.F.L. (3d) 81 (Ont. Surr. Ct.), McDermid Dist. Ct. J. concluded that section 6 of the *Family Law Act* does not address "multiple" wills. It only applies where there is a single will that is not being contested. Accordingly, a husband, who would have received substantial benefits under his wife's former will but who is excluded under a later will, may contest the later will and, nevertheless, file an election under subsection 6(9) of the *Family Law Act, 1986* to preserve his rights under section 5 in the event that the later will is upheld. Under these circumstances, the election applies only with respect to the second will. Should the husband's challenge of that will prove successful, his election does not prevent or restrict his entitlement under the first will. Form 1 in Ontario Regulation 605/86 under the *Family Law Act, 1986* which is technically deficient in that it is mandatory and does not permit a conditional election, should not be permitted to defeat the remedial nature of the Act, which was designed to enlarge rather than restrict the rights of spouses. The judge further observed that "an alternative suggestion, for future reference, might be to apply for an extension of time within which to file an election pursuant to [subsection] 6(10) of the [Family Law] Act until the issue as to the validity of the second will has been disposed of."

Subsection 6(4) of the Act provides that a surviving spouse who elects to take under the will or intestacy "shall also receive the other property to which he or she is entitled because of the first spouse's death". Such "other property" might include benefits under any life insurance policy taken out on the life of the deceased spouse or under a pension plan that provides death benefits to the surviving spouse, or damages awarded in a wrongful death action under Part V of the *Family Law Act, 1986*. Subsection 6(4) of the Act may be contrasted with subsection 6(6) and (6a) (enacted under *Family Law Amendment Act*, S.O. 1986, c. 35, subsection 2(1)), which apply to a spouse who elects to pursue an equalization claim. Such a spouse may assert rights as a beneficiary under a life insurance policy taken out on the life of the deceased spouse and owned by the deceased spouse or under a pension or similar plan that provides for a lump sum death benefit to the surviving spouse, but any payment under the policy or plan must be credited against the surviving spouse's entitlement under section 5, unless a written designation by the deceased spouse provides that the surviving spouse shall receive such payment in addition to the entitlement under section 5. The requisite designation must specifically address the relationship between the death benefits under the policy or plan and the surviving spouse's rights under section 5 of the Act. It must be clear that the deceased spouse intended these respective entitlements to be cumulative. The proceeds of any life insurance policy or a right thereto are to be ignored in calculating the net family property of each spouse for the purpose of determining any entitlement under section 5: *Family Law Act, 1986*, paragraph 4(2)4. Although this paragraph does not apply to death benefits paid under a "pension or similar plan", these benefits should also be excluded from the calculation of the net family property of either spouse by reason that the valuation date under subsection 4(1) is the date before the date of death. Where a surviving spouse elects to receive the entitlement under section 5 in the absence of a written designation by the deceased spouse entitling the survivor to additional payments under a life insurance policy, pension or similar plan, any such payments received in excess of the entitlement under section 5 may be recovered by the personal representative of the deceased spouse: *Family Law Act*, S.O. 1986, c. 4, subsection 6(6a), as enacted by subsection 2(1) of the *Family Law Amendment Act*, S.O. 1986, c. 35.

Pursuant to subsection 6(5) of the *Family Law Act, 1986*, a testator may expressly provide in his or her will that testamentary gifts shall be in addition to the surviving spouse's entitlement under section 5. In the absence of any such express provision, testamentary gifts to a surviving spouse who elects to receive his or her entitlement under section 5 are revoked and the will is to be interpreted as though the surviving spouse had predeceased the testator: subsection 6(7). When a surviving spouse is entitled to testamentary gifts in addition to the entitlement under section 5 by virtue of subsection 6(5) of the Act, the value of the testamentary gifts should not be included in the calculation of the surviving spouse's net family property for the purpose of determining the quantum of the equalization claim. They do not constitute excluded property under paragraph 4(2)1 ("gift or inheritance from a third person"), but the "valuation date" under subsection 4(1) in the event that death constitutes the triggering event is "the date before the date on which one of the spouses dies leaving the other spouse surviving". This definition implies, however, that the value of the testamentary gifts would be included in the calculation of the testator's net family property. It would, however, be open to the court to award the surviving spouse an amount that is more or less than half the difference between the net family properties of the two spouses, if equalization would be unconscionable having regard to "the part of a spouse's net family property that consists of gifts made by the other spouse": *Family Law Act, 1986*, clause 5(6)(c).

A spouse who elects to receive the entitlement under section 5 is deemed to have disclaimed any intestate succession rights that would otherwise arise under Part II of the *Succession Law Reform Act*, R.S.O. 1980, c. 488: *Family Law Act, 1986*, subsection 6(8).

Pursuant to clause 6(11)(a) and subsection 6(12) of the Act, a spouse's entitlement under section 5 has priority over third party testamentary gifts, excepting those made pursuant to a contract entered into by the deceased in good faith and for valuable consideration and insofar as the value of the gift does not exceed the consideration. The spousal entitlement under section 5 also takes priority over a third person's right of intestate succession under Part II of the *Succession Law Reform Act*, R.S.O. 1980, c. 488 (*Family Law Act, 1986*, S.O. 1986, c. 4, clause 6(11)(b)) and over any order made against the deceased spouse's estate for the support of family dependants under Part V of the *Succession Law Reform Act,* except an order in favour of a child of the deceased spouse: *Family Law Act, 1986,* clause 6(11)(c). The intestate succession rights of children or issue of the deceased spouse under Part II of the *Succession Law Reform Act* are accordingly subordinated to the rights of the surviving spouse under section 5 of the *Family Law Act, 1986.* But persons falling within the *extended* definition of "child" under clause 57(a) of the *Succession Law Reform Act* may pursue a claim for support against the deceased's estate under Part V and this presumably takes precedence over the surviving spouse's entitlement under section 5 of the *Family Law Act, 1986.* No corresponding privilege extends, however, to other dependants, such as a "common law wife" or a previously divorced spouse. The personal representative of the deceased spouse may, nevertheless, make reasonable advances to any "dependant" of the deceased spouse within the meaning of clause 57(d) of the *Succession Law Reform Act,* notwithstanding notice of an application by the surviving spouse under section 5 of the *Family Law Act, 1986,* subsection 6(16). Subject to this qualification, the personal representative of the deceased spouse is prohibited from distributing all or any of the deceased spouse's estate within six months of the death or after receiving notice of an application by the surviving spouse under section 5 of the Act, unless the surviving spouse gives written consent to the distribution or the court authorizes the distribution: *Family Law Act, 1986,* subsections 6(13) and (14). Contravention of these prohibitions renders the personal representative of the deceased spouse accountable for the improper distribution to the extent that it undermines or injuriously affects the surviving spouse's entitlement under section 5: *Family Law Act, 1986,* subsection 6(18). The personal representative will not be accountable, however, for any distribution made in the administration of the deceased spouse's estate if, pursuant to subsection 2(8) of the Act, the surviving spouse has been granted an extension of the normal period of six months for bringing an application under section 5 (see clause 7(3)(c)), provided that the distribution occurred before the date of the extension order and without notice of the application for such an order. In these circumstances, subsection 6(15) of the Act provides that the distributed property shall not be included in the calculation of the deceased spouse's estate. This subsection apparently precludes recourse by the surviving spouse not only against the personal representative of the deceased spouse who acted in good faith, but also against third persons who in good faith received all or part of the deceased spouse's estate. Even a partial distribution of the deceased spouse's estate presumably defeats the surviving spouse's claim under section 5, where the value of the undistributed property does not exceed the surviving spouse's net family property: *Family Law Act, 1986*, subsection 5(2). If, however, the residue of the deceased spouse's property after partial distribution still exceeds the net family property of the surviving spouse, an unequal sharing of the net family properties in favour of the surviving spouse might be justified pursuant to clauses 5(6)(c) or (h) of the *Family Law Act, 1986*.

Pursuant to subsection 16(19) of the Act, a surviving spouse may bring a motion for an order to suspend the administration of the deceased spouse's estate for such time and to such extent as the court may determine. This subsection might imply that the onus falls on the surviving spouse to protect his or her entitlement under section 5 and that the personal representative of the deceased spouse owes no obligation to the surviving spouse beyond that imposed by subsection 16(18) of the Act. A personal representative stands in the shoes of the deceased spouse and presumably owes no duty to the surviving spouse to advise that spouse of his or her statutory rights or options: compare *Hawkesley v. May*, [1956] 1 Q.B. 304, [1955] 3 All E.R. 353. A prudent personal representative would always be well advised, however, to obtain the written consent of the surviving spouse or the authorization of the court under clause 6(13)(a) or (b) or 6(14)(a) or (b) of the Act before distributing all or any of the deceased spouse's estate in contravention of the prohibitions imposed by subsection 6(13) or (14). In this context, a duly filed election under subsection 6(9) of the Act should not be perceived as a "written consent to the distribution". This is so regardless whether the surviving spouse elects to take his or her testate or intestate succession rights or to take his or her entitlement under section 5 of the Act. Otherwise, a surviving spouse who elects to take under the will or intestacy could be seriously prejudiced by dependants' claims for support against the deceased spouse's estate under Part V of the Act. And the entitlement of a surviving spouse who elects to take under section 5 of the Act, where, for example, no provision has been made for him or her in the deceased spouse's will, would be similarly prejudiced, if a duly filed election were deemed to constitute a written consent to the distribution of the estate.

Before exercising the statutory election or giving a written consent to the distribution of all or any of the deceased spouse's estate, the surviving spouse is presumably entitled to information respecting the extent and value of the deceased spouse's estate. It is uncertain, however, whether the personal representative of the deceased spouse must volunteer this information or await a demand for disclosure by the surviving spouse. A determination of the value of the deceased spouse's estate may present significant difficulties by reason of the absence of any statutory definition of value and, more particularly, by reason of the definition of "valuation date" in subsection 4(1) of the *Family Law Act, 1986*. Pursuant to this subsection, the "valuation date" for the purposes of an equalization claim under section 5 where death is the triggering event is "[t]he date before the date on which one of the spouses dies leaving the other spouse surviving". This appears to indicate that any impact of the spouse's death on the value of his or her assets or even on their extent, as, for example, where property is held under joint tenancy with the surviving spouse, is to be ignored in determining the deceased spouse's net family property for the purposes of an equalization claim under section 5. As one commentator has observed, the results of this interpretation may be patently absurd: see Maurice C. Cullity, "The Family Law Act, 1986; Estates and Estate Planning", published in The Law Society of Upper Canada Continuing Education Program, *The New Family Law Act — For Solicitors*, March 4, 1986, at 25-29. A personal representative of the deceased spouse would be acting at risk, however, in ignoring the implications of the above statutory definition by giving a realistic appraisal of the net worth of the deceased spouse following his or her death.

10.0 PROPERTY AND FINANCIAL STATEMENTS

Statement of property

8. In an application under section 7, each party shall serve on the other and file with the court, in the manner and form prescribed by the rules of the court, a statement verified by oath or statutory declaration disclosing particulars of,

    (a) the party's property and debts and other liabilities,
       (i) as of the date of the marriage,
       (ii) as of the valuation date, and
       (iii) as of the date of the statement;
    (b) the deductions that the party claims under the definition of "net family property";
    (c) the exclusions that the party claims under subsection 4(2); and
    (d) all property that the party disposed of during the two years immediately preceding the making of the statement, or during the marriage, whichever period is shorter.

Procedural requirements respecting the filing of financial statements are defined in Rules 70.14 and 71.04 of the Ontario Rules of Civil Procedure: see *infra*, APPENDIX. In the words of Fleury U.F.C.J. in *Menage v. Hedges*, unreported, June 8, 1987 (Ont. Unified Fam. Ct.):

> The Act does not state on whose shoulders lies the burden of establishing the value of the net family property. The only reference to onus of proof can be found in subsection 4(3) dealing with excluded property. . . . Because the property or debts being described are that of the deponent and presumably may have been or may still

be under his control, the primary onus of establishing the values referred to in the statement should reside on the deponent. In the absence of any contest by the opposing party, it may not be necessary for the deponent to call further evidence to justify the valuations arrived at, but where a real issue is raised as to the figures used, the onus is on the deponent to establish on a balance of probabilities the accuracy of his sworn statement. Because of the nature of claims made in proceedings of this type, it is only reasonable to consider each party as having to discharge the civil burden of proof concerning the value of his or her respective assets and debts.

Menage v. Hedden
burden of
justifying
"value" is on
person who
owns property

For the purpose of filing a financial statement, the ownership of property will be determined by reference to the title in which the property is registered: *Schaefer v. Schaefer* (1986), 38 A.C.W.S. (2d) 142 (Ont. S.C.). Where property is jointly owned by the spouses, half of the value should be reported in the respective financial statements of the spouses: *Schaefer v. Schaefer, supra*; see also *Skrlj v. Skrlj* (1986), 2 R.F.L. (3d) 305, at 310 (Ont. S.C.).

The objective of property and financial statements is to provide complete, up-to-date and meaningful information to the parties and the court. The valuation of property by reference to its book value or depreciated cost value does not satisfy the requirements of section 8 of the *Family Law Act, 1986*, or of Ontario Rule 70.14. What is required is the estimated market value or actual worth of the property at the relevant time: *Silverstein v. Silverstein* (1978), 20 O.R. (2d) 185, 87 D.L.R. (3d) 116, 1 R.F.L. (2d) 239, at 241-42 (S.C.) (Galligan J.): see text *supra*, 7.0 EQUALIZATION OF NET FAMILY PROPERTIES, subheading 7.6 "Value". Where a party has filed a statement that is less than frank and complete, the court may draw unfavourable inferences against that party: *Silverstein v. Silverstein, supra*, at 242; see also *Re Stoikiewicz and Filas* (1978), 21 O.R. (2d) 717, 7 R.F.L. (2d) 366, at 371 (Unified Fam. Ct.) (child support). The court may also award costs against a party whose failure to comply with the letter and spirit of section 8 or Ontario Rule 70.14 has resulted in unnecessary prolonging of the proceedings: *Silverstein v. Silverstein, supra*, at 242; *Payne v. Payne* (1982), 31 R.F.L. (2d) 211, at 217 (Ont. Unified Fam. Ct.); *Skrlj v. Skrlj, supra*. In addition, Ontario Rule 70.14(4) specifically provides that "[w]here a financial statement is required to be filed or delivered with a petition or counterpetition, or an answer to it, the registrar shall not accept the petition, counterpetition or answer for issuing or filing without the financial statement".

11.0 POWERS OF COURT

11.1 General observations

Powers of court
    9.—(1) In an application under section 7, the court may order,

(a) that one spouse pay to the other spouse the amount to which the court finds that spouse to be entitled under this Part;

(b) that security, including a charge on property, be given for the performance of an obligation imposed by the order;

(c) that, if necessary to avoid hardship, an amount referred to in clause (a) be paid in instalments during a period not exceeding ten years or that payment of all or part of the amount be delayed for a period not exceeding ten years; and

(d) that, if appropriate to satisfy an obligation imposed by the order,

   (i) property be transferred to or in trust for or vested in a spouse, whether absolutely, for life or for a term of years, or

   (ii) any property be partitioned or sold.

Financial information, inspections

(2) The court may, at the time of making an order for instalment or delayed payments or on motion at a later time, order that the spouse who has the obligation to make payments shall,

(a) furnish the other spouse with specified financial information, which may include periodic financial statements; and

(b) permit inspections of specified property of the spouse by or on behalf of the other spouse, as the court directs.

Variation

(3) If the court is satisfied that there has been a material change in the circumstances of the spouse who has the obligation to make instalment or delayed payments, the court may, on motion, vary the order, but shall not vary the amount to which the court found the spouse to be entitled under this Part.

"value" sharing in Ontario

Section 5 of the *Family Law Act, 1986*, which constitutes the basis of the statutory property sharing regime on marriage or death, is premised on a sharing of the value of property and not on a division of property *in specie*: see *Re Henry and Cymbalisty* (1986), 55 O.R. (2d) 51, at 55 (Unified Fam. Ct.); *Skrlj v. Skrlj* (1986), 2 R.F.L. (3d) 305, at 309 (Ont. S.C.); *Humphreys v. Humphreys* (1987), 7 R.F.L. (3d) 113 (Ont. S.C.); *Benke v. Benke*, unreported, December 10, 1986 (Ont. Dist. Ct.). It thus endorses an accounting procedure that will ordinarily result in a money judgment that leaves the title to property undisturbed. Section 9 of the *Family Law Act, 1986* nevertheless, provides a variety of means whereby a successful equalization claim may be satisfied. The court may select a combination of the various remedies provided by section 9 so that a fair and reasonable solution may be attained: *Kukolj v. Kukolj* (1986), 3 R.F.L. (3d) 359 (Ont. Unified Fam. Ct.); see also *Marsham v. Marsham* (1987), 7 R.F.L. (3d) 1 (Ont. S.C.).

Section 9 of the Act is expressly confined to applications involving the presumptive right to an equalization of the net family property of each spouse. This is clearly spelled out in the reference to "an application under section 7", which pursuant to subsection 7(1) of the Act involves a determination of spousal entitlement under section 5. Consequently, the powers conferred on the court by section 9 do not extend to applications under section 10 of the Act, which involve questions of ownership. Although section 10 confers certain powers on the court similar to those defined in section 9, they are by no means identical: see, however, section 11 which applies to orders made under both sections 9 and 10, *infra*, subheading 11.8 "Operating business or farm".

11.2 Order for payment

Clause 9(1)(a) of the *Family Law Act, 1986* expressly empowers the court to order one spouse to pay to the other spouse the amount to which that other spouse is entitled under Part I of the Act. This clause presupposes the payment of a <u>lump sum</u> in satisfaction of the rights accorded under section 5 of the Act.

11.3 Order for security

Clause 9(1)(b) empowers the court to order that security be given for the performance of any obligation imposed by any order of the court made pursuant to subsection 9(1). Such security may include a charge on property or on the proceeds of sale of designated property (*Jackson v. Jackson* (1986), 5 R.F.L. (3d) 8 (Ont. S.C.) (Kent L.J.S.C.)) and such a charge may presumably be made on "excluded property" within the meaning of subsection 4(2) of the *Family Law Act, 1986*. An order for security lies in the discretion of the court and is not available as of right. Where payment of the amount due is deferred or involves instalments pursuant to an order under clause 9(1)(c) of the Act, an order for security would appear to be appropriate: *Kukolj v. Kukolj* and *Benke v. Benke, infra*, subheading 11.4 "Deferred or instalment payments". An order for security may be varied or discharged pursuant to section 13 of the Act: see *infra*, subheading 13.0 "Variation and realization of security".

An order for "security" may be varied or discharged s. 13

11.4 Deferred or instalment payments

Where there is evidence that an order for immediate payment would create hardship, the court has a discretionary jurisdiction under clause 9(1)(c) of the Act to order that the due amount be paid in instalments over a maximum period of ten years or that all or any part of the due amount be deferred for a period not exceeding ten years: *Oliva v. Oliva* (1986), 2 R.F.L. (3d) 188 (Ont. S.C.); *Messier v. Messier* (1986), 5 R.F.L. (3d) 251 (Ont. Dist. Ct.); *Sheehan v. Sheehan*, unreported, March 31, 1987 (Ont. S.C.) (Flanigan L.J.S.C.) *infra*, and *Marsham v. Marsham*, unreported, May 5, 1987 (Ont. S.C.) subheading 11.5 "Transfers of property; partition and sale". The terms of any such order may be subsequently varied under subsection 9(3) of the Act but the court is expressly precluded from extending the ten-year period for payment by the express provisions of subsection 9(4). If Ontario courts grant "if and when" orders with respect to spousal pensions, the ten-year rule could present obstacles where the pension benefits will not mature or be fully realized within the ten-year period. The provisions of clause 9(1)(c) of the Act will only be met where the amount due is fully paid within the stipulated time period. It is not sufficient that such payments commence within that period but are not fully extinguished on the expiration thereof: compare *Porter v. Porter* (1986), 1 R.F.L. (3d) 12 (Ont. Dist. Ct.); see also *Kukolj v. Kukolj* (1986), 3 R.F.L. (3d) 359 (Ont. Unified Fam. Ct.), wherein the court declined to discount the value of the husband's employment pension by reason that it had not matured but authorized him to defer the equalization payment for a maximum of ten years, with the payment to be secured against the former matrimonial home. Clause 9(1)(c) of the *Family Law Act, 1986* is expressly confined, however, to circumstances where an order for payment is made. The ten-year maximum pay-out period has apparently no application where, pursuant to clause 9(1)(d) of the Act, the court orders that property be transferred to or in trust for a spouse: see *Marsham v. Marsham, supra.* Pension legislation has traditionally precluded the alienation, assignment or encumbering of a pension plan. In circumvention of such restrictions, courts have from time to time directed the spouse entitled to the pension to hold the other spouse's interest therein in trust with payments to be made on the basis of a designated formula upon the maturity of the pension plan: see, for example, *Rutherford v. Rutherford,* [1981] 6 W.W.R. 485, 30 B.C.L.R. 145, 23 R.F.L. (2d) 337 (C.A.); *George v. George,* [1983] 5 W.W.R. 606, 23 Man. R. (2d) 89, 149 D.L.R. (3d) 486, 35 R.F.L. (2d) 225 (C.A.); *Porter v. Porter supra;* and see *Marsham v. Marsham, supra.* Whether such use of a trust offends against the governing pension legislation would appear to depend upon whether clause 9(1)(d) of the *Family Law Act, 1986,* creates a paramount legislative authority that empowers the courts to override the express provisions of relevant pension legislation. Such authority was denied in *Clarke v. Clarke* (1986), 72 N.S.R. (2d) 387, 173 A.P.R. 387, 29 D.L.R. (4th) 492, 1 R.F.L. (3d) 29 (C.A.). Recent amendments to federal pension legislation and to the *Pension Benefits Act*, R.S.O. 1980, c. 373, could resolve this issue: see, for example, section 25 of the *Pension Benefits Standards Act, 1985*, S.C. 1986, c. 40, which came into force on January 1, 1987.

In *Benke v. Benke*, unreported, December 10, 1986 (Ont. Dist. Ct.), the court found that the husband could immediately discharge the equalization payment without undue hardship, but allowed him the option of deferring the payment for several months, subject to his providing security to the wife by way of a mortgage on his property. The court further directed that if the husband deferred payment, the mortgage would carry an interest rate of one-half per cent over prime and that the husband would be entitled to exercise a pre-payment privilege only on a monthly date when interest became due.

11.5 Transfers of property; partition and sale

Clause 9(1)(d) of the *Family Law Act, 1986* empowers the court to order that spousal entitlements under Part I of the Act shall be satisfied by property being transferred to or in "trust" for or vested in a spouse, whether absolutely, for life or for a term of years: see *Oliva v. Oliva* (1986), 2 R.F.L. (3d) 188 (Ont. S.C.); see also *McCutcheon v. McCutcheon* (1986), 2 R.F.L. (3d) 327 (Ont. Dist. Ct.), wherein the husband's interest in the matrimonial home and contents was vested in the wife purportedly under clause 34(1)(c) of the *Family Law Act, 1986*, which provision is applicable only in the context of a claim for support; and see *Sheehan v. Sheehan*, unreported, March 31, 1987 (Ont. S.C.) (Flanigan L.J.S.C.), wherein an equalization payment of $267,000 was ordered to be discharged by a tax free transfer of the matrimonial home and by a spousal roll-over of the husband's interest in his R.R.S.P., with the balance of $49,000 to be paid in cash over a period of two years. The court may alternatively order the partition and sale of *any* property. These judicial powers are discretionary and may be exercised "if appropriate to satisfy the obligation imposed by the order". Clause 9(1)(d) presupposes that a determination of a spousal monetary entitlement has been effectuated by the application of section 5 of the Act. Clause 9(1)(d) does not empower the court to order a division of specific property in lieu of undertaking the calculations required by sections 4 and 5, although such jurisdiction could be conferred on the court by a valid domestic contract, or presumably by minutes of settlement even though they do not comply with the statutory requirements that regulate domestic contracts. Consequential difficulties may accordingly ensue should the court wish to adopt the "if and when" approach to spousal pension benefits: see *supra*, 7.0 EQUALIZATION OF NET FAMILY PROPERTIES, subheading 7.4 "Pensions". Thus, Professor McLeod has observed (Annotation, *Porter v. Porter* (1986), 1 R.F.L. (3d) 12, at 14 (Ont. Dist. Ct.) (Kerr D.C.J.)):

> In order to avoid the difficulties of actuarial evidence and the difficulty of forcing someone to pay a cash award in respect of an asset he does not have and may never receive, most courts have adopted the "*George*" or "*Rutherford*" formula as in *Porter*. The difficulty with this approach in Ontario is that it does not appear to meet the statutory model since it does not give a dollar figure from which the deductions in s. 4(1) can be made. Further, it will only be in unusual cases that a *George* order will be able to be realized within the ten-year period dictated by the Act. In order to utilize the *George* formula, given the statutory scheme, it would be necessary to find that the wife was not entitled to any interest in the husband's pension on trust principles, that the husband had no premarital property or debts/liabilities to deduct under s. 4(1) and that the pension must be realizable within ten years of the decision. Since most people are rarely out of debt this will be difficult to attain. The alternative is for the court to treat the pension separate so long as the debts and other deductions can be covered by the other property owned by the husband. Although the Act in no way sanctions this separation of gross family property to determine net family property it may be the only way to make the best out of a bad situation and would accord with developments in other provinces.

And in *Marsham v. Marsham* (1987), 7 R.F.L. (3d) 1 (Ont. S.C.), Walsh J. concluded that while several provincial statutory regimes permit the use of the "if and when" approach "as a method to both value and settle the pension entitlement . . ., it clearly is not possible within the framework of the Ontario Act. Part I of the Act requires that all property owned by a spouse on the valuation date be valued in order to determine his or her net family property so that the amount required to equalize their net family properties can be ascertained. While it may be possible to satisfy all or part of the equalizing payment by an immediate transfer in trust to the other spouse of the pension benefits, nevertheless, in the first instance, the pension benefit must be valued for the purpose of determining the equalizing payment".

Difficulties may also arise with respect to the disposition of chattels: see *Re Henry and Cymbalisty* (1986), 55 O.R. (2d) 51, at 54-55 (Unified Fam. Ct.). Although courts were usually reluctant to order a division of chattels *in specie* in proceedings under the *Family Law Reform Act*, R.S.O. 1980, c. 152, a practice evolved whereby the court would induce the spouses to effectuate such a division by ordering a sale of the chattels in the event that no spousal agreement could be reached. The threat of realizing "fire-sale" prices under such an order provided a powerful incentive for settlement. It would appear that this practice is inconsistent with the statutory sharing regime established by section 5 of the *Family Law Act, 1986*. In *Humphreys v. Humphreys, supra*, Galligan J. categorically stated that the court has no power "to rearrange assets between the parties and compensate for any difference in value by way of an equalizing payment".

11.6 Financial information and inspections

It would appear that the power of the court to order financial disclosure or inspections of property pursuant to subsection 9(2) of the Act is confined to circumstances where the court makes an order for instalment or deferred payments under clause 9(1)(c) or on a motion to vary such an order brought pursuant to subsection 9(3) of the Act. This interpretation presupposes that the words "on motion at a later time" in subsection 9(2) indirectly refer to the "motion" permissible under subsection 9(3). Given this interpretation, a court could not invoke subsection 9(2) in the context of an order for security, including a charge on property, made pursuant to clause 9(1)(b) of the Act. This may well have been an oversight on the part of the legislature or the legislative draftsperson. It may not prove fatal, however, to an ancillary order for disclosure or inspection being made on the granting of an order to secure, such jurisdiction being exercisable as necessarily incidental to the court's power to order security to be provided.

11.7 Variation of order for instalment or deferred payments

Subsection 9(3) of the *Family Law Act, 1986* empowers the court to vary an order made pursuant to clause 9(1)(c) for instalment or deferred payments in the event of a material change in the circumstances of the spouse obligated by such order. No corresponding statutory jurisdiction is vested in the court to accommodate material changes in the circumstances of the entitled spouse, for example, the death of this spouse. The powers of variation are expressly restricted under subsection 9(3) in that the court cannot vary the amount to which a spouse is entitled. Furthermore, subsection 9(4) of the Act precludes the court for postponing any payment beyond the ten-year period specified in clause 9(1)(c) of the Act. The words "vary the order" in subsection 9(3) are broad in scope but in the overall context of the subsection appears to be confined to a variation of the terms of an order providing for instalment or deferred payments within the stipulated maximum ten-year period. This narrow but literal interpretation of subsection 9(3) would preclude the court, on an application to vary, from exercising powers to order any transfer or disposition of property corresponding to those exercisable on the original application pursuant to subclause 9(1)(d)(i) of the *Family Law Act, 1986*. Here again, there may well have been some degree of legislative oversight, but, in this context, it would not appear to be remediable by the exercise of any inherent jurisdiction

70

in the court. Subsection 9(3) also appears unduly restrictive in that it does not apparently envisage any variation of an order granted pursuant to clause 9(1)(a) or (d) of the Act. Although an order for the transfer, partition or sale of property under clause 9(1)(d) of the Act should ordinarily be final and irrevocable, different considerations may apply to an order for a lump-sum payment made pursuant to clause 9(1)(a) of the Act. Supervening events may well justify the variation of such an order by the substitution of an order for instalment or deferred payments. For the purpose of accommodating this possibility, an appropriate amendment of subsection 9(3) of the Act appears to be necessary. The variation or discharge of an order for security is expressly authorized by section 13 of the Act.

11.8 Operating business or farm

Operating business or farm
    11.—(1) An order made under section 9 or 10 shall not be made so as to require or result in the sale of an operating business or farm or so as to seriously impair its operation, unless there is no reasonable alternative method of satisfying the award.

Idem
    (2) To comply with subsection (1), the court may,
        (a) order that one spouse pay to the other a share of the profits from the business or farm; and
        (b) if the business or farm is incorporated, order that one spouse transfer or have the corporation issue to the other shares in the corporation.

Orders granted pursuant to the powers expressly conferred on the court by section 9 or 10 of the Act must avoid the sale of an operating business or farm or the serious impairment of its operation, unless there is no reasonable alternative method of satisfying the award: see *Benke v. Benke*, unreported, December 10, 1986 (Ont. Dist. Ct.), *supra*, subheading 11.4 "Deferred or instalment payments". The provisions of subsection 11(1) of the Act are mandatory and not permissive: *Postma v. Postma* (1987), 6 R.F.L. (3d) 50, at 62 (Ont. S.C.) (Carter L.J.S.C.). This contrasts with the discretionary powers of the court under subsection 11(2) to order a sharing of the profits from the business or farm and, if the business or farm is incorporated, to order the transfer of shares in the corporation in satisfaction of an award.

The provisions of subsection 11(1) do not preclude an order that will necessitate the disposition or impairment of an operating business or farm, where there is no practicable means of otherwise satisfying the award: *Postma v. Postma, supra*. In the context of a section 9 order, involving the presumptive right to equalization under section 5 of the Act, the court could presumably make an order for instalment or deferred payments and, if appropriate, order security to be provided, for the purpose of avoiding the disposition or impairment of an operating business or farm. It is doubtful, however, whether, on the determination of a question of ownership under section 10 of the Act, clause 10(1)(b) would entitle the court to grant compensation by way of instalment or deferred payments, except in accordance with the provisions of clause 11(2)(a) of the Act.

12.0 RESTRAINING ORDERS AND PRESERVATION ORDERS

Orders for preservation
12.—In an application under section 7 or 10, if the court considers it necessary for the protection of the other spouse's interests under this Part, the court may make an interim or final order,

    (a) restraining the depletion of a spouse's property; and
    (b) for the possession, delivering up, safekeeping and preservation of the property.

Unlike section 9 of the *Family Law Reform Act*, R.S.O. 1980, c. 152, which empowered the court to grant interim restraining orders or preservation orders "[i]n or pending an application", section 12 of the *Family Law Act, 1986* presupposes that an application has already been launched under section 7 or 10 of the Act. Section 12 also expressly empowers the court to make an interim or final order: see *de Champlain v. de Champlain* (1986), 2 R.F.L. (3d) 22 (Ont. S.C.), *supra*, 7.0 EQUALIZATION OF NET FAMILY PROPERTIES, subheading 7.13 "Excluded property — 7.13.3. Damages".

An interim order under section 12 may be granted by a Master of the Supreme Court of Ontario: *Schuster v. Schuster* (1986), 53 O.R. (2d) 665, 50 R.F.L. (2d) 256 (S.C.); *Angelopoulos v. Angelopoulos* (1986), 55 O.R. (2d) 101 (Ont. S.C.).

In the context of section 9 of the *Family Law Reform Act*, R.S.O. 1980, c. 152, interim preservation orders were more readily obtainable in respect of "family assets", such as the matrimonial home, household effects or the family cottage or boat, than in respect of business or commercial assets: see, for example, *Mageau v. Mageau* (1978), 22 O.R. (2d) 179, 92 D.L.R. (3d) 402, 8 R.F.L. (2d) 282 (S.C.). This practice may continue to prevail with respect to preservation orders, as distinct from restraining orders, under section 12 of the *Family Law Act, 1986*, notwithstanding the statutory abrogation of the former distinction between family and non-family assets that existed under the *Family Law Reform Act*, R.S.O. 1980, c. 152. Where the entitlement of a spouse under Part I of the *Family Law Act, 1986* can be otherwise secured, the court should refuse to grant a preservation order that might impair the effective management of a business or of commercial assets. In *Radosavljevic v. Radosavljevic* (1986), 57 O.R. (2d) 51, 3 R.F.L. (3d) 294 (S.C.), an application to vacate a restraining order was denied where the husband had conveyed the matrimonial home to a private company with intent to defeat his wife's realization of her equalization entitlement under Part I of the *Family Law Act, 1986*. The court, nevertheless, authorized a sale of the property by the company, subject to the posting of adequate security pending final disposition of the wife's claim. The court observed that the order granted pursuant to section 12 of the *Family Law Act, 1986* was not to be confused with a Mareva injunction. (*Mareva Compania Naviera S.A. v. Int'l Bulkcarriers S.A.*, [1975] 2 Lloyd's Rep. 509, [1980] 1 All E.R. 213).

Section 12 of the *Family Law Act, 1986* is preventive rather than curative in nature. Accordingly, it cannot be invoked to set aside transactions that have already been completed. Relief, if any, in these circumstances, must be found elsewhere, as, for example, under the provisions of the *Fraudulent Conveyances Act*, R.S.O. 1980, c. 176: see Maurice C. Cullity, "The Family Law Act, 1986: Estates and Estate Planning", The Law Society of Upper Canada Continuing Legal Education Program, *The New Family Law Act — For Solicitors*, March 4, 1986, at 36-39.

13.0 VARIATION AND REALIZATION OF SECURITY

Variation and realization of security
13.—If the court has ordered security or charged a property with security for the performance of an obligation under this Part, the court may, on motion,
   (a) vary or discharge the order; or
   (b) on notice to all persons having an interest in the property, direct its sale for the purpose of realizing the security or charge.

An order for security or for the charging of property granted pursuant to clause 9(1)(c) or 10(1)(d) of the *Family Law Act, 1986*, may be varied or discharged under section 13. In the alternative, the court may direct a sale of the property for the purpose of realizing the security, provided that notice of the motion to vary is given to all persons with an interest in the property.

14.0 RETROSPECTIVE OPERATION; PREJUDGMENT INTEREST

Application of Part
16.—(1) This Part applies to property owned by spouses,
  (a) whether they were married before or after this Act comes into force; and
  (b) whether the property was acquired before or after this Act comes into force.

Application of s. 14
(2) Section 14 applies whether the event giving rise to the presumption occurred before or after this Act comes into force.

Application of ss. 5-8
70.—(1) Sections 5 to 8 apply unless,
  (a) an application under section 4 of the *Family Law Reform Act* [R.S.O. 1980, c. 152], was adjudicated or settled before the 4th day of June, 1985; or
  (b) the first spouse's death occurs before the day this Act comes into force.

Extension of limitation period
(2) The limitation period set out in clause 7(3)(b) does not expire until six months after this Act comes into force.

Application of Part II
(3) Part II (Matrimonial Home) applies unless a proceeding under Part III of the *Family Law Reform Act* to determine the rights between spouses in respect of the property concerned was adjudicated or settled before the 4th day of June, 1985.

Interpretation of existing contracts
(4) A separation agreement or marriage contract that is validly made before the day this Act comes into force and that excludes a spouse's property from the application of sections 4 and 8 of the *Family Law Reform Act,*
  (a) shall be deemed to exclude that property from the application of section 5 of this Act; and
  (b) shall be read with necessary modifications.

Part I of the *Family Law Act, 1986*, applies to property owned by spouses, whether they were married before or after the date when the Act came into force, namely March 1, 1986: see *Vivier v. Vivier* (1987), 5 R.F.L. (3d) 450 (Ont. Dist. Ct.), *supra*, 6.0 TRIGGERING EVENTS FOR EQUALIZATION OF NET FAMILY PROPERTIES, subheading 6.2 "Limitation periods". In light of the extended definition of "spouse" in subsections 1(1) and (2) of the "Act", it is submitted that the word "married" in clause 16(1)(a) will not be literally construed. Although section 16 of the *Family Law Act, 1986* operates retrospectively, it will not necessarily be accorded an unlimited retroactive operation. Thus, in *Nelson v. Nelson*, unreported, July 17, 1986 (Ont. S.C.), Doyle J. observed:

> The valuation date in this matter is July 6th, 1982, when the parties separated but the amendments brought on by the present Act were not in force at the time. Counsel for the wife argues that the severance pay valued at $17,359.00 should be considered as part of the husband's net family property as it was at the very least contingent if not vested. It is to be noted that what was at separation contingent has since become a reality. The husband says that the severance pay no longer exists, it was spent in total, part of it prior to June 4, 1985, the date set out in s. 70(1)(a) of the Act. On June 4, 1985, he still had a value of $7,178.92.
>
> I cannot quite believe that the legislature intended the Act to have unlimited retroactivity. One could think of a separation occurring 25 years ago where a spouse with considerable assets at the time of separation might have lost his assets in an uncontrollable way and still be called upon after the Act comes into force to pay his spouse one half of his then net property value exceeding that of his wife. It is my view that the legislature intended retroactivity back to but not beyond June 4, 1985. The husband will therefore be credited with the sum of $7,178.92 as an asset.

Part I of the *Family Law Act, 1986* applies regardless of whether the property was acquired before or after the commencement of the Act. The presumptions arising pursuant to section 14 of the Act also apply even though the circumstances that give rise to the presumption occurred before the commencement of the Act: see text *supra*, 5.0 APPLICATIONS RESPECTING OWNERSHIP AND POSSESSION OF PROPERTY, subheading 5.2 "Presumptions".

An application based on sections 5 to 8 of the *Family Law Act, 1986* is precluded under subsection 70(1) by a prior application for a division of family or non-family assets under section 4 of the *Family Law Reform Act*, R.S.O. 1980, c. 152, if that application was adjudicated or settled before June 4, 1985. In the absence of a validly executed separation agreement or marriage contract that excludes the application of sections 4 and 8 of the *Family Law Reform Act, 1986, supra*, the adjudication or settlement of a claim under section 4 of that Act, which occurs after June 4, 1985, does not preclude subsequent proceedings being instituted on the basis of sections 5 to 8 of the *Family Law Act, 1986*. Minutes of settlement that have been approved by the court and include general or specific releases of claims under the *Family Law Reform Act* or presumably the *Family Law Act, 1986* would thus appear to be ineffective as a bar to subsequent proceedings by reason of the express provisions of clause 70(1)(a) and subsection 70(4) of the *Family Law Act, 1986*: compare *Monahan v. Monahan* (1986), 5 R.F.L. (3d) 73 (Ont. Dist. Ct.). The minutes of settlement would not be irrelevant, however, in the context of a subsequent application based on sections 5 to 8 of the *Family Law Act, 1986*. Indeed, they could be of decisive importance in the context of clause 5(6)(g) of the *Family Law Act, 1986*: see text *supra*, 8.0 UNEQUAL DIVISION OF NET FAMILY PROPERTIES, subheading 8.1.7 "Written agreement".

The meaning to be attributed to the term "adjudicated" in clause 70(1)(a) of the *Family Law Act, 1986* was addressed in *Wierzbicki v. Wierzbicki* (1986), 55 O.R. (2d) 77, at 81, 29 D.L.R. (4th) 78, at 81, 3 R.F.L. (3d) 82, at 88 (S.C.), wherein Callon J. observed:

> Whether or not s. 70(1)(*a*) of the *Family Law Act, 1986* applies in the present case depends upon the meaning of the word "adjudicated". If a claim is adjudicated when judgment is rendered, it is clear that s. 70(1)(*a*) applies to this action since judgment was released on April 4, 1986.
>
> There appears to be ample authority for the petitioner's submission that a claim is not adjudicated until it is finally decided and judgment has been rendered. It is not sufficient that the adjudicator may have made an unannounced or tentative decision: Black's Law Dictionary, 5th ed.; *Reidy v. Herry* (1897), 23 V.L.R. 508 at p. 510; *Words and Phrases Legally Defined*, 2nd ed., at pp. 23, 71-2; *Sutherland v. Spruce Grove* (1919), 44 D.L.R. 375, [1919] 1 W.W.R. 281, 14 Alta. L.R. 292 (Alta. C.A.).
>
> Although there are no cases interpreting the meaning of the word "adjudicated" in s. 70(1)(*a*), it is my conclusion that that section was intended to permit spouses to relitigate the division of family property even after the completion of trial and rendering of judgment. Although all of the evidence in the present action had been heard by April, 1985, the submissions of counsel were not made until September, 1985, and the action was, therefore, still before the court as of June 5, 1985, and had not yet been adjudicated. The respondent is, therefore, entitled to relitigate the division of family property in accordance with the provisions of the *Family Law Act, 1986*.

Section 16 of the *Family Law Act, 1986* takes on a particular significance with respect to prejudgment interest. Assume, for example, that spouses separated in 1974 and that no settlement or adjudication of their respective property entitlements has ever been achieved. If Part I of the *Family Law Act, 1986* is deemed retroactive as distinct from retrospective pursuant to section 16, the quantum of prejudgment interest could well exceed the quantification of the equalization entitlement under section 5. And if the observations of Potts J. in *Kelly v. Kelly* (1986), 50 R.F.L. (2d) 360, at 366, are correct (see *supra*, 8.0 UNEQUAL DIVISION OF NET FAMILY PROPERTIES, subheading 8.1.8 "Any other circumstances relating to the acquisition, disposition or management of property"), clause 5(6)(h) of the *Family Law Act, 1986* could not be invoked to ameliorate or eliminate any consequential unconscionability. The entitlement to prejudgment interest conferred by subsection 138(1) of the *Courts of Justice Act*, S.O. 1984, c. 11 is subject, however, to an overriding discretion conferred on the court by section 140 thereof. These sections provide as follows:

Prejudgment interest

138.—(1) A person who is entitled to an order for the payment of money is entitled to claim and have included in the order an award of interest thereon at the prejudgment interest rate, calculated.

    (a) where the order is made on a liquidated claim, from the date the cause of action arose to the date of the order; or

    (b) where the order is made on an unliquidated claim, from the date the person entitled gave notice in writing of his claim to the person liable therefor to the date of the order.

. . .

Postjudgment interest

139. . . .

Discretion of court

140. The court may, where it considers it just to do so, having regard to changes in market interest rates, the circumstances of the case, the conduct of the proceeding or any other relevant consideration,

    (a) disallow interest under section 138 or 139;

    (b) allow interest at a rate higher or lower than that provided in section 138 or 139;

    (c) allow interest for a period other than that provided in section 138, or 139

in respect of the whole or any part of the amount on which interest is payable under section 138 or 139.

In *Nuti v. Nuti* (1984), 4 O.A.C. 57 (Ont. C.A.), a wife was denied the right to interest on her property entitlement granted pursuant to the *Family Law Reform Act*, R.S.O. 1980, c. 152, having regard to the husband's right to purchase her interest in the non-family assets. And in *Gooder v. Gooder*, unreported, July 8, 1986 (Ont. Dist. Ct.), McCart D.C.J. observed:

> I am of the opinion that an award of pre-judgment interest has no place in an action under the *Family Law Act*, particularly in this case which has not been marked with the bitterness, rancour and lack of cooperation one so often finds in family disputes. I do not believe an award of pre-judgment interest would be in the spirit of the *Family Law Act* which recognizes the necessity of providing in law for the orderly and equitable settlement of the affairs of the spouses upon the breakdown of the partnership.

The issue of prejudgment interest will usually arise by reason of the effluxion of time between the valuation date and the date of adjudication. Different considerations would apply, however, if the presumptive right to an equalization of the net family property of each spouse automatically crystallizes upon the occurrence of the triggering event: see text, *supra*, 6.0 TRIGGERING EVENTS FOR EQUALIZA-TION OF NET FAMILY PROPERTIES, subheading 6.1 "General observations".

In *Skrlj v. Skrlj* (1986), 2 R.F.L. (3d) 305 (Ont. S.C.), the trial judge not only concluded that prejudgment interest was appropriate in ordering an entitlement under section 5 of the *Family Law Act, 1986* but also backdated the interest payments to a date preceding the commencement of the Act, namely, March 1, 1986. In addressing the issue of prejudgment interest, Galligan J. observed (at p. 315):

> I have been very concerned about the question of pre-judgment interest. I do not see specifically in the Family Law Act, 1986, where the court is called upon to consider interest. However, it seems to me that the pre-judgment interest provisions of the Courts of Justice Act should apply to payments ordered under the Family Law Act. There is of course some residual discretion in the Court under that Act and I see no reason in principle, subject to judicial discretion, why the pre-judgment interest provisions should not be considered in this type of case.
>
> In this case the husband has had the exclusive benefit of the moneys covered by the equalizing payment. I can think of no reason in justice or in common sense why he should not be required to return the interest that he had earned in the interim on that money. I am sure that he has earned interest on it. I specifically disbelieve him when he said that he just squandered that money. I have decided that the petitioner is entitled to pre-judgment interest.
>
> The issue is: at what rate, and over what period? The parties have had a history of keeping their money in savings accounts in trust companies. Filed as Ex. 14 is a schedule of interest rates payable on savings accounts. It is my opinion that the fair disposition of interest is to allow interest at the average rate over the period, taking the rates from Ex. 14. I have decided that pre-judgment interest will begin on 1st June 1982. That is the beginning of the first month following the respondent's cleaning-out of the joint savings account, Ex. 3. So, there will be interest on [the] equalizing payment at the average rate of interest as shown in Ex. 14, from 1st June 1982 to date.

However, in *Rawluk v. Rawluk* (1986), 55 O.R. (2d) 704, at 712, 29 D.L.R. (4th) 754, 3 R.F.L. (3d) 113 (S.C.), Walsh J. distinguished *Skrlj v. Skrlj, supra*, and declined to order prejudgment interest. Walsh J. observed:

> While my brother Galligan in *Skrlj, supra*, awarded prejudgment interest, it was on the basis that the moneys representing the equalization payment were joint funds taken by the husband on separation and that justice required he return to the wife the interest earned on that money. Such is not the case here. There are few, if any, moneys on deposit earning interest. The assets are mixed and complex, the payment most substantial, and given that the wife's right to an equalization payment itself arose only on March 1, 1986, I decline any award of prejudgment interest.

And in *Benke v. Benke*, unreported, December 10, 1986 (Ont. Dist. Ct.), Misener D.C.J. concluded that the wife was entitled to prejudgment interest pursuant to section 138 of the *Courts of Justice Act*, S.O. 1984, c. 11, but that it should not pre-date March 1, 1986, the date on which the *Family Law Act, 1986* came into force: see also *Crawford v. Crawford* (1987), 6 R.F.L. (3d) 308 (Ont. S.C.) (Sirois J.) and compare *Nelson v. Nelson, supra.*

In *Marsham v. Marsham*, unreported, May 5, 1987 (Ont. S.C.), wherein the wife was granted exclusive possession of the matrimonial home until June 30, 1990, Walsh J. declined to award *post-judgment* interest on the equalization payment but stipulated that the wife should not be charged with any occupation rent, provided she paid all carrying charges and maintained the home in a reasonable state of repair. And in *Humphreys v. Humphreys* (1987), 7 R.F.L. (3d) 113 (Ont. S.C.), Galligan J. refused to order pre-judgment interest "because the judgment relates to the value of an asset [namely, a pension] that Mr. Humphreys cannot realize upon until long in the future and could not have realized upon it in the past" and deferred any "post-judgment interest until the date of closing of the sale of the [former matrimonial home]."

The provisions of subsections 6(6) and (6a) of the *Family Law Act, 1986*, as enacted by section 2 of the *Family Law Amendment Act*, S.O. 1986, c. 35, which relate to death benefits under life insurance policies, pension plans or similar plans (see *supra*, 9.0 ENTITLEMENT ON DEATH), apply with respect to deaths that occurred before or after the coming into force of the Act: *Family Law Amendment Act*, S.O. 1986, c. 35, section 3.

PART II

MATRIMONIAL HOME

15.0 GENERAL

Part II of the *Family Law Act, 1986* supersedes Part III of the *Family Law Reform Act*, R.S.O. 1980, c. 152. The provisions of Part II of the *Family Law Act, 1986* regulate spousal possessory rights in the matrimonial home and the power to dispose of or encumber any interest in a matrimonial home. For the purposes of Part II, the definition of "spouse" in subsections 1(1) and (2) of the Act applies: see *supra*, PART I — FAMILY PROPERTY, subheading 3.0 DEFINITION OF "SPOUSE".

16.0 JURISDICTION

Definition of court

Definitions
   17. In this part,

"court"
"court" means a court as defined in subsection 1(1) but does not include the Provincial Court (Family Division);

Definitions
   1.—(1) In this Act,

"court"
"court" means the Provincial Court (Family Division), the Unified Family Court, the District Court or the Supreme Court;

The jurisdiction to entertain an application for relief under Part II of the *Family Law Act, 1986* is vested in the Unified Family Court, the District Court or the Supreme Court: see definition of "court in subsection 1(1) and section 17 of the *Family Law Act, 1986, supra*. Subject to possible qualification under subsections 34(1) and (2) of the *Family Law Act, 1986*, which apply to applications for support under Part III of the Act, the Provincial Court (Family Division) is constitutionally barred from exercising any jurisdiction over matters falling within the ambit of Part II of the *Family Law Act, 1986*: see *Reference re Section 6 of the Family Relations Act, S.B.C. 1978, c. 20*, [1982] 1 S.C.R. 62, 36 B.C.L.R. 1, [1982] 3 W.W.R. 1, 131 D.L.R. (3d) 257, 40 N.R. 206, 26 R.F.L. (2d) 113; *Re Lamb v. Lamb et al.*, [1985] 1 S.C.R. 851, 20 D.L.R. (4th) 1, 59 N.R. 166, 46 R.F.L. (2d) 1.

17.0 INDIAN LANDS

See *infra*, 25.0 POSSESSION ORDERS, 25.3 "Jurisdiction; constitutional implications".

18.0 DEFINITION OF "PROPERTY"

Definitions
   17. In this Part,

Part II applies to real and personal property

      ...

"property" means real or personal property.

Pursuant to the definition of "property" in section 17 of the *Family Law Act, 1986*, the provisions of Part II of the Act apply not only to real property but also to personal property. Part II accordingly extends to leasehold interests and to mobile homes, trailers and houseboats: *Smith v. Smith* (1985), 46 R.F.L. (2d) 323 (Ont. Dist. Ct.); *Caldwell v. Caldwell* (1978), 1 F.L.R.A.C. 143 (Ont. Dist. Ct.).

19.0 DEFINITION OF "MATRIMONIAL HOME"

Matrimonial home   *one of spouses*
   18.—(1) Every property in which a person has an interest and that is or, if the spouses have separated, was at the time of separation ordinarily occupied by the person and his or her spouse as their family residence is their matrimonial home.

Ownership of shares   *Co-operative housing shares*
   (2) The ownership of a share or shares, or of an interest in a share or shares, of a corporation entitling the owner to occupy a housing unit owned by the corporation shall be deemed to be an interest in the unit for the purposes of subsection (1).

Residence on farmland, etc.
   (3) If property that includes a matrimonial home is normally used for a purpose other than residential, the matrimonial home is only the part of the property that may reasonably be regarded as necessary to the use and enjoyment of the residence.

Subsection 18(1) of the *Family Law Act, 1986* requires two conditions to be satisfied before property can be characterized as a matrimonial home. The first condition requires that one of the spouses have an "interest" in the property. The nature of the interest to be held therein is not defined and would apparently include any interest that is recognized in law or equity, including a fee simple, a life estate or a leasehold interest. The ownership of shares in a co-operative housing scheme that entitles the shareholder to occupy a housing unit owned by the corporation constitutes an interest in the unit for the purposes of Part II of the Act: see subsection 18(2) and *Hartling v. Hartling*, [1979] 2 A.C.W.S. 555 (Ont. S.C.).

Subsection 18(1), which is central to the application of Part II of the *Family Law Act, 1986* and may also be of relevance to Part I with respect to the definition of "net family property" in subsection 4(1) (see *Folga v. Folga* (1986), 2 R.F.L. (3d) 358 (Ont. S.C.)) and in the context of paragraphs 4(2)1 and 4(2)5 of the Act, appears to be directed to the circumstance where only one spouse has an interest in the property. The language of subsections 19(2) and 20(2) of the Act and the judicial application of subsection 21(1) of the Act to joint tenancies (see, for example, *Kozub v. Timko* and *Sullivan v. Sullivan*; compare *Re Henry and Cymbalisty, infra*, heading 22.0 ALIENATION OF MATRIMONIAL HOME) may deny, however, such a restrictive interpretation being accorded to subsection 18(1).

The second condition arising under subsection 18(1) of the *Family Law Act, 1986* requires that the property be ordinarily occupied by both spouses as their family residence or that it had been so occupied immediately prior to the separation of the spouses: see *Folga v. Folga, supra*. Subsection 18(1) may result in more than one matrimonial home if, for example, the spouses are living, or at the time of separation were living, in an urban residence but also enjoyed the benefits of a summer cottage: *Schaefer v. Schaefer* (1986), 38 A.C.W.S. (2d) 142 (Ont. S.C.). A former residence that has ceased to be ordinarily occupied by the spouses as their matrimonial home and that was no longer so occupied immediately prior to their separation falls outside the ambit of subsection 18(1) of the *Family Law Act, 1986*. This appears to be so, even if that residence would have constituted a matrimonial home within the broader definition of subsection 39(1) of the *Family Law Reform Act*, R.S.O. 1980, c. 152, whereby any residence that had previously been occupied by the spouses as their family residence retained its character as a matrimonial home in the absence of a statutory designation under section 41 of the *Family Law Reform Act*: compare *Meszaros v. Meszaros* (1978), 22 O.R. (2d) 695 (S.C.). The retroactive provisions of clause 28(2)(b) of the *Family Law Act, 1986* clearly justify the above conclusion.

The phrase "ordinarily occupied . . . as their family residence" signifies more than the occasional occupation of a residence. In the words of Steinberg U.F.C.J. in *Taylor v. Taylor* (1978), 6 R.F.L. (2d) 341, at 350:

> The term "family residence" connotes something more than the simple occupation of a dwelling. It must be the residence around which a couple's normal family life revolves.

See also *C. v. C. (No. 1)* (1979), 11 R.F.L. (2d) 356 (Ont. Co. Ct.).

Where property which includes the matrimonial home is normally used for non-residential purposes, such as farming or business activities, the matrimonial home only includes that part of the property reasonably necessary to the use and enjoyment of the residence: *Family Law Act, 1986*, subsection 18(3); see *Meszaros v. Meszaros, supra; Youngblut v. Youngblut* (1979), 11 R.F.L. (2d) 249 (Ont. S.C.). The use of surrounding acreage for family recreation would not, however, trigger the operation of subsection 18(3) of the Act: see *Dowding v. Dowding* (1978), 1 F.L.R.A.C. 57 (Ont. S.C.).

20.0 POSSESSORY RIGHTS

See *infra*, 25.0 POSSESSION OF MATRIMONIAL HOME.

21.0 DESIGNATION OF MATRIMONIAL HOME

Designation of matrimonial home
20.—(1) One or both spouses may designate property owned by one or both of them as a matrimonial home, in the form prescribed by the regulations made under this Act.

Contiguous property
(2) The designation may include property that is described in the designation and is contiguous to the matrimonial home.

Registration
(3) The designation may be registered in the proper land registry office.

Effect of designation by both spouses
(4) On the registration of a designation made by both spouses, any other property that is a matrimonial home under section 18 but is not designated by both spouses ceases to be a matrimonial home.

Effect of designation by one spouse
(5) On the registration of a designation made by one spouse

only, any other property that is a matrimonial home under section 18 remains a matrimonial home.

Cancellation of designation

(6) The designation of a matrimonial home is cancelled, and the property ceases to be a matrimonial home, on the registration or deposit of,

    (a) a cancellation, executed by the person or persons who made the original designation, in the form prescribed by the regulations made under this Act;

    (b) a decree absolute of divorce or judgment of nullity;

    (c) an order under clause 23(e) cancelling the designation; or

    (d) proof of death of one of the spouses.

The provisions of section 20 of the *Family Law Act, 1986* differ significantly from those of its predecessor, section 41 of the *Family Law Reform Act*, R.S.O. 1980, c. 152 Pursuant to subsection 20(1) of the *Family Law Act*, either or both of the spouses may designate property owned by one or both of them as the matrimonial home. Such designation is to be made in the form prescribed by the regulation made pursuant to the Act. The designation may include property that is contiguous to the family residence (subsection 20(2)) and the designation may be registered in the appropriate land registry office (subsection 22(3)). The effect of such registration then depends upon whether the designation was made by both spouses or by one spouse acting unilaterally. In the former case, property other than that jointly designated as the matrimonial home no longer falls within the ambit of section 18 of the Act: subsection 20(4). Consequently, the provisions of Part II of the *Family Law Act, 1986* apply only to the jointly designated property. Property that has not been included in the joint designation can thus be freely disposed of or encumbered by the titleholder and occupational rights therein will be dependent upon title. The definition of "net family property" in subsection 4(1), and paragraphs 4(2)1 and 4(2)5 of the *Family Law Act, 1986*, which accord a special status to the matrimonial home in the determination of the net family property of a spouse for the purposes of an equalization claim, are also presumably confined to the property that has been jointly designated as the matrimonial home, provided that the registration of the joint designation preceded the "valuation date" as defined in subsection 4(1) of the Act: see definition of "matrimonial home" in subsection 4(1) of the *Family Law Act, 1986*. Different results ensue, however, where one spouse unilaterally designates particular property as the matrimonial home. Pursuant to subsection 20(5) of the Act, the registration of such a designation does not operate to take non-designated property outside the ambit of section 18. Consequently, Parts I and II of the *Family Law Act, 1986* continue to apply to both the designated and undesignated property that constitutes a matrimonial home within the meaning of section 18 of the Act. A duly registered unilateral designation may, nevertheless, be of significance as a means of deterring or preventing the titleholder from disposing of or encumbering the designated property in that the registration would constitute (notice) to any prospective purchaser for value that the spouse of the titleholder is asserting rights in respect of the property.

Any designation of property as a matrimonial home may be cancelled in accordance with the provisions of subsection 20(6) of the Act. Upon such cancellation, the property previously designated as the matrimonial home ceases to be a matrimonial home for the purposes of Part II of the Act, and presumably also for the purpose of Part I of the Act, if such cancellation precedes the valuation date, but the cancellation of a joint designation brings non-designated property back within the ambit of section 18 and consequently Parts I and II of the Act. The cancellation of a designation occurs on the registration or deposit of: (a) a cancellation, executed by the person or persons who made the original designation, in the form prescribed by the statutory regulations; (b) a final judgment of divorce or nullity; (c) an order of the court made pursuant to clause 23(e) of the Act or (d) proof of death of one of the spouses.

22.0 ALIENATION OF MATRIMONIAL HOME

Alienation of matrimonial home

21.—(1) No spouse shall dispose of or encumber an interest in a matrimonial home unless,

> **(a) the other spouse joins in the instrument or consents to the transaction;**
>
> **(b) the other spouse has released all rights under this Part by a separation agreement;**
>
> **(c) a court order has authorized the transaction or has released the property from the application of this Part; or**
>
> **(d) the property is not designated by both spouses as a matrimonial home and a designation of another property as a matrimonial home, made by both spouses, is registered and not cancelled.**

Setting aside transaction

(2) If a spouse disposes of or encumbers an interest in a matrimonial home in contravention of subsection (1), the transaction may be set aside on an application under section 23,

unless the person holding the interest or encumbrance at the time of the application acquired it for value, in good faith and without notice, at the time of acquiring it or making an agreement to acquire it, that the property was a matrimonial home.

Proof that property not a matrimonial home

(3) For the purpose of subsection (2), a statement by the person making the disposition or encumbrance,

    (a) verifying that he or she is not, or was not, a spouse at the time of the disposition or encumbrance;

    (b) verifying that the person is a spouse who is not separated from his or her spouse and that the property is not ordinarily occupied by the spouses as their family residence;

    (c) verifying that the person is a spouse who is separated from his or her spouse and that the property was not ordinarily occupied by the spouses, at the time of their separation, as their family residence;

    (d) where the property is not designated by both spouses as a matrimonial home, verifying that a designation of another property as a matrimonial home, made by both spouses, is registered and not cancelled; or

    (e) verifying that the other spouse has released all rights under this Part by a separation agreement,

shall, unless the person to whom the disposition or encumbrance is made had notice to the contrary, be deemed to be sufficient proof that the property is not a matrimonial home.

Idem, attorney's personal knowledge

(4) The statement shall be deemed to be sufficient proof that the property is not a matrimonial home if it is made by the attorney of the person making the disposition or encumbrance, on the basis of the attorney's personal knowledge.

Liens arising by operation of law

(5) This section does not apply to the acquisition of an interest in property by operation of law or to the acquisition of a lien under section 18 of the *Legal Aid Act* [R.S.O. 1980, c. 234].

Subsection 21(1) of the *Family Law Act, 1986*, S.O. 1986, c. 4, like its predecessor, subsection 42(1) of the *Family Law Reform Act*, R.S.O. 1980, c. 152, imposes a general prohibition against a spouse unilaterally disposing of or encumbering an interest in a matrimonial home: see *Clarkson v. Lukovich* (1986), 54 O.R. (2d) 609, 28 D.L.R. (4th) 277, 2 R.F.L. (3d) 392 (S.C.), wherein a divorced wife was held entitled to defend an action brought by a third party for specific performance of a pre-divorce contract for the purchase and sale of the matrimonial home, because her refusal to consent to the disposition was not unreasonably withheld and, furthermore, she was entitled to an exclusive interest in the matrimonial home pursuant to an oral agreement between the spouses. It has been held that a matrimonial home owned by the spouses as joint tenants falls within the ambit of the statutory prohibition and that the conveyance of a joint tenant's interest in the matrimonial home to a third party does not operate to sever the joint tenancy in the absence of compliance with the exclusionary provisions to clauses 21(1)(a) to (d): *Kozub v. Timko* (1984), 45 O.R. (2d) 588, 7 D.L.R. (4th) 509, 39 R.F.L. (2d) 146 (C.A.). Judicial opinion has been divided, however, on the question whether the severance of a joint tenancy in the matrimonial home can be unilaterally effectuated by a joint tenant executing a conveyance of his or her interest therein to himself or herself: see, for example, *Re Lamanna and Lamanna et al.* (1983), 27 R.P.R. 142, 32 R.F.L. (2d) 386, 145 D.L.R. (3d) 117 (Ont. S.C.); compare *Wierzbicki v. Wierzbicki* (1986), 55 O.R. (2d) 77, 29 D.L.R. (4th) 78, 3 R.F.L. (3d) 82 (S.C.) and *Re Van Dorp and Van Dorp* (1980), 30 O.R. (2d) 623 (Co. Ct.); see also *Knowlton v. Bartlett* (1983), 60 N.B.R. (2d) 271, 157 A.P.R. 271 (Q.B.) and see Derek Mendes da Costa, "Conveyance by One Joint Tenant to Self" (1984), 18 Law Society of Upper Canada Gazette 213. This difference of judicial opinion was recently addressed by the Ontario Court of Appeal in *Re Horne and Evans*, unreported, May 28, 1987, wherein it was held that a conveyance by one joint tenant to himself or herself for the purpose of severing a joint tenancy does not "dispose of" an "interest" in the matrimonial home within the meaning of section 42 of the *Family Law Reform Act*, R.S.O. 1980, c. 152 or section 21 of the *Family Law Act, 1986*, S.O. 1986, c. 4.

The statutory prohibition imposed by subsection 21(1) does not apply if the spouse without any interest in the matrimonial home joins in the instrument or consents to the disposition or encumbrance of the matrimonial home: clause 21(1)(a). The prohibition is also inapplicable where the non-titleholding spouse has released his or her rights under Part II of the Act under a separation agreement, as distinct from a marriage contract: clause 21(1)(b); see text *infra*, PART IV — DOMESTIC CONTRACTS, subheadings 31.0 "MARRIAGE CONTRACTS" and 33.0 "SEPARATION AGREEMENTS". A trustee in bankruptcy is not bound by the statutory prohibition and may transfer the husband's interest in the matrimonial home to his creditors whose loan to the husband was secured by a mortgage on the jointly owned matrimonial home: *Allesandro Building Corporation v. Rocca* (1986), 2 R.F.L. (3d) 32 (Ont. S.C.) (applying section 42 of the *Family Law Reform Act*, R.S.O. 1980, c. 152); see also *Re Neustaedter and Armitage* (1986), 56 O.R. (2d) 769, 32 D.L.R. (4th) 627 (S.C.), wherein it was held that a husband's beneficial interest in the matrimonial home owned under joint tenancy may be assigned to his trustee in bankruptcy and such an assignment does not contravene section 42 of the *Family Law Reform Act,* R.S.O. 1980, c. 152. Similarly, in *Re Ali (No. 1)* (1987), 57 O.R. (2d) 597, 5 R.F.L. (3d) 228 (S.C.), it was held that an assignment in bankruptcy is not a disposition within the meaning of section 21 of the *Family Law Act, 1986,* and does not require the consent of the spouse of the bankrupt. Such an assignment operates to sever the spousal joint tenancy in the matrimonial home and vests the interest of the bankrupt in the trustee. Consequently, the matrimonial home becomes owned by the spouse and the trustee as tenants in common. Although a tenant in common has a *prima facie* right to partition and sale, the court has a discretion to refuse an application for partition and sale where a sale would result in hardship. The spouse's possessory right in the matrimonial home conferred by subsection 19(1) of the *Family Law Act, 1986* is not terminated by the assignment in bankruptcy. The trustee in bankruptcy stands in no better position than the bankrupt and should commence proceedings under section 23 of the *Family Law Act, 1986* rather than, or in addition to, proceedings under the *Partition Act,* R.S.O. 1980, c. 369. In such proceedings, the court may be required to address the question of whether comparable accommodation or payment in lieu thereof is available to the spouse and children of the marriage.

A court order made pursuant to section 23 of the Act may override the statutory prohibition under section 21 and release the property from the application of Part II of the Act: clause 21(1)(c). In *Sullivan v. Sullivan* (1986), 2 R.F.L. (3d) 251 (Ont. Dist. Ct.), clause 23(b) of the *Family Law Act, 1986* was held inapplicable to a matrimonial home held under joint tenancy by the spouses, but a sale of the home was ordered pursuant to clause 21(1)(c) of the Act. However, in *Re Henry and Cymbalisty* (1986), 55 O.R. (2d) 51 (Unified Fam. Ct.), clauses 23(b) and 21(1)(c) were both interpreted as inapplicable to a matrimonial home held under joint tenancy. The court accordingly refused to order a transfer of the wife's interest in the matrimonial home to her husband, notwithstanding her undertakings in a duly executed domestic contract. In the words of Steinberg U.F.C.J., *supra,* at 56:
And see to like effect: *Rametta v. Rametta* (1987), 6 R.F.L. (3d) 294 (Ont. S.C.).

[handwritten margin notes: s. 23(b) s. 21(1)(c) can't be used if matrimonial home held under a "joint" tenancy]

> In my view, ss. 23 and 21(1)(*c*) can only be invoked so as to limit or cancel the right of possession of a non-consenting spouse in a matrimonial home. They cannot be interpreted so as to defeat a spouse's legal or equitable estate in a matrimonial home, no matter how unjustly or irrational he or she may be behaving in regards to the administration of the property.

The statutory prohibition is inapplicable where the property has not

So if both spouses have designated it as a home must use

been jointly designated by the spouses as a matrimonial home but other property has been so designated, and that designation has been registered and not cancelled: clause 21(1)(d). This explicit exclusion would appear to have been stipulated out of excessive caution, having regard to the provisions of subsections 20(1), (4) and (6) of the *Family Law Act, 1986, supra.*

21 (1)
a) consent
b) separation agreement
c) court order

s. 21 (2) set aside transaction if spouse disposes of or encumbers of a matrimonial home

If a spouse acts in contravention of subsection 21(1) in disposing of or encumbering an interest in a matrimonial home, the transaction may be set aside: subsection 21(2). This requires an application to be made under section 23 of the Act and the courts discretionary jurisdiction to set aside the transaction cannot be invoked against a third party who in good faith acquired rights in the home for value and without notice that the property was a matrimonial home: subsection 21(2). In the absence of actual or constructive notice to the contrary, a statement by the spouse making the disposition or encumbrance or by a person acting on his or her behalf under a power of attorney, which purports to verify particular circumstances that render the statutory prohibition inapplicable to the transaction, is sufficient to protect the interests of the *bona fide* purchaser for value: subsections 21(3) and (4): compare the requirements of subsection 42(3) of the *Family Law Reform Act*, R.S.O. 1980, c. 152, which expressly referred to "actual notice to the contrary" and see *Stoimenov v. Stoimenov* (1985), 50 O.R. (2d) 1, 44 R.F.L. (2d) 14 (C.A.),

person who made false statement is liable under s. 24 (1)(g)

revg (1983), 40 O.R. (2d) 69, 31 R.F.L. (2d) 173 (S.C.). The person who made the false statement may, nevertheless, be accountable pursuant to clause 24(1)(g) of the Act, which empowers the court to direct that other "real property" be substituted for the matrimonial home (compare section 17, *supra*) or that money may be set aside or security stand in its place.

Section 21 of the *Family Law Act, 1986* is expressly declared inapplicable to the acquisition of an interest in property by operation of law or to the acquisition of a lien under section 18 of the *Legal Aid Act*, R.S.O. 1980, c. 234: *Family Law Act, 1986*, subsection 21(5) and see *MacBride v. MacBride and Canco Employees (Hamilton) Credit Union Ltd. (Third Party)*, unreported, May 29, 1987 (Ont. Unified Fam. Ct.).

23.0 RIGHTS OF REDEMPTION AND NOTICE

Right of redemption and to notice

22.—(1) When a person proceeds to realize upon a lien, encumbrance or execution or exercises a forfeiture against property that is a matrimonial home, the spouse who has a right of possession under section 19 has the same right of redemption or relief against forfeiture as the other spouse and is entitled to the same notice respecting the claim and its enforcement or realization.

Service of notice

(2) A notice to which a spouse is entitled under subsection (1) shall be deemed to be sufficiently given if served or given personally or by registered mail addressed to the spouse at his or her usual or last known address or, if none, the address of the matrimonial home, and, if notice is served or given by mail, the service shall be deemed to have been made on the fifth day after the day of mailing.

Idem; power of sale

(3) When a person exercises a power of sale against property that is a matrimonial home, sections 32 and 33 of the *Mortgages Act* [R.S.O. 1980, c. 296] apply and subsection (2) does not apply.

Payments by spouse

(4) If a spouse makes a payment in exercise of the right conferred by subsection (1), the payment shall be applied in satisfaction of the claim giving rise to the lien, encumbrance, execution or forfeiture.

Realization may continue in spouse's absence

(5) Despite any other Act, when a person who proceeds to realize upon a lien, encumbrance or execution or exercises a forfeiture does not have any sufficient particulars of a spouse for the purpose and there is no response to a notice given under subsection (2) or under section 32 of the *Mortgages Act*, the realization or exercise of forfeiture may continue in the absence and without regard to the interest of the spouse and the spouse's rights under this section end on the completion of the realization or forfeiture.

Section 22 of the *Family Law Act, 1986* supersedes section 43 of the *Family Law Reform Act*, R.S.O. 1980, c. 152. Pursuant to subsection 22(1), a spouse with a right of possession under section 19 of the Act has the same right to notice and to redemption or relief against forfeiture as the titleholding spouse in the event that a third party seeks to realize upon a lien, encumbrance or execution against property that is a matrimonial home: see *Maritime Life Assurance Company v. Karapatakis* (1979), 24 O.R. (2d) 311, 10 C.P.C. 301, 7 R.P.R. 229, 9 R.F.L. (2d) 265 (S.C.). In exercising the rights conferred by subsection 22(1), a payment made by the spouse shall be applied in satisfaction of the claim giving rise to the lien, encumbrance, execution or forfeiture: subsection 22(4). Subsection 22(2) of the Act defines the means of providing due notice by way of personal service or registered mail and such notice takes effect on the fifth day after mailing. Pursuant to subsection 22(3), however, the notice requirements of subsection 22(2) do not qualify or supersede the provisions of sections 32 and 33 of the *Mortgages Act*, R.S.O. 1980, c. 296: compare *Re Kinross Mortgage Corporation v. Canada Mortgage and Housing Corporation* (1981), 128 D.L.R. (3d) 477, 18 R.P.R. 293 (Ont. S.C.). Subsection 22(5) provides that when a person, who seeks to realize upon a lien, encumbrance or execution or exercises a right of forfeiture, does not have sufficient particulars of a spouse to serve notice or there has been no response to any notice given, the realization or forfeiture may continue without regard to the interest of the spouse and the rights conferred on the spouse by section 22 terminate on the completion of the realization or forfeiture: compare *Maritime Life Assurance Company v. Karapatakis, supra.* In the alternative, an application may be brought under clause 23(c) to dispense with the notice required under section 22.

24.0 POWERS OF COURT RESPECTING ALIENATION

Powers of court respecting alienation
 23. **The court may, on the application of a spouse or person having an interest in property, by order,**
 (a) **determine whether or not the property is a matrimonial home and, if so, its extent;**
 (b) **authorize the disposition or encumbrance of the matrimonial home if the court finds that the spouse whose consent is required,**
 (i) **cannot be found or is not available,**
 (ii) **is not capable of giving or withholding consent, or**
 (iii) **is unreasonably withholding consent,**
 subject to any conditions, including provision of other comparable accommodation or payment in place of it, that the court considers appropriate;
 (c) **dispense with a notice required to be given under section 22;**
 (d) **direct the setting aside of a transaction disposing of or encumbering an interest in the matrimonial home contrary to subsection 21(1) and the revesting of the interest or any part of it on the conditions that the court considers appropriate; and**
 (e) **cancel a designation made under section 20 if the property is not a matrimonial home.**

Clauses 23(a), (b), (c) and (d) of the *Family Law Act, 1986* substantially correspond to clauses 44(a), (b), (c) and (d) of the *Family Law Reform Act*, R.S.O. 1980, c. 152. Clause 23(e) of the *Family Law Act, 1986* is a new provision.

The powers conferred on the court by section 23 of the Act are exercisable on the application of a spouse or any other person with an interest: see *Re Ali (No. 1)* (1987), 57 O.R. (2d) 597, 5 R.F.L. (3d) 228 (S.C.), *supra*, 22.0 "ALIENATION OF MATRIMONIAL HOME". For example, a person seeking to realize upon a lien, encumbrance or execution or to exercise a forfeiture against property that is a matrimonial home may invoke clause 23(c) of the Act to dispense with the statutory notice required under section 22. And third parties, such as persons who have entered into an agreement with one spouse for the purchase and sale of a matrimonial home, are entitled to invoke clause 23(b) of the Act: see *Re Menard and Butler* (1981), 21 R.P.R. 7 (Ont. Co. Ct.); *Gotkin v. Krawczyk et al.; Krawczyk Third Party* (1984), 27 A.C.W.S. (2d) 336 (Ont. S.C.).

Clause 23(a) of the Act empowers the court to determine whether or not property constitutes a matrimonial home and, if so, its extent. Although this section will ordinarily be invoked in the context of Part II of the *Family Law Act, 1986* it could also presumably be invoked in the context of paragraphs 4(2)1 and 4(2)5 of the Act.

Clause 23(b) of the Act empowers the court to dispense with the spousal consent required under subsection 21(1) as a precondition to the disposition or encumbrance of an interest in the matrimonial home: see *Sullivan v. Sullivan* (1986), 2 R.F.L. (3d) 251 (Ont. Dist. Ct.) and compare *Re Henry and Cymbalisty* (1986), 55 O.R. (2d) 51 (Unified Fam. Ct.), and *Rametta v. Rametta* (1987), 6 R.F.L. (3d) 294 (Ont. S.C.), *supra*, 22.0 "ALIENATION OF MATRIMONIAL HOME". Such dispensation may be ordered where the spouse whose consent is required cannot be found or is otherwise not available, is not capable of giving or withholding consent, or unreasonably withholds consent. The judicial dispensation may be made subject to any conditions that the court deems appropriate, including the provision of comparable accommodation or payment in substitution therefor. The words "comparable accommodation" in clause 23(b) are somewhat more restrictive than the words "suitable and affordable accommodation" which appear in clause 24(3)(e) of the *Family Law Act, 1986*.

Clause 23(d) empowers the court to set aside a transaction disposing of or encumbering an interest in the matrimonial home that contravenes the requirements of subsection 21(1) and to reinvest the interest or any part of it on such conditions as the court deems appropriate. This power cannot be exercised, however, against a *bona fide* purchaser for value without notice: see *Family Law Act, 1986*, subsections 21(2) and (3), *supra*. The victimized spouse may, nevertheless, invoke clause 24(1)(g) of the Act against the perpetrator of a false statement that was relied upon by the *bona fide* purchaser for value without notice. Pursuant to clause 24(1)(g), where a false statement has been made under subsection 21(3) of the Act, the person making the statement, or a person who acquired an interest in the matrimonial home with knowledge that the statement

93

was false and who thereafter conveyed that interest, may be ordered to substitute other real property for the matrimonial home or set aside money or security to stand in its place, subject to any conditions deemed appropriate by the court.

Clause 23(e) of the *Family Law Act, 1986* expressly empowers the court to cancel a designation of property as a matrimonial home made pursuant to section 20, if the property is not a matrimonial home.

Where conditions have been imposed on an order made pursuant to clauses 23(b) or (d) or clause 24(1)(g) of the Act, they may be discharged, varied or suspended on the motion of the person subject to the conditions, or his or her personal representative, if the court is satisfied that they are no longer appropriate: *Family Law Act, 1986*, subsection 25(2).

25.0 POSSESSION OF A MATRIMONIAL HOME

25.1 Possessory rights in matrimonial home

Possession of matrimonial home
  19.—(1) Both spouses have an equal right to possession of a matrimonial home.

Idem
  (2) When only one of the spouses has an interest in a matrimonial home, the other spouse's right of possession,
  (a) is personal as against the first spouse; and
  (b) ends when they cease to be spouses, unless a separation agreement or court order provides otherwise.

Section 19 of the *Family Law Act, 1986* supersedes section 40 of the *Family Law Reform Act*, R.S.O. 1980, c. 4.

Pursuant to subsection 19(1), both spouses have an equal right to possession of the matrimonial home, regardless of whether title is vested in one or both spouses. The statutory right conferred by subsection 19(1) applies without regard to the conduct of the spouses or the state of their marital relationship. The right of possession of a non-titled spouse appears to be dependent, however, upon that of the titled spouse. If the titled spouse has no right of possession, the non-titled spouse cannot assert a possessory right under subsection 19(1): see *Re Mauro* (1983), 41 O.R. (2d) 157, 45 C.B.R. (N.S.) 229, 32 R.F.L. (2d) 362 (S.C.); *Royal Bank of Canada v. Nicholson* (1981), 29 O.R. (2d) 141, 112 D.L.R. (3d) 364, 19 R.F.L. (2d) 84 (S.C.); compare *Re Ali (No. 1)* (1987), 57 O.R. (2d) 597, 5 R.F.L. (2d) 228 (S.C.), *supra*, 22.0 "ALIENATION OF MATRIMONIAL HOME".

Pursuant to subsection 19(2) of the Act, where only one spouse has an interest in the property, the possessory right of the other spouse is personal as against the spouse with the interest: *Re Henry and Cymbalisty* (1986), 55 O.R. (2d) 51, at 54 (Ont. Unified Fam. Ct.). It cannot be assigned to or assumed by third parties: *Chalmers v. Copfer* (1978), 7 R.F.L. (2d) 393 (Ont. Co. Ct.). Furthermore, in the absence of any contrary provision in a separation agreement or court order, the possessory right of the spouse without any interest in the matrimonial home terminates when the spouses cease to be spouses. This does not preclude an application being brought under section 10 of the Act to determine disputed questions of possession arising between former spouses.

A court may grant an order for exclusive possession of the [C-L] spouse matrimonial home that will survive the termination of the spousal *may get* relationship under the authority of section 24 or clause 34(1)(d) of the *Part II* *Family Law Act, 1986.* Clause 19(2)(b) of the Act expressly recognizes that *matrimonial home rights* a similar right may be conferred on the non-titled spouse by the *via s. 34* provisions of a separation agreement. *Quaere* whether the provisions of a (support) marriage contract could confer a corresponding right on the non-titled *order.* spouse, in light of the express provisions of subsection 2(10), clause 19(2)(b) and subsection 52(2) of the *Family Law Act, 1986.*

25.2 Order for possession of matrimonial home

Order for possession of matrimonial home
24.—(1) Regardless of the ownership of a matrimonial home and its contents, and despite section 19 (spouse's right of possession), the court may on application, by order,

> **(a) provide for the delivering up, safekeeping and preservation of the matrimonial home and its contents;**

24.—(1) (b) direct that one spouse be given exclusive possession of the matrimonial home or part of it for the period that the court directs and release other property that is a matrimonial home from the application of this Part;

> **(c) direct a spouse to whom exclusive possession of the matrimonial home is given to make periodic** *rent* **payments to the other spouse;**
> **(d) direct that the contents of the matrimonial home, or any part of them,**
> > **(i) remain in the home for the use of the spouse given possession, or**
> > **(ii) be removed from the home for the use of a spouse or child;**
> **(e) order a spouse to pay for all or part of the repair and maintenance of the matrimonial home and of**

95

other liabilities arising in respect of it, or to make periodic payments to the other spouse for those purposes;

(f) authorize the disposition or encumbrance of a spouse's interest in the matrimonial home, subject to the other spouse's right of exclusive possession as ordered; and

(g) where a false statement is made under subsection 21(3), direct,

    (i) the person who made the false statement, or

    (ii) a person who knew at the time he or she acquired an interest in the property that the statement was false and afterwards conveyed the interest,

to substitute other real property for the matrimonial home, or direct the person to set aside money or security to stand in place of it, subject to any conditions that the court considers appropriate.

Temporary or interim order

(2) The court may, on motion, make a temporary or interim order under clause 1(a), (b), (c), (d) or (e).

Order for exclusive possession: criteria

(3) In determining whether to make an order for exclusive possession, the court shall consider,

(a) the best interests of the children affected;

(b) any existing orders under Part I (Family Property) and any existing support orders;

(c) the financial position of both spouses;   *not a separation agreement*

(d) any written agreement between the parties;

(e) the availability of other suitable and affordable accommodation; and

(f) any violence committed by a spouse against the other spouse or the children.

Best interests of child

(4) In determining the best interests of a child, the court shall consider,

(a) the possible disruptive effects on the child of a move to other accommodation; and

(b) the child's views and preferences, if they can reasonably be ascertained.

Offence

(5) A person who contravenes an order for exclusive posses-

sion is guilty of an offence and upon conviction is liable,
  (a) in the case of a first offence, to a fine of not more than
      $1,000 or to imprisonment for a term of not more than
      three months, or to both; and
  (b) in the case of a second or subsequent offence, to a fine
      of not more than $10,000 or to imprisonment for a term
      of not more than two years, or to both.

Arrest without warrant
  (6) A police officer may arrest without warrant a person the
police officer believes on reasonable and probable grounds to
have contravened an order for exclusive possession.

Existing orders
  (7) Subsections (5) and (6) also apply in respect of contraventions, committed after this Act comes into force, of orders for
exclusive possession made under Part III of the *Family Law
Reform Act*.

Section 24 of the *Family Law Act, 1986* supersedes the provisions of
section 45 of the *Family Law Reform Act*, R.S.O. 1980, c. 152.

Section 24 of the *Family Law Act, 1986* confers a relatively broad
discretionary power on a court of competent jurisdiction to grant an
order for exclusive possession of the matrimonial home and/or its
contents to a non-titled spouse.

25.3 Jurisdiction: constitutional implications

Subject to possible qualification arising pursuant to clause 34(1)(d) and
subsection 34(2) in the context of support applications made under Part
III of the Act, the Provincial Court (Family Division) has no jurisdiction
to entertain an application under section 24: see definitions of "court" in
section 17 and subsection 1(1) of the Act; see also *Reference re Section 6 of
the Family Relations Act*, S.B.C. 1978, c. 20, [1982] 1 S.C.R. 62, 36 B.C.L.R.
1, [1982] 3 W.W.R. 1, 131 D.L.R. (3d) 257, 40 N.R. 206, 26 R.F.L. (2d)
113.

Although an order for exclusive possession of the matrimonial home
is relevant to support rights and obligations, it is not in and of itself a
support order. An application for exclusive possession of the matrimonial home under section 24 of the *Family Law Act, 1986* may accordingly
be joined with an application for support under the *Divorce Act, 1985*,
S.C. 1986, c. 4, and concurrent orders may be granted by the court
without offending the constitutional doctrine of paramountcy: *Re Lamb
and Lamb et al.*, [1985] 1 S.C.R. 851, 20 D.L.R. (4th) 1, 59 N.R. 166, 46
R.F.L. (2d) 1.

The provisions of section 24 of the *Family Law Act, 1986* have no application to a matrimonial home located on an Indian reserve by reason of the paramountcy of section 20 of the *Indian Act*, R.S.C. 1970, c. I-6: *Paul v. Paul et al.*, [1986] 1 S.C.R. 306, 1 B.C.L.R. 290, [1986] 3 W.W.R. 210, 26 D.L.R. (4th) 196, 65 N.R. 291, 50 R.F.L. (2d) 355; *Derrickson v. Derrickson et al.*, [1986] 1 S.C.R. 285, 1 B.C.L.R. 273, [1986] 3 W.W.R. 193, 26 D.L.R. (4th) 175, 65 N.R. 279, 50 R.F.L. (2d) 337; *Sandy v. Sandy* (1979), 27 O.R. (2d) 248, 107 D.L.R. (3d) 659, 13 R.F.L. (2d) 81 (C.A.).

25.4 Preservation orders

Clause 24(1)(a) of the *Family Law Act, 1986* empowers the court to grant an order for the delivering up, safekeeping and preservation of the matrimonial home and its contents. Although such an order may be made on a temporary or interim basis pursuant to subsection 24(2) of the Act, clause 24(1)(a), unlike section 47 of the *Family Law Reform Act*, R.S.O. 1980, c. 152, permits an order to be made on a permanent basis.

25.5 Duration of order; release of other property

Clause 24(1)(b) empowers the court to grant exclusive possession of a matrimonial home to one spouse for such a period as the court directs. An interim order or temporary order may be granted pursuant to subsection 24(2) of the Act. A permanent order could be declared operational during the joint lives of the "spouses" and perhaps even during the lifetime of the spouse granted exclusive possession of the matrimonial home: but see *Family Law Act, 1986*, subsection 26(2), *infra*; compare *Family Law Reform Act*, R.S.O. 1980, c. 152, which expressly empowered the court to grant exclusive possession of the matrimonial home to one spouse "for life". Such an order would not be terminated by the dissolution of the marriage.

An order may be granted for exclusive possession of only part of the matrimonial home: compare *Meleszko v. Meleszko* (1981), 24 C.P.C. 272, at 274 (Ont. S.C.) (Donkin, Master). In *Metcalf v. Metcalf* (1984), 47 O.R. (2d) 349, 40 R.F.L. (2d) 332 (Unified Fam. Ct.), Steinberg U.F.C.J. declared his willingness to make an order for exclusive possession of part of the matrimonial home in favour of both spouses that would reflect their current use of the premises. He was further prepared to reinforce the order by mutual restraining orders against each spouse.

Where an order for exclusive possession of the matrimonial home or part of it is granted to one spouse, clause 24(1)(b) empowers the court to release other property that is a matrimonial home under section 18 of the Act from the application of Part II, thus removing the constraints on alienation imposed by section 21 of the Act.

25.6 Order for periodic payments

A spouse who has been granted exclusive possession of the matrimonial home may be ordered to make periodic payments to the dispossessed spouse: *Family Law Act, 1986*, clause 24(1)(c). Such payments would, in effect, be a form of occupation rent: compare *Marsham v. Marsham, supra,* **PART I — FAMILY PROPERTY**, subheading 14.0 RETROSPECTIVE OPERATION; PREJUDGMENT INTEREST.

25.7 Contents of matrimonial home

Subclause 24(1)(d)(i) of the *Family Law Act, 1986* empowers the court to direct that all or part of the contents of the matrimonial home shall remain in the home for the use of the spouse granted exclusive possession of the home.

Subclause 24(1)(d)(i) is premised on the inter-relationship between exclusive possession of the home and the exclusive use and enjoyment of all or part of its contents. Subclause 24(1)(d)(ii) is not correspondingly circumscribed. Subclause 24(1)(d)(ii) empowers the court to order the removal of all or part of the contents of the matrimonial home for the use of a "spouse" or "child" as defined in subsections 1(1) and (2) of the *Family Law Act, 1986*. An application under subclause 24(1)(d)(ii) and an order consequential thereto may accordingly be made in the absence of any application or order for exclusive possession of the matrimonial home.

Clause 24(1)(d) relates to orders for the use of the contents of a matrimonial home. It does not empower the court to order an absolute transfer of such property. Such an order could be made, however, in the context of an equalization claim made pursuant to section 5 of the *Family Law Act, 1986*: see *ibid.,* subclause 9(1)(d)(i).

25.8 Order for repairs, maintenance, etc.

Clause 24(1)(e) of the *Family Law Act, 1986* empowers the court to order either spouse to pay for all or part of the repair or maintenance of the matrimonial home and of other liabilities arising in respect of it. Alternatively, the court may order periodic payments to be made for these purposes: see *Marsham v. Marsham, supra.* The words "other liabilities in respect of [the matrimonial home]" would clearly include mortgage payments, property taxes and insurance and perhaps include the indirect costs arising from the occupation of the home, such as heating, lighting and water: see *Langtvet v. Langtvet* (1978), 7 R.F.L. (2d) 224, at 233 (Ont. S.C.) (Killeen L.J.S.C.).

Clause 24(1)(e) is not conditioned on the existence of an order granting exclusive possession of the home to one spouse. Furthermore, where such an order is granted, an order under clause 24(1)(e) may be made against the spouse in possession (see *Langtvet v. Langtvet, supra; Campbell v. Campbell* (1979), 6 R.F.L. (2d) 392, at 396 (Ont. S.C.) (McBride, Master)) or against the dispossessed spouse, or the financial liabilities could be split between the spouses.

25.9 Disposition or encumbrance of matrimonial home

Where one spouse is granted an order for exclusive possession of the matrimonial home, clause 24(1)(f) of the *Family Law Act, 1986* empowers the court to authorize the disposition or encumbrance of the other spouse's interest in the home, subject to the rights conferred by the possession order. Clause 24(1)(f) supplements the provisions of clause 24(1)(b) of the Act, *supra*. An order made pursuant to clause 24(1)(f) appears to be final and irrevocable by reason of the exclusion of this clause from the provisions of subsection 24(2) (temporary or interim orders) and subsection 25(1) (variation orders) of the Act.

25.10 False statements made under subsection 21(3)

Clause 24(1)(g) of the *Family Law Act, 1986* regulates the effect of a false statement made under subsection 21(3) of the Act in relation to a disposition or encumbrance of the matrimonial home in contravention of the statutory requirement of spousal consent imposed by subsection 21(1) of the Act. The power of the court to set aside any such transaction under subsection 21(2) of the Act is not exercisable against a *bona fide* purchaser for value without notice. Clause 24(1)(g), nevertheless, protects a dispossessed non-titled spouse against the person making the false statement or any person who acquired an interest in the matrimonial home with knowledge of the falsity of the statement and thereafter conveyed that interest to another person. Pursuant to clause 24(1)(g), a party to the false statement may be ordered to substitute other *real* property (compare section 17, *supra*) for the matrimonial home or to set aside money or security to stand in place of it, subject to any conditions the court deems appropriate. If an order is made for the substitution of other real property, the court may presumably grant an exclusive possession order to the non-titled spouse in respect of that substituted property.

25.11 Temporary or interim orders

Subsection 24(2) of the *Family Law Act, 1986* empowers the court to make temporary or interim orders under clauses 24(1)(a), (b), (c), (d) and (e) of the Act. Although an application for an interim order presupposes that an application has been brought for a permanent order, no similar restriction applies to an application for a temporary order: see *Re Janssen and Janssen* (1979), 25 O.R. (2d) 213, at 216, 11 R.F.L. (2d) 274 (Co. Ct.). In *Clark v. Clark* (1984), 40 R.F.L. (2d) 92 (Ont. S.C.), the wife was granted a temporary exclusive possession order of a sailboat that was considered as an alternative matrimonial home.

An order for interim exclusive possession of the matrimonial home has traditionally been denied unless the applicant demonstrates that its continued shared use is a practical impossibility or that the well-being of the children is thereby threatened and the applicant is the preferred occupant on the balance of convenience: see *Rinta v. Rinta* (1980), 19 B.C.L.R. 287, 16 R.F.L. (2d) 187 (S.C.); *West v. West* (1982), 28 R.F.L. (2d) 375, at 378-79 (Ont. S.C.) (Cork, Master); *Barrett v. Barrett* (1982), 29 R.F.L. (2d) 13 (Ont. S.C.); *Campbell v. Campbell* (1979), 6 R.F.L. (2d) 392 (Ont. S.C.); see also *Bailey v. Bailey* (1987), 5 R.F.L. (3d) 354 (Ont. Dist. Ct.). At times, the Ontario courts appear to have imposed an unduly restrictive test in applying the criteria formerly defined in subsection 45(3) of the *Family Law Reform Act*, R.S.O. 1980, c. 152. The more general criteria defined in subsection 24(3) of the *Family Law Act, 1986* provide a broader base for the exercise of judicial discretion in applications for interim and permanent orders for exclusive possession of the matrimonial home: see *Pifer v. Pifer* (1986), 3 R.F.L. (3d) 167 (Ont. Dist. Ct.), *infra*, subheading 25.11 "Criteria for exclusive possession orders". In the final analysis, the question to be determined should be whether an order for exclusive possession in the matrimonial home would be fair, just and reasonable having regard to all the circumstances of the case: *Walker v. Walker*, [1978] 3 All E.R. 141, at 143 (C.A.) (Geoffrey Lane L.J.). In the words of Cumming-Bruce J. in *Bassett v. Bassett*, [1975] Fam. 76, [1975] 1 All E.R. 513, at 520-21 (C.A.), which were cited with approval by Ormrod L.J. in *Walker v. Walker, supra*, at 145:

> In my view, the approach of the court to these cases of application to expel a spouse from the matrimonial home should be strictly practical, having regard to the realities of family life. Where a mother is looking after a child or children, it is necessary to examine with the utmost care whether it is really practicable for the husband and wife to continue to live in the matrimonial home . . . I extract from the cases the principle that the court will consider with care the accommodation available to both spouses, and the hardship to which each will be exposed if an order is granted or refused, and then consider whether it is really sensible to expect a wife and child to endure the pressures which the continued presence of the other spouse will place on them. Obviously inconvenience is not enough. Equally obviously, the court must be alive to the risk that a spouse may be using the instrument of an injunction as a tactical weapon in the matrimonial conflict . . . In proceedings

pending suit it is unlikely that the court will be able to predict who will be living in the matrimonial home after all the problems of custody, finance and property adjustment have been determined. Where there are children, whom the mother is looking after, a major consideration must be to relieve them of the psychological stresses and strains imposed by the friction between their parents, as the long-term effect on a child is liable to be of the utmost gravity. This factor ought to weigh at least as heavily in the scales as the personal protection of the parent seeking relief.

An order for interim exclusive possession of the matrimonial home survives the presentation of a divorce petition. Being in the nature of an order affecting property interests, rather than an order for support, it falls outside the ambit of subsection 36(1) of the *Family Law Act, 1986,* formerly subsection 20(1) of the *Family Law Reform Act,* R.S.O. 1980, c. 152: *Bombier v. Bombier and Green* (1984), 42 R.F.L. (2d) 93 (Ont. S.C.).

25.12 Criteria for exclusive possession orders

Subsection 24(3) of the *Family Law Act, 1986* identifies the following six factors that must be considered on an application for exclusive possession:

(a) the best interests of the children affected;
(b) any existing orders under Part I of the *Family Law Act, 1986* and any existing support orders;
(c) the financial position of both spouses;
(d) any written agreement between the parties;
(e) the availability of other suitable and affordable accommodation;
(f) any violence committed by a spouse against the other spouse or children.

For the purposes of clause 24(3)(a) of the Act, subsection 24(4) requires the court to determine the best interests of a child having regard to

(a) the possible disruptive effects on the child of a move to other accommodation; and
(b) the child's views and preferences, if they can reasonably be ascertained.

The factors that the court must consider under subsections 24(3) and (4) of the *Family Law Act, 1986* in exercising the discretion conferred by subsection 24(1) of the Act are different and much broader in scope than those defined in subsection 45(3) of the *Family Law Reform Act,* R.S.O. 1980, c. 152, whereby the court's discretionary jurisdiction to grant an exclusive possession order was formerly narrowly circumscribed: *Pifer v.*

Pifer (1986), 3 R.F.L. (3d) 167 (Ont. Dist. Ct.). Subsection 45(3) of the *Family Law Reform Act*, R.S.O. 1980, c. 152, provided that "[a]n order under subsection (1) for exclusive possession may be made *only if*, in the opinion of the court, other provision for shelter is not adequate in the circumstances or it is in the best interests of a child to do so". The factors listed in subsection 24(4) of the *Family Law Act, 1986* are not necessarily exhaustive and do not exclude the court from considering many other factors such as the psychological stress to a child arising from persistent friction between the parents: see *Pifer v. Pifer*, *supra*. In *Plowman v. Plowman* (1973), 9 R.F.L. 160 (N.S.W.S.C.), the following considerations were considered relevant to the exercise of judicial discretion:

[margin note: s. 24(4) factors are not necess. exhaustive re "Best Interest of children"]

[margin note: Plowman]

(a) Can the wife be adequately housed elsewhere?
(b) Is money available either from the wife's own resources or from her husband's to provide that housing?
(c) For whom, husband or wife, is it less inconvenient to have to live away from the matrimonial home?
(d) What are the interests of any children of the parties and what order would be in their paramount interest?
(e) What are the proprietary rights of the spouses?
(f) Would a non-molestation order be an appropriate alternative to an order for expulsion?
(g) Is there a danger of improper methods being used, either by way of intimidation or fraud, to prevent the wife from pursuing her rights, if the spouses remain in the same house?
(h) The possible injustice of forcing a husband to establish another home for himself or otherwise accept inferior accommodation.

And in *Caines v. Caines* (1984), 42 R.F.L. (2d) 1 (Ont. Co. Ct.), Fleury Co. Ct. J. listed the following relevant considerations:

[margin note: Caines]

(a) Any agreement, formal or informal, between the parties as to the future use of the home.
(b) The date when the property was acquired.
(c) The historical ties of any parties to the property in question.
(d) The extent to which the property may have been acquired by one of the spouses by gift or by special efforts.
(e) The number of children who would continue to reside in the home.
(f) The financial ability of the parties to continue to maintain the property as well as to continue to dwell under separate roofs.
(g) The special character of the neighbourhood including such considerations as the presence of friends, relatives, members of a specific ethnic community.

(h) The need of the respondent for immediate funds.
(i) The impact of a move on the children's ability to attend school or university or to continue extra-curricular activities.
(j) The health of the children.
(k) The reaction of the children to the marriage breakdown and their need for continued stability.

In the words of Ormrod L.J. in *Samson v. Samson,* [1982] 1 All E.R. 780, at 783 (C.A.), "the court must concentrate on the practical issues involved in the case and make as sensible an order as is possible in the circumstances, having regard to the interests of all the parties, father, mother and the children".

An order for exclusive possession of the matrimonial home is a drastic order in that it is likely to cause hardship to the dispossessed spouse, but this is to be balanced against the hardship that would be sustained by an unsuccessful applicant: *Bassett v. Bassett,* [1975] Fam. 76, [1975] 1 All E.R. 513, at 517 (C.A.) (*per* Ormrod L.J.); see also *Re Ali (No. 1)* (1987), 57 O.R. (2d) 597, 5 R.F.L. (3d) 228 (S.C.), *supra,* 22.0 "ALIENATION OF MATRIMONIAL HOME". Inconvenience, however, is not enough to justify an exclusive possession order: *Bassett v. Bassett, supra,* at 521 (Cummings-Bruce J.). Where, for example, the children are healthy and well-adjusted and there is no difficulty in the custodial parent obtaining suitable accommodation in the same area, an application for an exclusive possession order should be dismissed: see *Allen v. Allen* (1981), 24 R.F.L. (2d) 152 (Ont. Co. Ct.); see also *Koziarz v. Koziarz* (1984), 39 R.F.L. (2d) 417 (Ont. S.C.); compare *Jaremkow v. Jaremkow* (1985), 48 R.F.L. (2d) 206 (Ont. Dist. Ct.).

The onus of proving that an order for exclusive possession of the matrimonial home is justified falls on the person seeking exclusive possession: see *Rondeau v. Rondeau and Laviolette* (1979), 12 R.F.L. (2d) 45 (Ont. Co. Ct.) and *Gies v. Gies* (1982), 30 R.F.L. (2d) 122 (Ont. Co. Ct.). In determining the availability of other suitable and affordable accommodation within the meaning of clause 34(3)(e) of the *Family Law Act, 1986,* the following criteria apply: (i) it need not match the present accommodation but must be reasonably suitable for the needs required and relate to the standard of living previously enjoyed, (ii) if it provides reasonable amenities, the court will ignore the niceties of its physical layout, and (iii) the financial ability to secure and maintain such alternative accommodation should be considered. In determining the best interests of the children with respect to alternative accommodation, the critical factors are the quality of the respective homes, their proximity to schools and other facilities, traffic hazards, and the effect of a change of environment on the children. Where the custodial parent's

104

financial circumstances make the purchase or rental of alternative accommodation impossible and there is no pressing need for the non-custodial parent to realize the equity in the matrimonial home, an order for exclusive possession in favour of the custodial parent is justified: *Gies v. Gies, supra.* In *Crane v. Crane* (1986), 3 R.F.L. (3d) 428 (Ont. S.C.), wherein the husband sought exclusive possession of the matrimonial home for a period of two years to permit the youngest child to complete Grade VIII, an order was denied on the ground that insufficient evidence had been adduced to satisfy the requirements of section 24 of the *Family Law Act, 1986.* And in *Rosenthal v. Rosenthal* (1986), 3 R.F.L. (3d) 126, at 136-38 (Ont. S.C.), McMahon L.J.S.C. concluded that the requirements of subsection 24(3) of the *Family Law Act, 1986* had not been satisfied where two of the three children were emancipated and the husband was contributing towards the college education of the third child. McMahon L.J.S.C. concluded that an exclusive possession order was not justified by reason only of the emotional stress of the applicant resulting from the marriage breakdown and that an order should be denied where it is apparent that there are insufficient funds available to permit the continued occupation of the home by one of the spouses.

The implications of a permanent order for exclusive possession of the matrimonial home upon the right of each spouse to realize any equalization claim under Part I of the *Family Law Act, 1986* should not be ignored: see *Rosenthal v. Rosenthal, supra*; compare *Nolet v. Nolet* (1985), 68 N.S.R. (2d) 370, 159 A.P.R. 370, 46 R.F.L. (2d) 388 (C.A.), varying (1985), 68 N.S.R. (2d) 375, 159 A.P.R. 375, 45 R.F.L. (2d) 203 (N.S.S.C.) (Richard J.).

Proof of any violence committed by one spouse against the other spouse or the children is expressly recognized by clause 24(3)(f) of the *Family Law Act, 1986* as of vital importance in determining whether an order for exclusive possession should be granted. It does not follow, however, that the conduct of either spouse is irrelevant, unless such conduct manifests some form of violence. This is self-evident where there are children involved because the court is expressly required to have regard to their best interests under clause 24(3)(a) and subsection 24(4) of the Act. But even where there are no children, the presence or absence of violence is only one factor to be considered and the relative hardship that would result to each spouse by the granting or refusal of an order for exclusive possession is to be considered in light of all the attendant circumstances, including their past conduct, whether of a violent or non-violent nature, and their respective financial condition: compare *Walker v. Walker,* [1978] 3 All E.R. 141, at 143 (C.A.) (Geoffrey Lane L.J.).

25.13 Penalties for contravention of exclusive possession order

Subsection 24(5) of the *Family Law Act, 1986* introduces significant penal sanctions that may be imposed for contravention of an order for exclusive possession. A person who is convicted of contravening an order for exclusive possession is liable in the case of a first offence to a fine not exceeding $1,000 and/or to imprisonment for a term not exceeding three months. In the event of a second or subsequent offence, the maximum penalty increases to $10,000 and/or imprisonment for two years.

Pursuant to subsection 24(6) of the Act, a police officer is expressly empowered to arrest without warrant a person the police officer believes, on reasonable and probable grounds, to have contravened an order for exclusive possession. The above penalty and arrest provisions also apply with respect to orders for exclusive possession that were granted pursuant to Part III of the *Family Law Reform Act*, R.S.O. 1980, c. 152: see *Family Law Act, 1986*, subsection 24(7).

26.0 VARIATION PROCEEDINGS

Variation of possessory order

25.—(1) On the application of a person named in an order made under clause 24(1)(a), (b), (c), (d) or (e) or his or her personal representative, if the court is satisfied that there has been a material change in circumstances, the court may discharge, vary or suspend the order.

Variation of conditions of sale

(2) On the motion of a person who is subject to conditions imposed in an order made under clause 23(b) or (d) or 24(1)(g), or his or her personal representative, if the court is satisfied that the conditions are no longer appropriate, the court may discharge, vary or suspend them.

Existing orders

(3) Subsections (1) and (2) also apply to orders made under the corresponding provisions of Part III of the *Family Law Reform Act* [R.S.O. 1980, c. 152].

26.1 Variation of possessory orders

Orders respecting the exclusive possession and use of the matrimonial home or its contents, which have been made pursuant to clause 24(1)(a), (b), (c), (d) or subsection (3) of the *Family Law Act, 1986*, are subject to judicial discharge, variation or suspension in the event of a material change in the circumstances. An application for this purpose may be brought by a person named in the order or by his or her personal representative: *Family Law Act, 1986*, subsection 25(1). Similar conditions apply to orders made under the corresponding provisions of Part III of the *Family Law Reform Act*, R.S.O. 1980, c. 152.

26.2 Variation of conditional orders respecting sale or encumbrance of matrimonial home

See *Family Law Act, 1986*, subsections 25(2) and (3), *supra*; see also text *supra*, 24.0 "POWERS OF COURT RESPECTING ALIENATION" and *supra*, subheading 25.10 "False statements made under subsection 21(3)".

27.0 EFFECT OF DEATH

27.1 Third party joint tenancy in matrimonial home; relevant statutory provisions

Joint tenancy in matrimonial home
26.—(1) If a spouse dies owning an interest in a matrimonial home as a joint tenant with a third person and not with the other spouse, the joint tenancy shall be deemed to have been severed immediately before the time of death.

Sixty day period after spouse's death
(2) Despite clauses 19(2)(a) and (b) (termination of spouse's right of possession), a spouse who has no interest in a matrimonial home but is occupying it at the time of the other spouse's death, whether under an order for exclusive possession or otherwise, is entitled to retain possession against the spouse's estate, rent free, for sixty days after the spouse's death.

27.2 Severance of third party joint tenancy in matrimonial home

Pursuant to subsection 26(1) of the *Family Law Act, 1986*, if a spouse dies owning an interest in the matrimonial home as a joint tenant with a person other than his or her spouse, the joint tenancy is deemed to be severed with a consequential loss of the right of survivorship immediately before the time of death. Accordingly, the value of the deceased's interest as a tenant in common is included in the calculation of his or her net family property for the purposes of an equalization claim brought against the deceased's estate pursuant to subsection 5(2) of the Act. Subsection 26(1) of the *Family Law Act, 1986* has no application to a joint tenant who died prior to the commencement of the Act, namely, March 1, 1986: *Re Vaillancourt et al.* (1986), 56 O.R. (2d) 453, 4 R.F.L. (3d) 263 (S.C.).

Pursuant to subsection 26(2) of the Act, a spouse who is occupying the matrimonial home without any proprietary interest therein at the time of the other spouse's death, is entitled to retain possession on a rent-free basis against the deceased spouse's estate for 60 days after the death. This right is exercisable, notwithstanding the provisions of clauses 19(2)(a) and (b) of the Act and regardless whether or not the possession right arose pursuant to an order for exclusive possession. The provisions of subsection 26(2) presumably override any order made pursuant to clause 24(1)(d) of the Act that required the spouse with exclusive possession to make periodic payments as occupation rent to the dispossessed spouse. Subsection 26(2) may imply that an order for exclusive possession granted pursuant to clause 24(1)(b) of the Act cannot be made for a period exceeding the joint lives of the spouses. Other interpretations of subsection 26(2) are viable, however, and the resolution of this question must, therefore, await judicial determination: see *supra*, 25.0 POSSESSION OF MATRIMONIAL HOME, subheading 25.5 "Duration of order; release of other property".

28.0 REGISTRATION OF ORDERS AGAINST LAND

Registration of order
27. Orders made under this Part or under Part III of the *Family Law Reform Act* [R.S.O. 1980, c. 152] are registrable against land under the *Registry Act* [R.S.O. 1980, c. 445] and the *Land Titles Act* [R.S.O. 1980, c. 230].

Orders granted pursuant to Part II of the *Family Law Act, 1986* or Part III of the *Family Law Reform Act*, R.S.O. 1980, c. 152, are registrable against land under the *Registry Act*, R.S.O. 1980, c. 445 and the *Land Titles Act*, R.S.O. 1980, c. 230.

29.0 SITUS OF MATRIMONIAL HOME; RETROSPECTIVE OPERATION OF PART II OF FAMILY LAW ACT

Application of Part
28.—(1) This Part applies to matrimonial homes that are situated in Ontario.

Idem
(2) This Part applies,
      (a) whether the spouses were married before or after this Act comes into force; and

(b) whether the matrimonial home was acquired before or after this Act comes into force.

The application of Part II of the *Family Law Act, 1986* is expressly confined to matrimonial homes that are situated in Ontario: subsection 28(1).

Pursuant to subsection 28(2) of the Act, Part II applies whether the spouses were married before or after March 1, 1986, and whether the matrimonial home was acquired before or after that date.

s. 28(1) says s Act applies only to homes made in Ontario

PART IV

DOMESTIC CONTRACTS

30.0 GENERAL

Part IV of the *Family Law Act, 1986* supersedes Part IV of the *Family Law Reform Act*, R.S.O. 1980, c. 152. Part IV endorses the concept of contractual autonomy by enabling persons to contract out of rights and obligations that would otherwise arise pursuant to the *Family Law Act, 1986*. Subsection 2(10) of the *Family Law Act, 1986* specifically provides that "[a] domestic contract dealing with a matter that is also dealt with in this Act prevails unless this Act provides otherwise": see *supra*, **PART I**, subheadings, 4.0 JURISDICTION, 4.4 Domestic Contracts and 7.0 EQUALIZATION OF NET FAMILY PROPERTIES, 7.13 Excluded property — 7.13.6 Property excluded by domestic contract. A significant qualification to the paramountcy of a domestic contract is found, however, in subsection 33(4) of the *Family Law Act, 1986*. This subsection empowers a court to set aside a provision for support or a waiver of the right to support in a domestic contract or paternity agreement, if the terms of the agreement result in unconscionable circumstances, or shift the prospective burden of supporting family dependants to the public purse, or the domestic contract or paternity agreement is in default at the time of an application for support under Part III of the *Family Law Act, 1986*. More stringent criteria regulate judicial disturbance of the terms of a separation agreement or minutes of settlement where spousal support is sought on or after divorce. In *Pelech v. Pelech* (1987), 7 R.F.L. (3d) 225 (S.C.C.); *Richardson v. Richardson* (1987), 7 R.F.L. (3d) 304 (S.C.C.) and *Caron v. Caron* (1987), 7 R.F.L. (3d) 274 (S.C.C.), *infra*, subheading 43.0 SPOUSAL AND CHILD SUPPORT, it was held that the terms of a comprehensive financial settlement, freely entered into by the spouses with independent legal advice, should not be disturbed by the exercise of the court's discretionary jurisdiction to order spousal support pursuant to section 11 of the *Divorce Act*, R.S.C. 1970, c. D-8, where the settlement is not unconscionable in a substantive law sense, unless there has been a radical change in circumstances since the settlement and that change was causally connected with a pattern of economic dependence engendered by the marriage relationship.

111

Section 51 of the Act defines a domestic contract to mean "a marriage contract, separation agreement or cohabitation agreement". This definition applies for all purposes of the Act pursuant to the supplementary definition of "domestic contract" in subsection 1(1) of the Act.

Except insofar as the *Family Law Act, 1986* expressly provides to the contrary, the general principles of the law of contract apply to "domestic contracts" within the meaning of the *Family Law Act, 1986*. Non-compliance with the explicit requirements of the *Family Law Act, 1986* does not necessarily preclude an action on the agreement at common law.

31.0 MARRIAGE CONTRACTS

Definitions
51. In this Part,

. . .

"domestic contract" means a marriage contract, separation agreement or cohabitation agreement;

"marriage contract" means an agreement entered into under section 52.

. . .

Marriage contracts
52.—(1) A man and a woman who are married to each other or intend to marry may enter into an agreement in which they agree on their respective rights and obligations under the marriage or on separation, on the annulment of dissolution of the marriage or on death, including,

     (a) ownership in or division of property,
     (b) support obligations;
     (c) the right to direct the education and moral training of their children, but not the right to custody of or access to their children; and
     (d) any other matter in the settlement of their affairs.

Rights re matrimonial home excepted
(2) A provision in a marriage contract purporting to limit a spouse's rights under Part II (Matrimonial Home) is unenforceable.

Persons may enter into marriage contracts before or during their marriage, provided that in the latter circumstance they are still

112

cohabiting at the time of the execution of the agreement: see *infra*, subheading 33.0 "SEPARATION AGREEMENT". Marriage contracts cannot be entered into by cohabitants of the same sex nor by persons living in a permanent common law relationship: see *infra*, 32.0 "COHABITATION AGREEMENTS". In light of the extended definition of "spouse" in subsections 1(1) and (2) of the *Family Law Act, 1986*, marriage contracts may be entered into by parties to a void or voidable marriage or by parties to a validly celebrated polygamous marriage.

Pursuant to subsection 52(1) of the *Family Law Act, 1986*, the parties to a marriage contract may regulate their respective legal rights and obligations during the marriage, or on separation, annulment or dissolution of the marriage or on death. A valid marriage contract that regulates "the ownership" and "division of property" takes precedence over the statutory property entitlements conferred by Part I of the *Family Law Act, 1986: ibid.*, subsection 2(10), *supra*. Specific property may also be excluded from a spouse's net family property pursuant to paragraph 4(2)6 of the Act. A marriage contract may also preclude an order for support being granted under Part III of the Act, subject to the court's discretionary jurisdiction to override the contract under the conditions specified in subsection 33(4) of the *Family Law Act, 1986* or under section 56 of the Act. Subsection 33(4) is expressly confined to support applications under the *Family Law Act, 1986*. Different considerations may be deemed relevant to applications for support by way of corollary relief in divorce proceedings: compare *Pelech v. Pelech, Richardson v. Richardson* and *Caron v. Caron, supra*, subheading 30.0 "GENERAL" and *infra*, subheading 43.0 "SPOUSAL AND CHILD SUPPORT", wherein the Supreme Court of Canada addressed the impact of separation agreements and minutes of settlement — as distinct from marriage contracts — on spousal support applications brought on after divorce.

If spouses wish to predetermine their property entitlement on marriage breakdown or death, declarations of ownership may be insufficient of themselves to exclude an equalization claim under section 5 of the *Family Law Act, 1986*: see *Kerr v. Kerr* (1983), 41 O.R. (2d) 704, 147 D.L.R. (3d) 384, 35 R.F.L. (2d) 363 (C.A.), affg (1981), 32 O.R. (2d) 146, 121 D.L.R. (3d) 221, 22 R.F.L. (2d) 19 (S.C.) and compare *Lotton v. Lotton* (1979), 25 O.R. (2d) 1, at 8, 99 D.L.R. (3d) 745, 11 R.F.L. (2d) 112 (C.A.).

A marriage contract, unlike a separation agreement, cannot limit the rights conferred on a spouse by Part II of the *Family Law Act, 1986: ibid.*, subsection 52(2). Pursuant to section 19 of the Act, both spouses have an equal right to possession of the matrimonial home in the absence of a separation agreement or court order to the contrary. Furthermore, neither spouse can unilaterally dispose of or encumber an interest in the matrimonial home in the absence of authority conferred by a separation agreement or court order. Subsection 52(2) of the *Family Law Act, 1986* does not, however, preclude a marriage contract from determining rights of ownership in the home or excluding the home or its value from any equalization claim based on section 5 of the Act: compare *Lotton v. Lotton, supra*. The language of the marriage contract should, however, be carefully drawn so as to make it clear that possessory interests remain unaffected by its terms. In *Ramboer v. Ramboer* (1979), 11 R.F.L. (2d) 320 (Ont. S.C.), for example, a marriage contract was declared void pursuant to subsection 51(2) of the *Family Law Reform Act*, S.O. 1978, c. 2, where the husband paid a lump sum "in full satisfaction and payment of the wife's interest in the home". The wife was accordingly entitled to an equal share in the value of the matrimonial home pursuant to subsection 4(1) of the *Family Law Act, 1986*. A different conclusion would presumably have been reached if the terms of the marriage contract had not inextricably intertwined possessory, proprietary and division rights in the general release. The language of subsection 51(2) of the *Family Law Reform Act* and of its successor, subsection 52(2) of the *Family Law Act, 1986*, S.O. 1986, c. 4, with the express reference to "[a] *provision* in a marriage contract", clearly envisages the possibility of severing the offending provision from the contract as a whole, if this is practicable under the terms of the marriage contract. It may be significant that an offending provision was rendered void by subsection 51(2) of the *Family Law Reform Act*, which was applied in *Ramboer v. Ramboer, supra*, but is now merely unenforceable pursuant to subsection 52(2) of the *Family Law Act, 1986*.

Clause 52(1)(c) of the *Family Law Act, 1986* precludes the parties to a marriage contract from determining prospective rights to the custody of or access to their children. A marriage contract may, nevertheless, define the right to direct the education and moral upbringing of the children. Any such provision is, however, subject to the court's discretionary jurisdiction under section 56 of the *Family Law Act, 1986* to disregard the provision where the best interests of the child are not thereby served.

32.0 COHABITATION AGREEMENTS

Definitions
51. In this Part,

. . .

"domestic contract" means a marriage contract, separation agreement or cohabitation agreement;

"cohabitation agreement" means an agreement entered into under section 53.

. . .

114

Cohabitation agreements

53.—(1) A man and a woman who are cohabiting or intend to cohabit and who are not married to each other may enter into an agreement in which they agree on their respective rights and obligations during cohabitation, or on ceasing to cohabit or on death, including,

[handwritten margin note: s. s. rights overridden by contract s. 2(10)]

(a) ownership in or division of property;
(b) support obligations;
(c) the right to direct the education and moral training of their children, but not the right to custody of or access to their children; and
(d) any other matter in the settlement of their affairs.

Effect of marriage on agreement

(2) If the parties to a cohabitation agreement marry each other, the agreement shall be deemed to be a marriage contract.

Cohabitation agreements may be entered into by persons of the opposite sex who are cohabiting or intend to cohabit but who are not married and have no present intention to marry. The mere fact that two persons of the opposite sex are sharing accommodation does not, of itself, constitute cohabitation. Subsection 1(1) of the *Family Law Act, 1986* specifically defines "cohabit" as meaning "to live together in a conjugal relationship, whether within or outside marriage". Some indication of the factors relevant to determining whether parties are cohabiting may be gleaned from judicial interpretation of the meaning of the phrase "living separate and apart" in paragraph 4(1)(e) of the *Divorce Act*, R.S.C. 1970, c. D-8: see, for example, *Cooper v. Cooper* (1972), 10 R.F.L. 184 (Ont. S.C.); *Dupere v. Dupere* (1975), 9 N.B.R. (2d) 554, 1 A.P.R. 554, 19 R.F.L. 270 (S.C.), affd 10 N.B.R. (2d) 148, 4 A.P.R. 148 (C.A.).

Cohabitation agreements may regulate the rights and obligations of the respective parties during cohabitation or on the cessation of cohabitation or on death. Such agreements, like marriage contracts, may pre-determine the ownership or division of property, support rights and obligations, the right to direct the education or moral upbringing of children and any other matter in the settlement of the cohabitants' affairs: see *supra*, heading 31.0 "MARRIAGE CONTRACTS". The property rights of unmarried cohabitants fall outside the ambit of Part I of the *Family Law Act, 1986* by reason of the definition of "spouse" in subsection 1(1) of the Act. Subject to the terms of a valid cohabitation agreement, therefore, unmarried cohabitants may only invoke the more limited rights conferred upon them by established principles of common law or equity, which include rights arising by way of resulting or constructive trusts: see *Pettkus v. Becker*, [1980] 2 S.C.R. 834, 117 D.L.R. (3d) 257, 34 N.R. 384, 19 R.F.L. (2d) 165; *Sorochan v. Sorochan*, [1986] 5

[handwritten margin notes: unmarried co-hab's use "con-trust" no s. s rights, not a spouse or use; a co-hab, s 53 agreement to get s. s, s. 34 rights]

115

W.W.R. 289, 29 D.L.R. (4th) 1, 2 R.F.L. (3d) 225 (S.C.C.); and *Anderson v. Luoma* (1986), 50 R.F.L. (2d) 127 (B.C.S.C.). Part II of the *Family Law Act, 1986*, which regulates possessory rights in the matrimonial home and the disposition or encumbering of any interest therein, is also inapplicable to unmarried cohabitants, although corresponding rights may be conferred by the provisions of a valid cohabitation agreement. The restrictive definition of "spouse" in subsection 1(1) of the *Family Law Act, 1986*, which applies for the purposes of Parts I and II of the Act, is expanded in the context of support rights and obligations arising pursuant to Part III of the Act. Section 29 of the Act defines "spouse" for the purpose of Part III as follows:

Definitions
29. In this Part,

. . .

"spouse" means a spouse as defined in subsection 1(1), and in addition includes either of a man and woman who are not married to each other and have cohabited,
> **(a) continuously for a period of not less than three years, or**
> **(b) in a relationship of some permanence, if they are the natural or adoptive parents of a child.**

Where unmarried cohabitants fall within the above definition, the court has jurisdiction in an application for support to grant an interim or final order for the transfer of property or for exclusive possession of the matrimonial home: *Family Law Act, 1986*, clauses 34(1)(c) and (d). The rights of the owner of the family residence may thus be qualified in the exercise of the court's jurisdiction over support under these provisions. Subject to above qualifications, unmarried cohabitants are unprotected by Parts I, II and III of the *Family Law Act, 1986*. A financially dependent cohabitant is, therefore, well advised to protect his or her economic security by the execution of a cohabitation agreement as defined in section 53 of the *Family Law Act, 1986*.

If the parties to a cohabitation agreement subsequently marry each other, the agreement is deemed to be a marriage contract pursuant to the express provisions of subsection 53(2) of the *Family Law Act, 1986*: see *Re Vaillancourt et al.* (1986), 56 O.R. (2d) 453, 4 R.F.L. (3d) 263 (Ont. S.C.). Whether such metamorphosis would render unenforceable any provisions of the cohabitation agreement that purported to regulate rights falling within the ambit of Part II of the *Family Law Act, 1986* is a matter for speculation in light of subsection 52(2) of the Act: see *supra*, subheading 31.0 "MARRIAGE CONTRACTS".

33.0 SEPARATION AGREEMENTS

Definitions
  51. In this Part,

· · ·

"**domestic contract**" means a marriage contract, separation agreement or cohabitation agreement;

· · ·

"**separation agreement**" means an agreement entered into under section 54.

Separation agreements
  54. A man and a woman who cohabited and are living separate and apart may enter into an agreement in which they agree on their respective rights and obligations, including,

  (a) ownership in or division of property;
  (b) support obligations;
  (c) the right to direct the education and moral training of their children;
  (d) the right to custody of and access to their children; and
  (e) any other matter in the settlement of their affairs.

[handwritten margin notes: "separate and apart" Same criteria as under Divorce Act s. 8(2)(a)]

Separation agreements may be entered into by persons of the opposite sex who have cohabited and are living separate and apart. The term "cohabit" is defined in subsection 1(1) of the *Family Law Act, 1986* as meaning "to live together in a conjugal relationship, whether within or outside marriage". The words "living separate and apart" in section 54 of the Act apparently bear the same meaning as that accorded by the courts to these words in the context of paragraph 4(1)(e) of the *Divorce Act*, R.S.C. 1970, c. D-8. Accordingly, the *factum* of separation and an *animus separandi* must co-exist before spouses or other persons can be found to be "living separate and apart": compare *Herman v. Herman* (1969), 3 D.L.R. (3d) 551 (N.S.S.C.). Continued residence under the same roof does not preclude a finding that the parties are living separate and apart, provided that they are living independent lives while sharing common accommodation: compare *Cooper v. Cooper* (1972), 10 R.F.L. 184 (Ont. S.C.); *Dupere v. Dupere* (1975), 9 N.B.R. (2d) 554, 1 A.P.R. 554, 19 R.F.L. 270 (S.C.), affd 10 N.B.R. (2d) 148, 4 A.P.R. 148 (C.A.). Furthermore, isolated or casual acts of post-separation sexual intercourse do not preclude a finding that the parties are living separate and apart: compare *Deslippe v. Deslippe* (1974), 4 O.R. (2d) 35, 47 D.L.R. (3d) 30, 16 R.F.L. 38 (C.A.); *Leaderhouse v. Leaderhouse*, [1971] 2 W.W.R. 180, 17 D.L.R. (3d) 315, 4 R.F.L. 174 (Sask. Q.B.).

At common law, spouses could enter into valid separation agreements before withdrawing from cohabitation, provided that a cessation of cohabitation was imminent. The language of sections 52 and 54 of the *Family Law Act, 1986* suggests that such agreements are now to be characterized as marriage contracts. The difference between marriage contracts and separation agreements is not, however, merely a matter of form. Clause 52(1)(c) and subsection 52(2) of the *Family Law Act, 1986* preclude a marriage contract from regulating custody and access rights and render unenforceable any provision thereof relating to the limitation of possessory or disposition rights in the matrimonial home under Part II of the Act. No corresponding qualifications apply to separation agreements: see clauses 54(d), 19(2)(b) and 21(1)(b) of the *Family Law Act, 1986*. Where separation is imminent, therefore, the execution, as distinct from the drafting of an agreement, should be deferred until the parties have, in fact, ceased cohabitation. Otherwise, there may be serious impediments to a complete and final settlement of all outstanding issues.

Where a valid separation agreement has been executed, its terms prevail over rights that might otherwise have arisen under Parts I *and* II of the *Family Law Act, 1986*: see *Puopolo v. Puopolo* (1986), 2 R.F.L. (3d) 73 (Ont. S.C.); compare *supra*, subheading 31.0 "MARRIAGE CONTRACTS". Spousal support claims under Part III of the *Family Law Act, 1986* may also be barred by the provisions of a separation agreement where there is no vitiating factor such as duress or undue influence and no inequality of bargaining power at the time of the execution of the agreement: *Puopolo v. Puopolo, supra; Salonen v. Salonen* (1986), 2 R.F.L. (3d) 273 (Ont. Unified Fam. Ct.). Separation agreements, like marriage contracts, fall subject, however, to the possible application of subsection 33(4) of the *Family Law Act, 1986: ibid*. As to the implications of the terms of a separation agreement or of minutes of settlement on an application for support on or after divorce, see *Pelech v. Pelech, Richardson v. Richardson* and *Caron v. Caron, supra*, subheading 30.0 "GENERAL" and *infra*, subheading 43.0 "SPOUSAL AND CHILD SUPPORT".

Although a separation agreement, unlike a marriage contract, may purport to regulate the right to custody of and access to children, clause 54(d) of the *Family Law Act, 1986* is subject to the overriding provisions of subsection 56(1), whereby the court may disregard any custody or access provision in a domestic contract where such a course of action is in the best interests of a child.

34.0 FORMAL REQUIREMENTS OF DOMESTIC CONTRACT

Form of contract

55.—(1) A domestic contract and an agreement to amend or

118

rescind a domestic contract are **unenforceable** unless made in writing, signed by the parties and witnessed.

. . .

Subsection 55(1) of the *Family Law Act, 1986* is the successor to subsection 54(1) of the *Family Law Reform Act*, R.S.O. 1980, c. 152. There is, however, one marked difference between these two provisions. Non-compliance with the formal requirements of subsection 54(1) of the *Family Law Reform Act, 1986, supra*, rendered the domestic contract void. Pursuant to subsection 55(1) of the *Family Law Act, 1986*, such non-compliance does not invalidate the domestic contract but merely renders it unenforceable. Consequently, the equitable doctrine of part performance might possibly be invoked in appropriate circumstances to render a domestic contract enforceable, notwithstanding non-compliance with the statutory formalities set out in subsection 55(1): compare *Steadman v. Steadman*, [1974] 2 All E.R. 977 (H.L.).

The provisions of subsection 55(1) of the *Family Law Act, 1986* are inapplicable to negotiated settlements entered into by the solicitors for the respective parties after the institution of legal proceedings: *Geropoulos v. Geropoulos* (1982), 35 O.R. (2d) 763, at 769, 133 D.L.R. (3d) 121, 26 R.F.L. (2d) 225 (C.A.); *Campbell v. Campbell* (1986), 52 O.R. (2d) 206, at 209-10, 47 R.F.L. (2d) 392, at 396-98 (S.C.). In the latter case, Steele J. further concluded that the relevant statutory provisions "do not require that the signature of each party be expressly witnessed but only that the agreement be witnessed".

[Handwritten margin notes: s. 55(1) renders domestic contract unenforceable not void. "minutes" of settlement not rendered ineffective by s. 55(1)]

35.0 CAPACITY TO ENTER INTO DOMESTIC CONTRACTS

Capacity of minor
55.—(2) A minor has capacity to enter into a domestic contract, subject to the approval of the court, which may be given before or after the minor enters into the contract.

Agreement on behalf of mentally incompetent person
(3) If a person is mentally incompetent,
(a) the person's committee, if any, unless the person's spouse is the committee;
(b) in all other cases, the Public Trustee,
may enter into a domestic contract or give any waiver or consent under this Act on the mentally incompetent person's behalf, subject to the prior approval of the court.

In the province of Ontario, a person attains the age of majority and ceases to be a minor on reaching the age of 18 years: *Age of Majority and Accountability Act*, R.S.O. 1980, c. 7, section 1. Subsection 55(2) of the *Family Law Act, 1986* confers a qualified capacity on minors to enter into a marriage contract, cohabitation agreement or separation agreement, in that any such contract or agreement is subject to the approval of the court, either before or after its execution.

The committee of a mentally incompetent person is expressly empowered to enter into a domestic contract on behalf of the person under such disability and may also give any waiver or consent required by the *Family Law Act, 1986*. Such powers cannot be exercised by the spouse of the disabled person even though such spouse is the committee. In such a case, or where no committee has been appointed, the Public Trustee may act on behalf of a mentally incompetent person. In all cases, however, the domestic contract, waiver or consent is subject to the *prior* approval of the court: *Family Law Act, 1986*, subsection 55(3).

36.0 BEST INTERESTS OF CHILD

Contracts subject to best interests of child

56.—(1) In the determination of a matter respecting the support, education, moral training or custody of or access to a child, the court may disregard any provision of a domestic contract pertaining to the matter where, in the opinion of the court, to do so is in the best interests of the child.

Subsection 56(1) of the *Family Law Act, 1986* confers a broad discretionary jurisdiction on the court to disregard the provisions of a domestic contract relating to the support, education, moral training or custody of or access to a child, where the best interests of the child are not thereby served.

Examples of circumstances wherein the courts have in the past ordered child support, notwithstandng the limitations purportedly imposed by a domestic contract, may be found in *Barlow v. Barlow* (1978), 8 R.F.L. (2d) 6 (Ont. Prov. Ct.) (application under *Family Law Reform Act*, R.S.O. 1978, c. 2); *Richardson v. Richardson* (1987), 7 R.F.L. (3d) 304 (S.C.C.) (application under *Divorce Act*, R.S.C. 1970, c. D-8); and *Hansford v. Hansford and Batchelor*, [1973] 1 O.R. 116, 30 D.L.R. (3d) 392, 9 R.F.L. 233 (S.C.) (application under *Divorce Act*, R.S.C. 1970, c. D-8).

The right of a court to override the provisions of a spousal agreement respecting custody or access has long been established. No spousal agreement can deprive the court of its traditional responsibility for the custody and guardianship of children: *Voegelin v. Voegelin* (1980), 15 R.F.L. (2d) 1 (Ont. Co. Ct.); *Statia v. Statia* (1981), 29 Nfld. & P.E.I.R. 464, 82 A.P.R. 464 (P.E.I.S.C.). In matters of custody and access, the courts are clearly entitled to override the terms of a spousal agreement, if the terms of the agreement do not harmonize with the welfare or best interests of the child: *Liang v. Liang* (1979), 5 R.F.L. (2d) 103 (Ont. S.C.). Opinions may differ, however, as to how a child's welfare or best interests will be served in controversial situations and the wishes of the parents may be entitled to considerable weight: *Liang v. Liang, supra.*

37.0 *DUM CASTA* CLAUSES

Dum casta clauses
   56.—(2) A provision in a domestic contract to take effect on separation whereby any right of a party is dependent upon remaining chaste is unenforceable, but this subsection shall not be construed to affect a contingency upon marriage or cohabitation with another.

Idem
   (3) A provision in a domestic contract made before this section comes into force whereby any right of a party is dependent upon remaining chaste shall be given effect as a contingency upon marriage or cohabitation with another.

   The rights and obligations of the parties to a domestic contract cannot be made contingent upon the chastity of either party following separation. Any provision to such effect is unenforceable pursuant to subsection 56(2) of the *Family Law Act, 1986*. It is quite permissible, however, for the terms of a domestic contract to take account of any subsequent marriage or cohabitational relationship. A domestic contract does not offend subsection 56(2) of the *Family Law Act, 1986*, if, for example, periodic "spousal" support is payable only until the payee's marriage or remarriage or non-marital cohabitation with another person: see *Caron v. Caron* (1987), 7 R.F.L. (3d) 274 (S.C.C.) (application under *Divorce Act*, R.S.C. 1970, c. D-8).
   The provisions of subsections 56(2) and (3) of the *Family Law Act, 1986* are consistent with pre-existing judicial practices. It is no longer the practice of the courts to incorporate a *dum casta* clause in an order for periodic support: see *Re Seeman* (1976), 13 O.R. (2d) 414, 71 D.L.R. (3d) 204, 28 R.F.L. 275 (S.C.) and *Sleigh v. Sleigh* (1979), 23 O.R. (2d) 336, 95 D.L.R. (3d) 552 (Ont. S.C.). It is not unusual, however, for a court to order periodic spousal support to be payable until the payee's marriage, remarriage or non-marital cohabitation in circumstances similar to marriage: see, for example, *Gelgoot v. Gelgoot* (1977), 1 R.F.L. (2d) 204 (Ont. S.C.).

38.0 SETTING ASIDE DOMESTIC CONTRACT

Setting aside domestic contract

56.—(4) A court may, on application, set aside a domestic contract or a provision in it,   *doesn't say income*

    (a) **if a party failed to disclose to the other significant assets, or significant debts or other liabilities, existing when the domestic contract was made;**

    (b) **if a party did not understand the nature or consequences of the domestic contract; or**

    (c) **otherwise in accordance with the law of contract.**

Barriers to remarriage

(5) The court may, on application, set aside all or part of a separation agreement or settlement, if the court is satisfied that the removal by one spouse of barriers that would prevent the other spouse's remarriage within that spouse's faith was a consideration in the making of the agreement or settlement.

Idem

(6) Subsection (5) also applies to consent orders, releases, notices of discontinuance and abandonment and other written or oral arrangements.

Application of subss. (4, 5, 6)

(7) Subsections (4), (5) and (6) apply despite any agreement to the contrary.

The jurisdiction of a court to set aside a domestic contract or any provision thereof pursuant to the application of established principles of the Law of Contract is expressly recognized by clause 56(4)(c) of the *Family Law Act, 1986*. Judicial opinion has been divided in the past as to the effect of non-disclosure on a domestic contract: see *Farquar v. Farquar* (1983), 43 O.R. (2d) 423, 1 D.L.R. (4th) 244, 35 R.F.L. (2d) 287, at 299 (C.A.) (*per* Zuber J.A.) and compare dissenting judgment of Matas J.A. in *Tutiah v. Tutiah* (1985), 36 Man. R. (2d) 12, 48 R.F.L. (2d) 337, at 356-59 (C.A.). The consequential uncertainty would now appear to be resolved by clause 56(4)(a) of the *Family Law Act, 1986*, which empowers the court to set aside the domestic contract or a provision thereof, if a party failed to disclose significant assets, debts or other liabilities in existence when the domestic contract was made. The court should first determine whether a failure to disclose within the meaning of clause 56(4)(a) is proven. Only where such non-disclosure is established, can the court be called upon to exercise its statutory discretion. The fact of non-disclosure does not, *per se,* compel the court to set aside all or part of the domestic contract. In *Demchuk v. Demchuk* (1986), 1 R.F.L. (3d) 176 (Ont. S.C.), an application to rescind or amend a separation agreement executed prior to the commencement of the *Family Law Act, 1986*, was coupled with a claim for lump sum and periodic spousal support under subsection 11(1) of the *Divorce Act*, R.S.C. 1970, c. D-8. In denying relief to the claimant, Clarke J. reached the following conclusions. The positive duty of disclosure imposed by clause 56(4)(a) of the *Family Law Act, 1986* has retrospective effect pursuant to section 60. Non-disclosure, whether consensual or innocent, falls within the ambit of clause 56(4)(a) and waiver of full disclosure is not permissible by virtue of subsection 56(7). Full disclosure presupposes the identification of all significant assets and their value. The trial judge, nevertheless, refused to exercise the statutory discretion to re-open the agreement having regard to the attendant circumstances of the case, including the absence of concealment of the husband's pension and deferred profit sharing plan, the absence of material misrepresentation, duress or unconscionable circumstances in the making of the agreement, the neglect of the wife to pursue full legal disclosure and her subsequent failure to expeditiously seek a variation, the absence of any catastrophic change in the wife's situation that would compel judicial intervention, the substantial benefits received by the wife pursuant to the agreement, the social desirability of a "clean break" following the discharge of the obligations imposed by the agreement, the wife's attainment of financial self-sufficiency and the husband's willingness to assume continuing responsibility for the cost of the children's post-secondary education. The trial judge further concluded that interference with the terms of the separation agreement was unwarranted because the pension and deferred profit sharing plan was not a "significant asset" at the time when the agreement was entered into. Accordingly, the court upheld the separation agreement and refused to order spousal support pursuant to subsection 11(1) of the *Divorce Act*, R.S.C. 1970, c. D-8. The trial judge also concluded that clause 56(4)(a) of the *Family Law Act, 1986* does not impose a reverse onus. Although each party is now under a positive and absolute duty to disclose, the party who seeks to rescind the separation agreement in whole or in part must demonstrate that the other party has failed to discharge that duty.

The duty to disclose the value, and not merely the extent, of significant assets must be realistically applied by the courts. In the absence of any definition of "value" in the *Family Law Act, 1986*, opinions may differ as to its meaning, and even if this is agreed upon, there may be legitimate differences of opinion respecting the manner of determining the value of particular assets. Accordingly, it is submitted that clause 56(4)(a) of the *Family Law Act, 1986* will be satisfied, if the court concludes that the valuation of an asset was not inherently misleading and constituted a realistic estimate in light of established valuation practices: see *supra*, EQUALIZATION OF NET FAMILY PROPER-TIES, subheading "Value".

Subsection 56(5) of the *Family Law Act, 1986* empowers the court to set aside all or part of a separation agreement in circumstances where one party has brought pressure to bear on the other by means of the former party's control over the latter's freedom to remarry within his or her religious faith: see also *Family Law Act*, S.O. 1986, c. 4, subsections 2(4), (5), (6) and (7); see *Glass v. Glass*, unreported, February 23, 1987 (Ont. S.C.) (Cork, Master); see also *Morris v. Morris*, [1974] 2 W.W.R. 193, 42 D.L.R. (3d) 550, 14 R.F.L. 163 (Man. C.A.), leave to appeal to Supreme Court of Canada granted: [1974] 3 W.W.R. 479, 51 D.L.R. (3d) 77, 15 R.F.L. 234; compare *Brett v. Brett*, [1969] 1 W.L.R. 487, [1969] 1 All E.R. 1007 (C.A.); and see *Koepell v. Koepell* (1956), 138 N.Y. Supp. 366 (N.Y. Sup. Ct.) and D.P. Jones and A. Bissett-Johnson, "Re Morris and Morris: A Case Comment" (1977), 23 McGill L.J. 110. It is open to question how far, if at all, subsection 56(5) of the *Family Law Act, 1986* qualifies the doctrine of unconscionability previously established by judicial decisions: see generally, Michel G. Picher, "The Separation Agreement as an Unconscionable Transaction: A Study in Equitable Fraud" (1972), 7 R.F.L. 257. Questions may also arise as to the constitutional validity of subsection 56(5) in light of section 15 of the *Canadian Charter of Rights and Freedoms*. It is submitted, however, that any constitutional challenge of subsection 56(5) is likely to prove unsuccessful: see J. Syrtash, "Removing Barriers to Religious Remarriage in Ontario: Rights and Remedies" with "Memorandum of Law" by J. Whyte (1987), 1 Can. Fam. Law Qtly 309.

39.0 RIGHTS OF DONORS OF GIFTS

Rights of donors of gifts

57. If a domestic contract provides that specific gifts made to one or both parties may not be disposed of or encumbered without the consent of the donor, the donor shall be deemed to be a party to the contract for the purpose of enforcement or amendment of the provision.

Section 57 of the *Family Law Act, 1986* qualifies the common law doctrine of privity of contract by protecting the rights of a donor who has imposed conditions on specific gifts made to one or both parties, whereby any disposition or encumbrance of the property requires the donor's consent. In these circumstances, the parties to a domestic contract cannot bilaterally circumvent the donor's interest. Should they attempt to do so by the terms of a domestic contract, the donor has the

124

locus standi to enforce the terms of the gift or amend the provisions of the domestic contract.

40.0 CONTRACTS MADE OUTSIDE ONTARIO

Contracts made outside Ontario

58. The manner and formalities of making a domestic contract and its essential validity and effect are governed by the proper law of the contract, except that,

    (a) a contract of which the proper law is that of a jurisdiction other than Ontario is also valid and enforceable in Ontario if entered into in accordance with Ontario's internal law;

    (b) subsection 33(4) (setting aside provision for support or waiver) and section 56 apply in Ontario to contracts for which the proper law is that of a jurisdiction other than Ontario; and

    (c) a provision in a marriage contract or cohabitation agreement respecting the right to custody of or access to children is not enforceable in Ontario.

Section 58 of the *Family Law Act, 1986* substantially corresponds to section 57 of the *Family Law Reform Act*, R.S.O. 1980, c. 152. In the absence of a *bona fide* choice of law clause in the domestic contract, the proper law of the contract is the system of law that has the most real and substantial connection with the contract. The proper law of a contract ordinarily governs its essential validity and effect. Pursuant to the provisions of clause 58(a) of the *Family Law Act, 1986*, however, the validity and enforceability of a domestic contract will be upheld, notwithstanding non-compliance with a foreign proper law, if the contract is valid and enforceable according to the laws applicable in Ontario. Pursuant to clause 58(b) of the Act, domestic contracts, which are governed by a foreign proper law, cannot circumvent the application of subsection 33(4) or of section 56 of the *Family Law Act, 1986*: see *supra*, subheadings 30.0 "GENERAL", 36.0 "BEST INTERESTS OF CHILD" and 37.0 "*DUM CASTA* CLAUSES". Such contracts are also subject to limitation under clause 56(c) of the Act, whereby a provision in a marriage contract or cohabitation agreement that purports to regulate custody and access rights is unenforceable in Ontario.

41.0 PATERNITY AGREEMENTS

Paternity agreements

59.—(1) If a man and a woman who are not spouses enter into an agreement for,

    (a) the payment of the expenses of a child's prenatal care and birth;

    (b) support of a child; or

    (c) funeral expenses of the child or mother,

on the application of a party, or a children's aid society, to the Provincial Court (Family Division) or the Unified Family Court, the court may incorporate the agreement in an order, and Part III (Support Obligations) applies to the order in the same manner as if it were an order made under that Part.

Absconding respondent

(2) If an application is made under subsection (1) and a judge of the court is satisfied that the respondent is about to leave Ontario and that there are reasonable grounds to believe that the respondent intends to evade his or her responsibilities under the agreement, the judge may issue a warrant in the form prescribed by the rules of the court for the respondent's arrest.

Bail

(3) Section 134 (interim release by justice of the peace) of the *Provincial Offences Act* [R.S.O. 1980, c. 400], applies, with necessary modifications, to an arrest under the warrant.

Capacity of minor

(4) A minor has capacity to enter into an agreement under subsection (1) that is approved by the court, whether the approval is given before or after the minor enters into the agreement.

Application to existing agreements

(5) This section applies to paternity agreements that were made before the day this Act comes into force.

42.0 PRE-EXISTING CONTRACTS

Application of Act to existing contracts

60.—(1) A domestic contract validly made before the day this Act comes into force shall be deemed to be a domestic contract for the purposes of this Act.

Contracts entered into before coming into force of Act

(2) If a domestic contract was entered into before the day this Act comes into force and the contract or any part would have been valid if entered into on or after that day, the contract or part is not invalid for the reason only that it was entered into before that day.

Idem

(3) If property is transferred, under an agreement or understanding reached before the 31st day of March, 1978, between spouses who are living separate and apart, the transfer is effective as if made under a domestic contract.

Section 60 of the *Family Law Act, 1986* is the successor to section 59 of the *Family Law Reform Act*, R.S.O. 1980, c. 152. Pursuant to subsection 60(1) of the *Family Law Act, 1986* a marriage contract, cohabitation agreement or separation agreement validly made before March 1, 1986, is deemed to be a domestic contract for the purposes of the Act. Such a contract or agreement will accordingly prevail over the rights conferred by the *Family Law Act, 1986*, except insofar as the Act provides otherwise: subsection 2(10), discussed *supra*. Having regard to the fundamental differences between the *Family Law Act, 1986* and the *Family Law Reform Act*, R.S.O. 1980, c. 152, subsection 70(4) of the *Family Law Act, 1986* expressly provides as follows:

Interpretation of existing contracts

70.—(4) A separation agreement or marriage contract that is validly made before the day this Act comes into force and that excludes a spouse's property from the application of sections 4 and 8 of the *Family Law Reform Act*,

> **(a) shall be deemed to exclude that property from the application of section 5 of this Act; and**
> **(b) shall be read with necessary modifications.**

Subsection 60(2) of the *Family Law Act, 1986* upholds the validity of prior domestic contracts entered into in contemplation of the Act, provided that such contracts would have been valid if entered into after the commencement of the *Family Law Act, 1986*.

Subsection 60(3) of the *Family Law Act, 1986* is directed to transfers of property that occurred before the commencement of the *Family Law Reform Act*, S.O. 1978, c. 2: see *Cushman v. Cushman* (1979), 10 R.F.L. (2d) 305 (Ont. S.C.).

43.0 SPOUSAL AND CHILD SUPPORT

Setting aside domestic contract

33.—(4) The court may set aside a provision for support or a waiver of the right to support in a domestic contract or paternity agreement and may determine and order support in an application under subsection (1) although the contract or agreement

contains an express provision excluding the application of this section,

> (a) if the provision for support or the waiver of the right to support results in "unconscionable" circumstances;
>
> (b) if the provision for support is in favour of or the waiver is by or on behalf of a dependant who qualifies for an allowance for support out of public money; or
>
> (c) if there is default in the payment of support under the contract or agreement at the time the application is made.

Subsection 33(4) of the *Family Law Act, 1986* confers a limited discretionary jurisdiction on the court to set aside a provision for spousal or child support in a domestic contract or paternity agreement *and* to determine the right to and quantum of support, if any, in an application under Part III of the Act, notwithstanding that the contract or agreement purports to exclude any such right. The discretionary jurisdiction of the court is exercisable pursuant to the subsection: (a) if the provision for support of the waiver of support results in unconscionable circumstances; (b) where the provision for support, if any, is in favour of a dependent spouse or child who qualifies for public assistance; or (c) if there is default in the payment of support under the contract or agreement at the time when an application is made pursuant to section 33 of the *Family Law Act, 1986*. It is submitted that clause 33(4)(a) of the Act may be invoked by either spouse, where the contract or agreement is unconscionable: compare *Porter v. Porter* (1979), 23 O.R. (2d) 492, 8 R.F.L. (2d) 349 (S.C.) and *Gergely v. Gergely* (1979), 11 R.F.L. (2d) 221, at 230 (Ont. S.C.).

Subsection 33(4) of the *Family Law Act, 1986* is supplemented by subsection 56(1) of the Act, which empowers the court to disregard any provision respecting child support in a domestic contract, where such a course of action is justified in light of the best interests of the child. The provisions of the *Family Law Act, 1986* have no direct application to corollary claims for spousal or child support in divorce proceedings: *McMeekin v. McMeekin* (1978), 21 O.R. (2d) 72, 89 D.L.R. (2d) 418 (S.C.).

Clause 15(5)(c) of the *Divorce Act, 1985*, S.C. 1986, c. 4, expressly requires the court to have regard to "any . . . agreement or arrangement relating to the support of the spouse or child" in making an order for spousal or child support. It is submitted that clause 15(5)(c) does not materially change the legal position as defined by the courts under the *Divorce Act*, R.S.C. 1970, c. D-8, (compare *Brockie v. Brockie* (1987), 5 R.F.L. (3d) 440, at 444 (Man. Q.B.) (Bowman J.) and see text, *infra*) and

s. 34 FLA gives indication when
court may overturn domestic K
re: support

P p. 111 N.A. book

[43]

s. 15(5)a N.A. *Domestic Contracts*
offers no guidelines - Brockie said agreement is
one factor among many so

support old Act ... if applies to new Act

that the following principles will be applied to applications for support
made pursuant to section 15 of the *Divorce Act, 1985*. ... any agreement relating to
support .... of the spouse.

A freely negotiated and informed waiver of spousal rights in a
separation agreement or in minutes of settlement that are incorporated
in a divorce judgment cannot oust the discretionary jurisdiction of the
court to order spousal support on or after divorce: *Pelech v. Pelech*,
unreported, June 4, 1987 (S.C.C.); *Hyman v. Hyman*, [1929] A.C. 601, 98
L.J. (P.) 81, 141 L.T. 329, 45 T.L.R. 444 (H.L.); see Julien D. Payne,
"Proposals for Reform of the Law Relating to Separation and
Maintenance Agreements" (1968), 33 Sask. R. 1. A critical distinction
must be made, however, between the existence of the discretionary
jurisdiction and the circumstances wherein it is proper for that
discretionary jurisdiction to be exercised. Where the parties have
negotiated their own agreement, freely and on the advice of legal
counsel, as to how their financial affairs should be settled, and the
agreement is not unconscionable in the substantive law sense, it should
be respected by reason of (1) the importance of finality in the financial
affairs of former spouses and (2) judicial deference to the right of
individuals to take responsibility for their own lives and their own
decisions. Only where an applicant seeking support or an increase in
support establishes that he or she has suffered a radical change in
circumstances since the execution of the separation agreement or
minutes of settlement and that radical change flowed from a pattern of
economic dependence engendered by the marriage, should the court
exercise its relieving power to order (increased) spousal support.
Otherwise, the obligation to support an indigent former spouse should
be the communal responsibility of the state. The fact that a former
spouse is impoverished and in receipt of public assistance, with little or
no prospect of improvement in his or her economic condition, is
insufficient in itself to warrant judicial disturbance of a negotiated
settlement by way of an order for spousal support, if there is no causal
connection between the former spouse's present economic status and the
prior marital relationship: *Pelech v. Pelech* (1987), 7 R.F.L. (3d) 225
(S.C.C.); *Richardson v. Richardson* (1987), 7 R.F.L. (3d) 304 (S.C.C.); and
Caron v. Caron (1987), 7 R.F.L. (3d) 274 (S.C.C.). The same criteria apply
to both an original application for support and an application to vary
minutes of settlement that have been incorporated in a previous divorce
judgment: *Richardson v. Richardson*, unreported, June 4, 1987 (S.C.C.)
(Wilson J., with Dickson C.J., McIntyre, Lamer and Le Dain JJ.,
concurring; but compare dissenting judgment of La Forest J.).

Significantly different considerations apply to child support rights and
obligations where a spousal settlement prejudicially affects the financial
well-being of the children: *Richardson v. Richardson, supra; Pelech v.
Pelech, supra; Jull v. Jull* (1985), 34 Alta. L.R. (2d) 252, 14 D.L.R. (4th)

Brockie says
agreement is
merely one factor
among many
to be taken
into account.

So if wife
looked after
home & kids
cty no skills
and "radical
change" in
circumstances
occur later
they are related
to marriage
it "may" rise
overturn
(2) K otherwise
stays same i.e.
"causally
connected"
between
present "need"
and marriage

Parallel
p. 211 Payne
on Divorce
(3) she said
must be
causal
connection
between "need"
and marriage
otherwise
state looks
after her
(4) If
agreement
or settlement
aren't final
and binding
Court can
discretionary
order support

P
R doesn't
C apply to
child
support

129

309, 42 R.F.L. (2d) 113 (C.A.). Child support, like access, is the right of the child: *Richardson v. Richardson, supra (per* Wilson J.). Children are not parties to the spousal agreement and neither parent has the authority to waive or restrict the statutory support obligations that each parent owes to dependent children: *Krueger v. Taubner* (1975), 17 R.F.L. 86, at 88 (Man. Q.B.); affd 17 R.F.L. 267, 50 D.L.R. (3d) 159 (Man. C.A.); *MacKenzie v. MacKenzie* (1976), 9 Nfld. & P.E.I.R. 176, 25 R.F.L. 354, *sub nom. MacKenzie v. MacKenzie and Monaghan* at 355-356 (P.E.I.S.C.); *Roy v. Chouinard*, [1976] C.S. 842 (Que.). The court is always free to intervene and determine the appropriate level of support for a child: *Richardson v. Richardson, supra (per* Wilson J.). Indeed, the court has a duty to scrutinize any agreement to ensure that the children are not prejudiced by it: *Kravetsky v. Kravetsky*, [1976] 2 W.W.R. 470, 63 D.L.R. (3d) 733, 21 R.F.L. 211 (Man. C.A.). If a child is being inadequately provided for, the concern of the court is to be addressed through an order for (increased) child support, even if the custodial parent may indirectly benefit from such an order. Spousal support, however, should not be ordered or increased simply because the spouse has custody of a child. The duty to support a child is an obligation owed to the child and not to the other parent and should be discharged, where necessary, through an order for child support and not an order for (increased) spousal support: *Richardson v. Richardson*, unreported, June 4, 1987 (S.C.C.).

44.0 INCORPORATION OF PROVISIONS OF DOMESTIC CONTRACT IN ORDER UNDER FAMILY LAW ACT, 1986

Incorporation of contract in order
2.—(9) A provision of a domestic contract in respect of a matter that is dealt with in this Act may be incorporated in an order made under this Act.

Subsection 2(9) of the *Family Law Act, 1986* expressly provides that a provision of a domestic contract respecting a matter that is dealt with by the Act may be incorporated in an order made pursuant to the Act. Insofar as the domestic contract regulates matters pertaining to property rights or entitlements under Part I or possessory or dispositional rights in the matrimonial home under Part II of the *Family Law Act, 1986* such incorporation may only be ordered by the Unified Family Court, the District Court or the Supreme Court: see definitions of "court" in subsection 4(1) and section 17 of *Family Law Act, 1986*; compare subsection 34(2); see also *Reference re Section 6 of Family Relations Act, S.B.C. 1978, c. 20*, [1982] 1 S.C.R. 62, [1982] 3 W.W.R. 1, 131 D.L.R. (3d) 257, 40 N.R. 206, 36 B.C.L.R. 1, 26 R.F.L. (2d) 113; *Re Lamb and Lamb et al.,* [1985] 1 S.C.R. 851, 20 D.L.R. (4th) 1, 59 N.R. 166, 46 R.F.L. (2d) 1. The provisions of a domestic contract respecting spousal or child support may, however, be incorporated in a judgment of the Provincial Court (Family Division): see definition of "court" in subsection 1(1) of the *Family Law Act, 1986.*

45.0 INCORPORATION OF PROVISIONS OF DOMESTIC CONTRACT IN DIVORCE JUDGMENT

The definition of "court" in subsection 2(1) of the *Divorce Act, 1985,* S.C. 1986, c. 4, designates a particular court in each province or territory to exercise jurisdiction under the Act. For the province of Ontario, jurisdiction is vested in "the trial division or branch of the Supreme Court of the Province . . . and includes such other court in the province the judges of which are appointed by the Governor General as is designated by the Lieutenant Governor in Council of the province as a court for the purposes of this Act". This provision permits the Lieutenant Governor in Council to designate a Unified Family Court, which is presided over by federally appointed judges, as a court of competent jurisdiction for the purposes of the *Divorce Act, 1985.* The requirement that any designated court shall be presided over by federally appointed judges reflects the constitutional limitations imposed on both the Parliament of Canada and the provincial legislatures by section 96 of the *Constitution Act, 1867*: see *McEvoy v. Attorney General for New Brunswick and Attorney General of Canada,* [1983] 1 S.C.R. 704, 148 D.L.R. (3d) 25, *sub nom. Re Court of Unified Criminal Jurisdiction; McEvoy v. Attorney General of New Brunswick and Attorney General of Canada* (1983), 46 N.B.R. (2d) 219, 121 A.P.R. 219. Section 96 of the *Constitution Act, 1867* does not, however, preclude provincial legislation that vests concurrent divorce jurisdiction in District Court judges in their capacity of Local Judges of the Supreme Court: *Re Supreme Court Amendment Act 1964 (B.C.); Attorney General of British Columbia v. McKenzie* (1965), 51 D.L.R. (2d) 623 (S.C.C.); *Reference Re Constitutional Validity of Section 11 of the Judicature Amendment Act, 1970 (No. 4),* [1971] 2 O.R. 521, 18 D.L.R. (3d) 385 (Ont. C.A.).

The *Divorce Act, 1985,* like its predecessor, *The Divorce Act,* R.S.C. 1970, c. D-8, is silent on matters relating to property rights or entitlements and perhaps necessarily so by virtue of section 92(13) of the *Constitution Act, 1867,* which confers exclusive legislative jurisdiction over "Property and Civil Rights" on the provinces. The jurisdiction of a court to incorporate the provisions of a domestic contract in a divorce judgment is accordingly fettered. The court has a discretionary jurisdiction to incorporate the terms of a separation agreement, with or without amendment, in the divorce judgment, but this jurisdiction is limited to those corollary relief matters that fall within the ambit of the *Divorce Act, 1985*. The court may, therefore, incorporate in the divorce judgment the provisions of a separation agreement insofar as they relate to spousal and child support or custody and access, but there is no jurisdiction to include covenants respecting the ownership or distribution of real or personal property. Where the provisions of a separation agreement are properly incorporated in a divorce judgment, the spouses must look to the judgment, which supersedes the separation agreement. The agreement continues to be operative and enforceable, however, in so far as its provisions cannot be legitimately incorporated in the divorce judgment, being matters falling outside the jurisdiction of the court under the *Divorce Act, 1985*: see *Oeming v. Oeming and Al Oeming Investments Limited* (1984), 43 R.F.L. (2d) 175 (Alta. Q.B.); *Re Finnie and Rae* (1977), 16 O.R. (2d) 54, 77 D.L.R. (3d) 330 (Ont. S.C.); *Campbell v. Campbell*, [1976] 5 W.W.R. 513, 27 R.F.L. 40 (Sask. Q.B.); compare *Horne v. Roberts*, [1971] 4 W.W.R. 663, 5 R.F.L. 15, *sub nom. Re Roberts*, 20 D.L.R. (3d) 719 (B.C.S.C.).

46.0 FILING, ENFORCEMENT AND VARIATION OF SUPPORT PROVISIONS OF DOMESTIC CONTRACT

Domestic contract, etc., may be filed with court

35.—(1) A person who is a party to a domestic contract or paternity agreement may file the contract or agreement with the clerk of the Provincial Court (Family Division) or of the Unified Family Court together with the person's affidavit stating that the contract or agreement is in effect and has not been set aside or varied by a court or agreement.

Effect of filing

(2) A provision for support or maintenance contained in a contract or agreement that is filed in this manner,

> **(a) may be enforced; and**   use scoE
> **(b) may be varied under section 37 and increased under section 38,** (indexing)

as if it were an order of the court where it is filed.

(4) can out — var — ind

Setting aside available

(3) Subsection 33(4) (setting aside in unconscionable circumstances, etc.) applies to a contract or agreement that is filed in this manner.

Filing and enforcement available despite waiver

(4) Subsection (1) and clause (2)(a) apply despite an agreement to the contrary.

Existing contracts, etc.
   (5) Subsections (1) and (2) also apply to contracts and
agreements made before this Act comes into force.

Existing arrears
   (6) Clause (2)(a) also applies to arrears accrued before this Act
comes into force. *but s. 50 limitation period — 2 years.*

   Subsection 35(1) of the *Family Law Act, 1986* empowers a party to a
domestic contract or paternity agreement to file the contract or
agreement with the clerk of the Provincial Court (Family Division) or of
the Unified Family Court with an accompanying affidavit stating that the
contract or agreement is still in effect and has not been set aside or
varied by court order or agreement. Upon such filing, any provision for
spousal or child support in the domestic contract may be enforced in the
same manner as a support order. The enforcement power conferred by
clause 35(2)(a) is expressly confined to support rights and obligations
and has no application to any provision of the domestic contract relating
to such matters as property entitlements or dispositional rights in the
matrimonial home. Subsection 35(1) and clause 35(2)(a), being discretionary, do not preclude a party to a domestic contract from pursuing
a contractual remedy in the event of non-compliance with support
provisions of a domestic contract. Any action arising from default under
the domestic contract may fall subject, however, to the limitation
provisions of subsection 50(2), as qualified by subsection 2(8), of the
Family Law Act, 1986. Pursuant to clause 35(2)(b) of the Act, the support
provisions of a duly filed domestic contract may be varied under section
37 of the Act. An application under this section may be made by either
party and the court may discharge, vary or suspend the support
provisions of the domestic contract, either prospectively or retroactively,
with consequential remission of all or part of any arrears or interest
thereon. Clause 35(2)(b) also provides for an increase in the quantum of
support provided under a duly filed domestic contract or paternity
agreement by means of a court-ordered indexation of the amount based
on the Consumer Price Index. The jurisdiction of the court to index
support payments and the definition of the indexing factor to be used
are specifically defined in subsections 34(5) and (6) and in section 38 of
the *Family Law Act, 1986*. In *Mintz v. Mintz*, unreported, August 29, 1986
(Ont. S.C.), Sutherland J. observed:

(marginal notes: s. 35(2)(a) limited to "support" rights only. doesn't cover property entitlements)

(marginal notes: s. 50 limitation period of 2 years; 2(8) extension of time)

(marginal notes: Court may "index" the support order; s. 34(5); s. 35(2)(b); s. 38(1))

> As to future indexing of the support order, s. 39 of the *Family Law Act* makes s. 38 of
> that *Act* applicable to orders made under Part II of the *Family Law Reform Act*.
> Subsection 38(1) of the *Family Law Act* authorizes the dependant to apply to the
> court for indexing in accordance with s-s. 34(5). It is provided in the last-mentioned
> subsection that the court may provide that the amount payable shall be increased
> annually on the order's anniversary date by the defined indexing factor of the

previous year. However s-s. 38(2) makes indexing mandatory on applications with respect to orders covered by s. 39 or s. 37 unless the respondent shows that his income, assets and means have not increased by the indexing factor as defined. The respondent has satisfied me that his income has not increased but not that his assets have not increased (counting the reductions in mortgage indebtedness) by an amount greater than that produced by the application of the indexing factor to the support obligations. The subsection is quite harsh on respondents in that it obligates a respondent who has had no increase in income but who has saved some of his income and so increased his assets, and so his means, to submit to indexing whereas another person with no increase in income and a wasteful expenditure of assets could escape indexing. The application having been made and the respondent not having satisfied all three branches of the exculpatory proviso, an order for indexing of future support payments will issue.

The provisions of subsection 33(4) of the Act, which fetter the jurisdiction of a court to interfere with the support provisions of a domestic contract or paternity agreement, continue to apply, however, where the contract or agreement is filed with the Provincial Court (Family Division) or the Unified Family Court: *Family Law Act, 1986*, subsection 35(3). *Quaere*, however, whether subsection 35(3) is intended to apply not only to an application to vary under section 37 but also to an application for an indexed increase under section 38.

The statutory powers of the court exercisable under section 37 of the Act cannot be ousted by the terms of any domestic contract or paternity agreement: subsection 37(4). The overall provisions of the domestic contract or paternity agreement will, nevertheless, remain significant in the exercise of the court's discretionary jurisdiction.

Domestic contracts or paternity agreements that were entered into prior to March 1, 1986, fall subject to the aforementioned statutory provisions, as do arrears that have accrued prior to that date: *Family Law Act, 1986*, subsections 35(5) and (6).

134

PRECEDENTS

The author acknowledges with deep appreciation the drafting of the following draft separation agreements by Glen Kealey, Barrister and Solicitor, Ottawa, Ontario. These agreements are specifically directed to recurring practical problems that face the Family Law practitioner. The agreements are intended to provide guidelines for practising lawyers and do not purport to release any legal advisor from assuming a personal responsibility for protecting the interests of his or her client.

INTERIM SEPARATION AGREEMENT
THIS INTERIM SEPARATION AGREEMENT made the day of April, 1987

B E T W E E N:

JACK NIMBLE
hereinafter called the "husband"

AND:

JILL NIMBLE
hereinafter called the "wife"

1. DEFINITIONS
(a) "Divorce Act" means the Divorce Act 1985, S.C. 1986, c. 4;
(b) "Family Law Act" means the Family Law Act, S.O. 1986, c. 4;
(c) "matrimonial home" means the premises at 5 Heart Throb Lane, Ottawa, Ontario;
(d) "property" means "property" as defined in s. 4(1)(b) of the Family Law Act.

2. BACKGROUND
(a) The parties married each other in the City of Ottawa, in the Province of Ontario, on the 10th day of November, 1967.
(b) They have two children namely Ann Nimble, born June 17th, 1977 and Tom Nimble, born December 5th, 1978.
(c) The parties have been living separate and apart since October 1st, 1986. The husband has paid to his wife for support since October 1st, 1986 the amount of ONE THOUSAND TWO HUNDRED ($1,200.00) DOLLARS per month.
(d) The parties are negotiating a final settlement of all claims arising out of their marriage. Accordingly, they are entering into this interim agreement pending a final agreement or court order.

3. AGREEMENT
Each party agrees with the other to be bound by the provisions of this agreement.

4. DOMESTIC CONTRACT

This agreement is entered into pursuant to s. 54 of the Family Law Act and each party acknowledges that it is a domestic contract which prevails over other matters provided for in this Act and its successors.

5. EFFECTIVE DATE

This agreement will take effect on the date it is executed by the last of the husband and the wife signing his or her name to the agreement.

6. SEPARATE AND APART

During the term of this agreement the parties will continue to live separate and apart from each other and neither party will directly or indirectly harass, molest, disturb or annoy the other, or interfere with the other in any manner whatsoever.

7. CUSTODY AND ACCESS

The wife shall have custody of the children of the marriage subject to reasonable and generous access to the husband.

8. INTERIM SUPPORT

During the currency of this agreement the husband shall pay to the wife as interim support for herself and the two children the following amounts:

    (a) on the 1st day of October 1986 and on the 1st day of each month thereafter until the termination of this agreement the sum of ONE THOUSAND TWO HUNDRED ($1,200.00) DOLLARS per month.

The parties acknowledge and agree that all support payments made by the husband in accordance with this paragraph including such payments as preceded the operative date of this agreement shall be deducted by him and included by the wife in the calculation of his and her taxable income and shall be considered as having been paid and received pursuant to the provisions of subsections 56.1(3) and 60.1(3) of the Income Tax Act.

9. INTERIM POSSESSION OF THE MATRIMONIAL HOME

    (a) During the currency of this agreement the wife shall have interim exclusive possession of the matrimonial home without payment of occupation rent until June 30th, 1987 or until it is sold whichever is later.

    (b) The parties agree that the matrimonial home shall be listed for sale on or before April 30th, 1987 with a closing date as soon as possible after June 30th, 1987.

(c) All matters relating to the listing for sale and the sale shall be the subject of discussion and agreement. In the event the parties are unable to agree with respect to any issue regarding the listing of the sale or the sale any such issue shall be determined by a court of competent jurisdiction.

(d) The wife shall be solely responsible for the following expenses from October 1st, 1986 until the termination of the within interim separation agreement:

    i/ the mortgage payments on the matrimonial home (principal, interest and taxes);

    ii/ all household expenses and utility expenses including telephone, heat, light, water and electricity.

(e) The husband and wife during the period from October 1st, 1986 until the termination of this interim separation agreement shall equally share the costs of any major repairs, including painting, to the matrimonial home. No major repairs to the matrimonial home shall be undertaken without the written consent of both the husband and the wife. Neither spouse shall unreasonably withhold his or her consent to necessary major repairs. A major repair shall be deemed to be any repair in excess of $150.00. The wife shall be solely responsible for any individual repairs costing $150.00 or less.

10. EXISTING O.H.I.P., SUPPLEMENTARY MEDICAL & DENTAL, LIFE INSURANCE AND DEATH BENEFITS

During the currency of this agreement the husband shall keep in effect for the benefit of the wife and children the above existing plans unencumbered, and without alteration.

11. ORTHODONTAL EXPENSES

During the currency of this agreement the husband and wife shall share equally any orthodontal expenses incurred by either child not covered by any insurance plan.

12. INDEPENDENT LEGAL ADVICE

The parties acknowledge that they have signed this agreement having received independent legal advice relating to their rights and obligations.

13. AGREEMENT WITHOUT PREJUDICE TO RIGHTS OF PARTIES

None of the rights of either party shall be permanently waived or compromised by this agreement. During the currency of this agreement all the rights that either party had immediately before the effective date of this agreement shall be in suspension except for the rights conferred by or arising from this interim separation agreement. Upon termination of this agreement all rights that the parties had immediately prior to the effective date of this agreement shall revive including rights with respect to:

(a) custody and access;
(b) child support and spousal support including the right to dispute liability for any claim to support and the amount of any such claim;
(c) possession of the matrimonial home, its contents and any other property;
(d) the equalization or division of their net family properties; and
(e) any other right with respect to making or defending any claim with respect to support, property or any other matter.

14. DURATION OF AGREEMENT

Termination of this agreement shall be on the earlier of the following dates:

(a) the date of execution of a final agreement; or
(b) June 30th, 1987.

TO EVIDENCE HIS AGREEMENT, the husband has signed this agreement on   , 19   , under seal before a witness.

SIGNED, SEALED AND
   DELIVERED   )
   in the presence of   )
)
_____   )   _____
Witness as to the signature   )   JACK NIMBLE
of JACK NIMBLE   )

TO EVIDENCE HER AGREEMENT, the wife has signed this agreement on   , 19   , under seal before a witness.

SIGNED, SEALED AND
   DELIVERED   )
   in the presence of   )
)
_____   )   _____
Witness as to the signature   )   JILL NIMBLE
of JILL NIMBLE   )

PERMANENT SEPARATION AGREEMENT

THIS SEPARATION AGREEMENT made this 30th day of December 1987 at Ottawa, Ontario, Canada

B E T W E E N:

ROMEO SMITH
called the husband throughout

AND:

JULIET SMITH
called the wife throughout

1. DEFINITIONS
   (a) *"Divorce Act"* means the Divorce Act, 1985, S.C. 1986, c. 4, as amended, and any successor;
   (b) *"Family Law Act"* means the Family Law Act, 1986, S.O. 1986, c. 4, as amended, and any successor;
   (c) *"Arbitrations Act"* means the Arbitrations Act, R.S.O. 1980, c. 25, as amended, and any successor;
   (d) *"Trustee Act"* means the Trustee Act, R.S.O. 1980, c. 512, as amended, and any successor;
   (e) *"Succession Law Reform Act"* means the Succession Law Reform Act, R.S.O. 1980, c. 488, as amended, and any successor;
   (f) *"Income Tax Act"* means the Income Tax Act, S.C. 1970-71-72, c. 63, as amended, and any successor;
   (g) *"matrimonial home"* means the residence located at _____, Ontario, more particularly described in Appendix "A" attached hereto;
   (h) *"cottage"* means the property located at _____, Ontario, more particularly described in Appendix "B" attached hereto;
   (i) *"property"* is defined in accordance with s. 4(1) of the *Family Law Act*.

140

2. BACKGROUND AND GENERAL PROVISIONS

(a) The paragraph titles in this Agreement shall not be construed to change the meaning of the paragraphs but are for convenience only.

(b) The proper law of this Agreement shall be the law of the Province of Ontario. This Agreement shall also be deemed to be valid and in force in accordance with the law of any other jurisdiction.

(c) The spouses intend all of their rights and obligations with respect to their domestic situation to be governed by this Agreement.

(d) The spouses agree that this Agreement is valid and enforceable in the Province of Ontario and that they intend it to be a domestic contract in accordance with the *Family Law Act* and that it be legally binding.

(e) The spouses were married to each other on April 1st, 1966. Throughout this Agreement they are called respectively the wife and husband and collectively the spouses. In the event that their marriage is dissolved, the terms wife and husband shall be construed to mean former wife and former husband.

(f) The husband and wife have two children of the marriage within the meaning of the *Divorce Act* (hereinafter referred to as the children) who are Judith Smith born June 4th, 1975 and Sol Smith born August 17th, 1972.

(g) The spouses executed a marriage contract in the Province of Quebec dated April 8th, 1966. The spouses hereby terminate this marriage contract and declare that it is not in force and effect.

(h) The spouses have been living separate and apart since November 15th, 1986. They acknowledge that each has been ordinarily resident in Ontario within the meaning of s. 3(1) of the *Divorce Act* since November 15th, 1986.

(i) With respect to s. 8(3)(b)(ii) of the *Divorce Act* the spouses acknowledge that since separation they cohabited for a single period of less than 90 days.

(j) The parties agree to continue to live separate and apart and to settle by this Agreement all the rights and obligations which they have or might otherwise acquire with respect to each other and their children.

(k) The spouses executed an interim separation agreement dated March 1st, 1987 which they hereby terminate and declare that it is no longer in force and effect.

3. FREEDOM FROM THE OTHER

Neither the husband nor the wife shall directly or indirectly harass, molest, annoy or interfere with the other or use any means to persuade or try to persuade the other to cohabit with him or her nor engage any agent to keep the other under surveillance. Neither the husband nor the wife shall, except in an emergency, telephone the other's place of employment or address any correspondence to the other's place of employment.

4. JOINT CUSTODY

(a) The husband and wife shall have joint custody of the children. The children shall reside on an approximate equal time basis, including summer holidays, Jewish holidays and March school breaks, with the husband and wife, in accordance with Appendix "C" attached hereto.

(b) The husband and wife agree and undertake that the children's best interests shall at all times be paramount. The husband and wife shall continue to instil in the children love and respect for both parents and for the grandparents. Neither the husband nor the wife shall by any act, omission or innuendo directly or indirectly attempt to alienate the children from a parent or grandparent or any other person.

(c) The husband and wife shall have the right to communicate with the children by telephone or letter at all reasonable times provided that such communications shall not unduly interfere with the wife or the husband.

(d) The husband and wife agree that there shall be full disclosure between them on all matters affecting the welfare, health and education of the children. They agree that they shall confer as often as necessary to attempt to resolve any problems concerning the aforementioned matters.

(e) The husband and wife agree to provide each other with reasonable notice of the special occasions they would like to spend with the children, and to make every reasonable effort to accommodate the other's request. If special occasions, holidays, activities become available to the children, the husband and wife shall maintain a reasonable and flexible position respecting such special occasions.

(f) The husband and wife agree that, if either of them cohabit with a member of the opposite sex, this shall not affect the rights of that spouse to have the children live with and visit him or her.

(g) If the spouses cannot agree on any issue regarding their children and in particular if one of the spouses decides to move more than 50 kilometers from the City of Ottawa and a new parenting arrangement is not agreed upon, they agree to immediately seek mediation with an experienced professional mediator practising in the City of Ottawa in order to reach an appropriate parenting arrangement. If they cannot agree on the choice of mediator, they will accept a decision from their solicitors as to the choice of a mediator and the terms of the mediation. They agree to pay the costs of mediation as the mediator may recommend. The mediator may be a Family Law Commissioner of the Supreme Court of Ontario or any other judicial officer in Ontario acting in a mediation capacity. If the spouses are unable to resolve their dispute through mediation, either spouse may apply to a court of competent jurisdiction to determine any issue relating to the children.

(h) If either spouse with custody intends to be away from the children overnight, such spouse shall offer the other spouse the right to care for the children during such absence.

(i) The spouses agree that the children shall continue to be instructed in the Jewish faith.

(j) The husband and wife shall immediately advise the other of any change of address or telephone number.

(k) Neither spouse shall remove any of the children from the City of Ottawa for a period in excess of 14 days without the written consent of the other spouse or the approval of a court of competent jurisdiction after at least 30 days' notice to the other spouse of such court hearing.

5. NAMES OF CHILDREN

Neither spouse shall change the names of the children without the written consent of the other spouse.

6. WIFE SUPPORT

(a) The husband (or his estate if he be deceased) shall pay to the wife for her support during her life the following monthly sums in advance on the 1st day of the month:

i/ effective January 1st, 1988 to and including December 1st, 1988 the sum of ONE THOUSAND ($1,000.00) DOLLARS;

ii/ effective January 1st, 1989 to and including December 1st, 1989 the sum of EIGHT HUNDRED ($800.00) DOLLARS;

iii/ effective January 1st, 1990, to and including December 1st, 1990 the sum of SIX HUNDRED ($600.00) DOLLARS per month;

iv/ effective January 1st, 1991, the wife's entitlement to spousal support shall permanently cease;

143

v/ notwithstanding anything to the contrary herein contained, payments for wife support shall permanently cease in the event the wife remarries or cohabits with another person for a period or periods totalling more than 30 days.

(b) Subject to the above payments in paragraph 6(a), each of the spouses:

i/ releases all rights to claim or obtain interim support or permanent support pursuant to the Family Law Act or the Divorce Act from the other.

ii/ releases the other from all obligations to pay interim support or permanent support pursuant to the Family Law Act or the Divorce Act;

iii/ The spouses acknowledge and agree that they shall be financially independent and shall not require financial support from the other.

iv/ The spouses intend this Agreement to be a final settlement of all claims for spousal support. Neither spouse shall seek to incorporate its provisions respecting spousal support in any order or judgment. The spouses acknowledge that each of them may enjoy or suffer radical or catastrophic changes in their respective income, assets, debts and expenses, in the cost of living or in their health, or changes of fortune by reason of unforeseen factors. Nevertheless they agree that under no circumstances will any change, direct or indirect, foreseen or unforeseen, give either the right to claim any alteration in the spousal support provision of this agreement. The wife acknowledges that she may be required to encroach in whole or in part on her assets for her own support.

7. RETROACTIVE CHILD SUPPORT

Effective December 1st, 1986 and on the 1st day of each month thereafter, the husband shall pay in advance to the wife the sum of THREE HUNDRED ($300.00) DOLLARS per month per child (being a total of $600.00 each month) for child support. The spouses acknowledge and agree that all child support payments made by the husband pursuant to this Agreement on or after December 1st, 1986, shall be deemed deductible by him and includable by the wife in the calculation of their income for tax purposes. Such payments shall be considered as having been paid and received pursuant to the provisions of sub-section 56.1(3) and 60.1(3) of the Income Tax Act.

Such payments for the support of each child shall continue until one of the following events occurs:

    (a) the child ceases to reside full time with the wife. The child shall be deemed to "reside full time with the wife" if the child lives away from the wife's residence for the purpose of attending an educational institution, working in the summer or taking a vacation, but otherwise resides with the wife;

    (b) the child becomes 18 years of age and ceases to be in full time attendance at an educational institution;

    (c) the child becomes 22 years of age;

    (d) the child marries;

    (e) the wife dies;

    (f) the husband dies.

8. POSTDATED CHEQUES

    (a) The husband shall forthwith deliver to the wife:

        i/ a series of thirty six (36) monthly postdated cheques for the payments of wife support pursuant to paragraph 6 herein;

        ii/ a series of twelve (12) monthly postdated cheques for the period 1 December 1987 to 1 November 1988, inclusive of both dates, for the payment of child support pursuant to Paragraph 7 herein. Thereafter the husband shall provide from time to time a further series of twelve (12) monthly postdated cheques for child support in accordance with Paragraphs 7, 9, and 10 herein;

    (b) If any cheque for the payment of wife support or child support is not honoured for any reason, the husband shall pay to the wife as an administrative charge or as liquidated damages, but not as a penalty, the sum of TWENTY FIVE ($25.00) DOLLARS for each such cheque.

9. VARIATION OF CHILD SUPPORT — Consumer Price Index

Payments of child support shall be adjusted annually in accordance with the lesser of:

    (a) the annual percentage increase, if any, in the Consumer Price Index for Canada for prices of all items at December 1st, 1987, namely, _____ points, or

    (b) the percentage increase in the husband's gross income from employment; the base shall be his gross income from employment as at December 1st, 1987, namely _____.

The first of such adjustments shall be effective December 1st, 1988 and shall be based on the annual percentage increase in the Consumer Price Index for Canada for prices of all items as reported for the period December 1st, 1987 to December 1st, 1988 or in the percentage increase in the husband's gross income from employment from December 1st, 1987 to December 1st, 1988.

EXAMPLE: Assume between December 1st, 1987 and December 1st, 1988 the annual percentage increase in the Consumer Price Index for Canada for prices of all items was 4%. Assume between December 1st, 1987 and December 1st, 1988 the husband's gross income from employment increased 3%. Effective December 1st, 1988 and thereafter until any subsequent increase the husband shall pay to the wife for the support of the children the sum of $600.00 per month plus 3% of same i.e. $618.00.

10. VARIATION OF CHILD SUPPORT — HUSBAND'S DISABILITY OR RETIREMENT

(a) Except for variations of child support pursuant to paragraph 9 herein, the amount for child support pursuant to paragraph 7 herein may only be varied if:

    i/ the husband for reasons beyond his control and without his default is unable to engage in regular, full-time employment; or

    ii/ the husband, after attaining the age of sixty (60) years, is not engaged in regular, full-time employment.

(b) Any dispute with respect to paragraph 10(a) may be determined at the instance of either the husband or the wife by a single arbitrator acting pursuant to the Arbitrations Act. This paragraph shall be deemed a submission pursuant to the Arbitrations Act.

(c) The right to vary child support shall not include the right to forgive all or part of any arrears that may have accumulated.

11. WAIVER OF RIGHT TO INDEX SUPPORT PAYMENTS

(a) The spouses hereby confirm that child support payments shall be indexed in accordance with paragraph 9 herein and not in accordance with the Family Law Act or any other statute.

(b) The spouses agree with respect to indexing of child support and wife support payments as follows:

    i/ each waives all claims and rights that he or she has or may have to require that any amount payable for child support or wife support under this Agreement be increased annually, or at any time, by an indexing factor as provided in the Family Law Act or in any other statute;

    ii/ neither shall apply at any time to the Provincial Court (Family Division) or to any other court of competent jurisdiction to vary or index the child support or wife support provisions of this Agreement pursuant to section 35(2)(b) of the Family Law Act or any other statute.

12. MATERIAL CHANGE IN CIRCUMSTANCES

(a) The spouses intend paragraph 4 of this Agreement to be final except for variation by reason of a material change in circumstances.

(b) If a material change in circumstances occurs, only the provisions in paragraph 4 of this Agreement may be varied.

(c) The spouse wanting the variation shall notify the other in writing of the variation sought and the spouses may then confer with each other personally or through their solicitors to settle the issue of variation.

(d) If no Agreement has been reached thirty clear days after notice has been given under paragraph 12(c), the spouses may, if they both agree, seek mediation with a mediator practising in the City of Ottawa, in an attempt to resolve any dispute.

(e) The spouses agree to pay the costs of the mediator as the mediator may recommend.

(f) The spouses may attend before any judicial officer including a judge or Family Law Commissioner in an attempt to resolve any dispute.

(g) If the spouses are unable to resolve any dispute through mediation, either spouse may apply to a court of competent jurisdiction to vary any provision in this Agreement relating to custody or access.

13. MEDICAL AND HEALTH EXPENSES

(a) The husband warrants that he is maintaining in force for the benefit of the children a plan of insurance established under the Ontario Health Insurance Plan, together with an extended health care plan available through his employer. Such plan or plans (or reasonable substitutes) are hereinafter referred to as the Health Plans.

(b) The husband agrees to continue such Health Plans for the children for as long as they qualify for coverage and are eligible to receive support.

(c) If the husband fails to maintain such Health Plans he shall pay all costs which would ordinarily be paid thereby.

(d) Notwithstanding anything to the contrary contained in paragraph 13(c), if the husband changes employment and an extended health care plan is not available through his employer, or if the husband is self employed, or if his present employer ceases to provide this benefit, the husband shall not be obliged to continue such coverage; if any of these events occur, the husband shall forthwith provide his wife with written notice of any termination of coverage.

(e) The spouses agree to share equally any special medical and health expenses incurred on behalf of the children which are not covered by any insurance or benefit plan. Without limiting the generality of the foregoing, such medical expenses shall include all dental, orthodontal, prescription drug, eyeglass and contact lens expenses. If either spouse has a plan which covers any such expenses, that spouse shall maintain such plan for the benefit of the children for as long as they qualify for coverage and are eligible to receive support.

14. POST-SECONDARY EDUCATIONAL EXPENSES FOR CHILDREN

The husband shall pay any post-secondary educational expenses incurred by or on behalf of either child for as long as such child is eligible to receive support. Such payments shall include the cost of books, tuition, fees and other charges. Notwithstanding anything to the contrary herein contained, the maximum amount that the husband shall be required to pay for such expenses in any calendar year shall not exceed $5,000.00 whether the expenses are for one or both of the children.

15. CULTURAL, SPORTS' EXPENSES OF THE CHILDREN

The husband and wife shall share equally the cultural and sports' expenses of either child for as long as such child is eligible to receive support. Without limiting the generality of the foregoing, such expenses shall include piano lessons, ski passes, ski clothing and ski equipment.

16. SUMMER CAMP COSTS

The husband shall be solely responsible for the payment of summer camp costs incurred on behalf of either child as long as such child is eligible to receive support. Notwithstanding anything to the contrary herein contained, the maximum the husband shall be liable to pay for summer camp costs in any calendar year shall not exceed $2,000.00 whether the expenses are for one or both children.

17. LIFE INSURANCE AND DEATH BENEFITS

(a) Each spouse shall, either privately or through his employer, keep in force life insurance and death benefit plans (hereinafter referred to as Death Benefit Plans) that provide an unencumbered minimum amount of FIFTY THOUSAND ($50,000.00) DOLLARS for each child.

(b) Each spouse shall designate the other spouse under the Death Benefit Plans as a trustee for the children.

(c) Each, if requested by the other, shall provide written evidence that such Death Benefit Plans are in good standing.

(d) Each shall keep such Death Benefit Plans in force notwithstanding any change of employment.

(e) If either spouse fails to keep in force such Death Benefit Plans then the said amount of coverage together with all costs incurred on a solicitor client basis in enforcing this obligation shall be a first charge on the estate of the defaulting spouse.

(f) If either spouse defaults in the payment of the premiums or expenses of any Death Benefit Plans, the other spouse may pay any of such premiums or expenses and recover them together with all costs on a solicitor and client basis.

(g) Notwithstanding anything to the contrary herein contained, neither spouse shall be obliged to maintain Death Benefit Plans for a child who is not eligible for support. Each spouse agrees to give to the other any consents that may be required to enable the other to deal with any such Death Benefit Plans as he or she sees fit with respect to any child who ceases to be eligible for support.

(h) The spouses acknowledge and agree that the above provisions are intended to provide the children with financial assistance in the event of the death of either spouse. Neither spouse shall have any further claim against the other's estate for support except as set out above.

18. INCOME TAX ON SPECIAL EXPENSES

Payments made pursuant to paragraphs 13, 14, 15, 16 and 17 herein shall not be includable in the taxable income or deductible from the taxable income of either spouse.

19. FAMILY ALLOWANCE CHEQUES

Subject to applicable statutory provisions or regulations the wife shall continue to be entitled to receive all payments pursuant to the Family Allowances Act or any other similar allowances, payments or benefits in respect of both children.

20. PERSONAL PROPERTY

(a) The husband and wife acknowledge and agree that:
   i/ all their personal property has been divided between them to their mutual satisfaction;
   ii/ each is entitled to the personal property now in his or her possession free from any claim by the other.

(b) Notwithstanding anything to the contrary herein contained, the items listed in Appendix D attached hereto, which items are presently located in the matrimonial home, shall be deemed the sole property of the husband. The husband shall remove these items from the matrimonial home at his expense on or before January 10th, 1988.

21. PHOTOGRAPHS, RECORDS
The spouses acknowledge that:
- (a) included in their household contents were many photographs, slides, family video movies, audio cassettes, tape recordings, and records;
- (b) they have divided such items to their mutual satisfaction;
- (c) each is the sole owner of such items in his or her possession;
- (d) notwithstanding anything to the contrary herein contained, each spouse at his or her expense shall be entitled to make reproductions, copies or duplicates of any such item in the other spouse's possession.

22. PAINTING — "SUNSET AT DUCK LAKE"
- (a) Notwithstanding anything to the contrary herein contained, the spouses acknowledge that the husband and wife have an equal ownership interest as joint tenants with right of survivorship in the painting by Arthur Lismer titled "Sunset at Duck Lake" (hereinafter referred to as the Painting).
- (b) As long as both spouses are alive the Painting shall not be sold.
- (c) The husband shall have the sole right to the possession, use and enjoyment of the Painting in even numbered years commencing in 1988. The wife shall have the sole right to the possession, use and enjoyment of the Painting in odd numbered years.

23. CHESS SET
Notwithstanding anything to the contrary herein contained, the spouses acknowledge that the husband is the sole owner of an ivory chess set known as "The Crusaders" (hereinafter referred to as the Chess Set). The husband quit claims his interest in the Chess Set to his son Sol, subject to reserving to himself a life interest in the Chess Set. The husband shall execute a will to give effect to this provision.

24. SNOWMOBILE
The husband warrants and represents:
- (a) that he is the sole owner of a Skidoo No. 1234567 (hereinafter referred to as the Snowmobile);
- (b) that the Snowmobile is unencumbered by any debt, liability, lien, charge or mortgage;

(c) that the Snowmobile is in good running condition.

The husband quit claims his interest in the Snowmobile to the wife.

25. BMW AUTOMOBILE LEASE

The wife acknowledges that Eureka Investments Limited is the lessee of the 1987 BMW bearing Ontario Licence Plate "FAT CAT". The wife shall continue to have the sole use of the BMW until the expiry of the lease on December 31st, 1990, without payment of the monthly lease expense. The wife shall continue to be solely liable for all expenses incurred in respect of the BMW except for the monthly lease expense. Without limiting the generality of the foregoing, such expenses shall include all expenses for the maintenance, repair, operation, license and insurance for the BMW. The husband or his nominee or Eureka Investments Limited shall be liable to make all monthly lease payments with respect to the BMW. The wife shall not have the right to exercise any option at any time to purchase the BMW.

26. DIVISION OF NET FAMILY PROPERTIES

(a) The spouses acknowledge that each has been advised of his or her rights concerning the equalization or reapportionment of their net family properties under the Family Law Act.

(b) Each spouse acknowledges that the benefits he or she has received prior to the date of this Agreement, together with other benefits granted pursuant to this Agreement fully satisfy all entitlements each spouse has or may have to an equalization or reapportionment of their net family properties.

27. MATRIMONIAL HOME — EQUALIZATION PAYMENT

The husband shall forthwith at his expense quit claim his interest in the Matrimonial Home to the wife. The wife shall forthwith pay to the husband the sum of FORTY TWO THOUSAND ($42,000.00) DOLLARS as a final adjustment to the equalization or reapportionment of their net family properties pursuant to s. 5 of the Family Law Act.

28. MATRIMONIAL HOME — OCCUPATION RENT

The wife acknowledges that she has had the sole use of the Matrimonial Home since the date of separation, namely November 15th, 1986. The husband shall not be liable with respect to any claims for taxes, charges or any expenses incurred in respect of the Matrimonial Home since November 15th, 1986. The wife shall indemnify the husband and save him harmless with respect to any such claims. The wife shall not be liable to pay any occupation rent to the husband.

29. COTTAGE

    (a) The spouses acknowledge that the husband is the sole owner of the Cottage. The wife quit claims any interest in the Cottage to the husband.

    (b) Notwithstanding anything to the contrary herein contained, the wife shall have a license for the exclusive possession and use of the Cottage for herself and the children for fourteen consecutive days between July 1st and August 30th to and including the year 1998 without payment of occupation rent.

    (c) Notwithstanding anything to the contrary herein contained, in the event of a sale of the Cottage prior to 1999, the husband shall have the right to terminate forthwith the wife's license to occupy the Cottage.

30. PRIVATE PENSION PLANS

Neither spouse shall make any claim to any employment pension plan of the other nor to any profit sharing plan, Registered Retirement Savings Plans; Registered Home Ownership Savings Plans, Registered Retirement Income Fund, Registered Education Savings Plans or any similar plan or plans. The spouses acknowledge that they do not wish to obtain any actuarial or other valuations with respect to any such plans.

31. CANADA PENSION PLAN

Each spouse shall be entitled to apply under the Canada Pension Plan or similar plans for a division of pension credits.

32. EUREKA INVESTMENTS LIMITED

The wife acknowledges that the husband has an ownership interest in Eureka Investments Limited (hereinafter referred to as Eureka) but that she has never had any ownership interest in Eureka. The wife quit claims and releases to the husband any interest she may have in Eureka pursuant to the Family Law Act or any other statute or law. The wife acknowledges that she has received from Eureka a salary of approximately $500.00 per week and that her employment with Eureka has been terminated effective December 31, 1987. The wife acknowledges that she has received reasonable and fair:

    (a) notice of termination;

    (b) compensation for her services provided to Eureka.

The wife releases her husband and Eureka from any claim with respect to any rights she may have with respect to the services she has provided to Eureka.

33. SKYHIGH REAL ESTATE DEVELOPMENT — RELEASE

(a) The spouses agree as follows:

    i/ The husband is a partner with his brother Aaron in Skyhigh Real Estate Development (hereinafter called the Partnership). There are no other partners in the Partnership.

    ii/ The wife lent the husband the sum of $20,000.00 secured by a promissory note dated January 1st, 1986.

    iii/ The husband applied the sum of $20,000.00 as part of the down payment on a vacant lot (hereinafter called the Lot), which Lot is more particularly described in Appendix "E" attached hereto. The lot is owned by the Partnership.

    iv/ The wife has not been paid any part of the principal or interest on the note.

(b) As part of the financial adjustment between the spouses in this Agreement, the wife hereby releases the husband, the husband's brother Aaron and the Partnership from any obligation in respect of the note and waives any right with respect to payment of principal or interest on the note.

(c) The wife releases her right to any interest she may have in the Lot.

34. THE SWANK GOLF CLUB

(a) The spouses acknowledge:

    i/ that the husband has been a member of The Swank Golf Club (hereinafter referred to as the Club) for twenty years and that he has paid for a family membership in the Club which expires on December 31st, 1988;

    ii/ that the husband is on the Club's board of directors and has been an active competitive golfer in the Club;

    iii/ that he has used the Club frequently for business purposes.

(b) The wife agrees and undertakes that she will make no use of the Club either as a member or as a guest. The husband agrees to continue to pay the Club's family membership to permit the children full privileges until such time as neither child is eligible to receive support.

35. RESUMPTION OF COHABITATION

(a) If the spouses cohabit as husband and wife for a period or periods totalling no more than 90 days, with reconciliation as the primary purpose of the cohabitation, the terms of this Agreement will not be affected, except insofar as the spouses agree in writing to suspend the payment of wife support or child support during such period or periods of resumed cohabitation.

(b) If the spouses cohabit as husband and wife for a period or periods totalling more than 90 days, with reconciliation as the primary purpose of the cohabitation, the terms of this Agreement shall be rendered void, except that nothing in this paragraph will affect or invalidate any payment, conveyance or act made or done pursuant to this Agreement.

36. NO CONDONATION

Nothing in this Agreement constitutes condonation by the husband or the wife of any conduct, which would entitle the husband or wife to a divorce judgment.

37. GET

The spouses acknowledge that they are members of the Jewish faith. Each spouse shall forthwith do all things necessary to obtain a Get. The husband shall pay any expenses or costs incurred in obtaining a Get.

38. OWNERSHIP OF FAMILY DOG "PEPPER"

The spouses agree that the family dog "Pepper" is owned by the children. "Pepper" will alternate between the residences of the children in accordance with their time sharing arrangements with the spouses. "Pepper's" expenses shall be shared equally by the spouses.

39. NONDISCLOSURE OF ASSETS

(a) The husband and wife acknowledge and agree that they have made full disclosure of their assets in their sworn Financial Statements. The husband's Financial Statement sworn _____, 19____, is attached hereto as Appendix "F". The wife's Financial Statement sworn _____, 19____, is attached hereto as Appendix "G".

(b) The husband and wife shall own equally as tenants in common any assets (valued as at the date of separation namely November 15th, 1986) which are not disclosed in Appendix "F" and Appendix "G".

(c) A non-disclosing party shall indemnify the other for all reasonable costs incurred to discover the existence of any undisclosed asset and to determine its value. Such costs shall include the fees and disbursements incurred for legal, accounting and valuation expenses.

40. DEBTS AND OBLIGATIONS

   (a) The spouses acknowledge and agree that all of their debts up to and including the date of execution of this Agreement have been accounted for and apportioned between them.

   (b) Neither spouse shall contract in the name of the other nor in any way bind the other for any debts or obligations.

   (c) If debts or obligations are incurred by either spouse on behalf of the other before or after the date of this Agreement, he or she shall indemnify the other from all such debts or obligations and any related damages or costs.

41. RELEASE OF RIGHTS IN EACH OTHER'S ESTATE

Except for any rights expressly given to either spouse pursuant to the terms of this Agreement, and in particular subject to paragraphs 6 and 17 above, each spouse hereby releases and discharges all claims and rights that he or she has or may have under the laws of any jurisdiction against the other and the estate of the other and in particular under the *Family Law Act* and the *Succession Law Reform Act,* including all claims and rights:

   (a) to a share in the estate of the other should the other die intestate;

   (b) to any property of the other or any allowance or payment as a dependant from the estate of the other;

   (c) to act under the *Trustee Act* as an administrator of the estate of the other, and

   (d) to an amount representing the equalization or reapportionment of their net family properties.

42. RIGHTS ON DEATH

Except for any rights expressly given to either spouse pursuant to the terms of this Agreement, in the event of the death of one spouse, nothing in this Agreement shall be deemed to constitute a waiver of rights to:

   (a) any property devised or bequeathed by the deceased to the other under the terms of the deceased's Will; or

   (b) any insurance or death benefits to which the survivor may be entitled as beneficiary.

43. WAIVER OF RIGHTS UNDER PART II OF THE FAMILY LAW ACT

Except for any rights expressly given to either spouse pursuant to the terms of this Agreement, the husband and the wife each releases any rights either of them may have or afterwards acquire pursuant to Part II of the *Family Law Act* with respect to any property owned by the other.

44. PROPERTY RELEASE

(a) Except for any rights expressly given to either party pursuant to the terms of this Agreement, the husband and the wife hereby release and discharge all claims and rights against the other and rights to all or any part of the property of the other that he or she has or may acquire during his or her lifetime under the laws of any jurisdiction, and in particular in Ontario under the *Family Law Act* including all claims and rights to:

    i/ ownership of any property of the other;

    ii/ division of any property of the other;

    iii/ compensation for contributions of any kind, both direct and indirect, monetary and non-monetary, made to property of the other;

    iv/ an interest in property of the other for contributions of any kind, both direct and indirect, monetary and non-monetary;

    v/ an interest in property of the other by way of support;

    vi/ an amount representing the equalization or reapportionment of their net family properties; and

    vii/ any claim to property, based on any trust including a constructive trust, or resulting trust.

(b) This section is a complete defence to any action brought by either the husband or the wife to assert a claim to any interest in property, wherever situate, in which the other has or had an interest.

45. GENERAL RELEASE

(a) The husband and wife each accepts the provisions of this Agreement in satisfaction of all claims and causes of action each now has including, but not limited to, claims and causes of action for maintenance, support, interim maintenance or interim support, child maintenance or support, possession of, division of, or title to property, or any other claim arising out of the marriage of the husband and wife, except for claims and causes of action:

    i/ arising under this Agreement, or

    ii/ for a divorce judgment.

(b) Nothing in this Agreement shall bar any action or proceeding by either the husband or the wife to enforce any of the terms of this Agreement.

46. LEGAL FEES & DISBURSEMENTS

The husband shall forthwith contribute the sum of ONE THOUSAND ($1,000.00) DOLLARS towards part payment of the wife's legal fees and disbursements for the negotiation and drafting of this Agreement. The wife hereby irrevocably authorizes and directs the husband to pay the sum of ONE THOUSAND ($1,000.00) DOLLARS directly to her solicitors, Messrs. Jones & Jones.

47. EXECUTION OF OTHER DOCUMENTS

The husband and wife shall execute and deliver to the other any document that the other reasonably requires to give effect to this Agreement.

48. WARRANTIES AND UNDERSTANDINGS

(a) The husband and wife each warrant that there are no oral or written representations, collateral Agreements or conditions affecting this Agreement except as expressed herein.

(b) This Agreement constitutes the entire understanding of the spouses and supersedes any prior understandings or Agreements between the spouses.

(c) This Agreement may be amended only by a further written Agreement signed by the spouses and witnessed.

(d) If any term of this Agreement is held to be invalid or unenforceable, such term shall be severable and not affect the validity or enforcement of the other terms of this Agreement.

49. BINDING ON HEIRS

This Agreement is binding on the executors, heirs, administrators and assigns of each spouse.

50. INDEPENDENT LEGAL ADVICE

(a) Each spouse acknowledges that he or she:
   i/ received independent legal advice;
   ii/ read the entire Agreement carefully;
   iii/ understands his or her rights and obligations under this Agreement and the nature and consequences of this Agreement;
   iv/ has made full and complete disclosure of his or her financial position, including but not limited to his or her income, assets, expenses, debts or other liabilities;
   v/ acknowledges that the terms of this Agreement are fair and reasonable having regard to the circumstances of the spouses;
   vi/ is signing this Agreement voluntarily, and not under duress, without any undue influence, or threats or coercion by the other.

TO EVIDENCE HIS AGREEMENT, the husband has signed this Agreement on   , 19   , under seal before a witness.

SIGNED, SEALED AND
   DELIVERED   )
   in the presence of   )
)
_____)   _____
Witness as to the signature)   ROMEO SMITH
of ROMEO SMITH   )

TO EVIDENCE HER AGREEMENT, the wife has signed this Agreement on   , 19   , under seal before a witness.

SIGNED, SEALED AND
   DELIVERED   )
   in the presence of   )
)
_____)   _____
Witness as to the signature)   JULIET SMITH
of JULIET SMITH   )

CERTIFICATE OF INDEPENDENT LEGAL ADVICE

I, John Doe, of the City of Ottawa, in the Regional Municipality of Ottawa-Carleton, Solicitor, DO HEREBY CERTIFY:

(a) that I was consulted by (my client) named in the annexed Agreement, dated the 30th day of December, 1987, as to his(her) obligations and rights under the said Agreement;

(b) that I acted solely for him(her) and explained fully to him(her) the nature, effect and consequences of the said Agreement;

(c) that he(she) did this day acknowledge and declare that he(she) fully understood the nature, effect and consequences thereof;

(d) that he(she) did execute the said Agreement in my presence and did acknowledge and declare and it appeared to me that he(she) was executing the said Agreement of his(her) own volition and without fear, threats, compulsion or undue influence by (the other spouse) or any other person.

DATED this   day of   , 198 .

_____

John Doe — Solicitor

AFFIDAVIT OF EXECUTION

JUDICIAL DISTRICT	)	I,
OF OTTAWA-CARLETON	)	of the
	)	in the
	)	MAKE OATH AND SAY:

1. THAT I was personally present and did see the within Agreement duly signed, sealed and executed by _____, one of the parties thereto.
2. THAT the said Agreement was executed by the said party at _____, in the _____.
3. THAT I know the said party.
4. THAT I am a subscribing witness to the said Agreement.

SWORN BEFORE ME at the City)	
of Ottawa, in the Regional)	
Municipality of Ottawa-)	
Carleton, this day of)	
, 198)	_____
)	
A Commissioner, etc.)	

APPENDIX A

FAMILY LAW ACT, 1986

(S.O. 1986, c. 4,)
as amended by the FAMILY LAW AMENDMENT
ACT, 1986 (S.O. 1986, c. 35)

**An Act to revise the
Family Law
Reform Act**

TABLE OF CONTENTS

Preamble   Whereas it is desirable to encourage and strengthen the role of the family; and whereas for that purpose it is necessary to recognize the equal position of spouses as individuals within marriage and to recognize marriage as a form of partnership; and whereas in support of such recognition it is necessary to provide in law for the orderly and equitable settlement of the affairs of the spouses upon the breakdown of the partnership, and to provide for other mutual obligations in family relationships, including the equitable sharing by parents of responsibility for their children;

Therefore, Her Majesty, by and with the advice and consent of the Legislative Assembly of the Province of Ontario, enacts as follows:

Definitions   **1.**—(1) In this Act,

"child"   "child" includes a person whom a parent has demonstrated a settled intention to treat as a child of his or her family, except under an arrangement where the child is placed for valuable consideration in a foster home by a person having lawful custody; *no jurisd for { Part I { Part II*

"cohabit"   "cohabit" means to live together in a conjugal relationship, whether within or outside marriage; *s. 96*

"court"   "court" means the Provincial Court (Family Division), the *judges* Unified Family Court, the District Court or the Supreme Court;

"domestic contract"   "domestic contract" means a domestic contract as defined in Part IV (Domestic Contracts);

"parent"   "parent" includes a person who has demonstrated a settled intention to treat a child as a child of his or her family, except under an arrangement where the child is placed for valuable consideration in a foster home by a person having lawful custody;

"paternity agreement"   "paternity agreement" means a paternity agreement as defined in Part IV (Domestic Contracts);

"spouse"   "spouse" means either of a man and woman who,

(c-1) spouse allowed in Part III support

    (a) are married to each other, or

    (b) have together entered into a marriage that is voidable or void, in good faith on the part of the person asserting a right under this Act.

Polygamous marriages   (2) In the definition of "spouse", a reference to marriage includes a marriage that is actually or potentially polygamous,

163

if it was celebrated in a jurisdiction whose system of law recognizes it as valid.

Staying
application

2.—(1) If, in an application under this Act, it appears to the court that for the appropriate determination of the spouses' affairs it is necessary or desirable to have other matters determined first or simultaneously, the court may stay the application until another proceeding is brought or determined as the court considers appropriate.

All
proceedings
in one court

(2) Except as this Act provides otherwise, no person who is a party to an application under this Act shall make another application under this Act to another court, but the court may order that the proceeding be transferred to a court having other jurisdiction where, in the first court's opinion, the other court is more appropriate to determine the matters in issue that should be determined at the same time.

Applications in
Supreme or
District Court

(3) In the Supreme or District Court, an application under this Act may be made by action or application.

Statement re
removal of
barriers to re-
marriage

(4) A party to an application under section 7 (net family property), 10 (questions of title between spouses), 33 (support), 34 (powers of court) or 37 (variation) may serve on the other party and file with the court a statement, verified by oath or statutory declaration, indicating that,

    (a) the author of the statement has removed all barriers that are within his or her control and that would prevent the other spouse's remarriage within that spouse's faith; and

    (b) the other party has not done so, despite a request.

Idem

(5) Within ten days after service of the statement, or within such longer period as the court allows, the party served with a statement under subsection (4) shall serve on the other party and file with the court a statement, verified by oath or statutory declaration, indicating that the author of the statement has removed all barriers that are within his or her control and that would prevent the other spouse's remarriage within that spouse's faith.

Dismissal, etc.

(6) When a party fails to comply with subsection (5),

    (a) if the party is an applicant, the proceeding may be dismissed;

    (b) if the party is a respondent, the defence may be struck out.

Exception

(7) Subsections (5) and (6) do not apply to a party who does not claim costs or other relief in the proceeding.

See s. 7(3) lim periods | *1. 2(8) extension of time*

Extension of times

(8) The court may, on motion, extend a time prescribed by this Act if it is satisfied that,

    (a) there are *prima facie* grounds for relief;

    (b) relief is unavailable because of delay that has been incurred in good faith; and

    (c) no person will suffer substantial prejudice by reason of the delay.

Incorporation of contract in order

(9) A provision of a domestic contract in respect of a matter that is dealt with in this Act may be incorporated in an order made under this Act.

Act subject to contracts

(10) A domestic contract dealing with a matter that is also dealt with in this Act prevails unless this Act provides otherwise.

D-C can't exclude pension rights under federal Pension Act

s. 33(4), s. 52(2) *s. 56(1)* → *overturn domestic contract re support* *s. 56(4)*

Registration of orders

(11) An order made under this Act that affects real property does not affect the acquisition of an interest in the real property by a person acting in good faith without notice of the order, unless the order is registered in the proper land registry office.

Divorce Act s. 15(5) agreement no criteria on overturning support in domestic contract so S.C.C. p. 129 give criteria when to overturn support provision in a domestic contract.

Mediation

3.—(1) In an application under this Act, the court may, on motion, appoint a person whom the parties have selected to mediate any matter that the court specifies.

s. Mediate — private stat for recn under OA

Support *Custody*

s. 35 SLRA custody, access power closed

Consent to act

(2) The court shall appoint only a person who,

    (a) has consented to act as mediator; and

    (b) has agreed to file a report with the court within the period of time specified by the court.

Duty of mediator

(3) The mediator shall confer with the parties, and with the children if the mediator considers it appropriate to do so, and shall endeavour to obtain an agreement between the parties.

s. 3 FLA open, closed signposts

Full or limited report

(4) Before entering into mediation, the parties shall decide whether,

    (a) the mediator is to file a full report on the mediation, including anything that he or she considers relevant; or

    (b) the mediator is to file a limited report that sets out only the agreement reached by the parties or states only that the parties did not reach agreement.

Filing and copies of report

(5) The mediator shall file with the clerk or registrar of the court a full or limited report, as the parties have decided, and shall give a copy to each of the parties.

Admissions, etc., in the

(6) If the parties have decided that the mediator is to file a limited report, no evidence of anything said or of any

165

course of mediation

admission or communication made in the course of the mediation is admissible in any proceeding, except with the consent of all parties to the proceeding in which the mediator was appointed. *← parties may "jointly" waive privilege*

Fees and expenses

(7) The court shall require the parties to pay the mediator's fees and expenses and shall specify in the order the proportions or amounts of the fees and expenses that each party is required to pay.

Idem, serious financial hardship

(8) The court may require one party to pay all the mediator's fees and expenses if the court is satisfied that payment would cause the other party or parties serious financial hardship.

PART I
FAMILY PROPERTY

Definitions

4.—(1) In this Part,

"tribunal"

"court" means a court as defined in subsection 1(1), but does not include the Provincial Court (Family Division);

"fmv" or "fair value"

"matrimonial home"

"matrimonial home" means a matrimonial home under section 18 and includes property that is a matrimonial home under that section at the valuation date; *value owr — not post v-d*

deduction claimed even if property ceased to exist on v-date

In Ontario "values" of property are shared

"net family property"

post v-d prop. excluded " " " but s.10 may divide it

"net family property" means the value of all the property, except property described in subsection (2), that a spouse owns on the valuation date, after deducting,

v-off Va If pre-assets g matrimonial home dec

{ nfp is "value" sharing scheme

Cons " trust if unfair use 5(6) unequal division

(a) the spouse's debts and other liabilities, and

√ matrimonial home,

s. 4(5) if "deficit" in nfp≠0

"value" as of date of m.

(b) the value of property, other than a matrimonial home, that the spouse owned on the date of the marriage, after deducting the spouse's debts and other liabilities, calculated as of the date of the marriage;

is spouse alive shor value equ mate No

"property"

"property" means any interest, present or future, vested or contingent, in real or personal property and includes,

Oliva
5 p. 10
step method
1 value
2 value - deduct marital date
3 deduct 3,2 frm1
4 equalize it
5 Use s. 5(6) ?

(a) property over which a spouse has, alone or in conjunction with another person, a power of appointment exercisable in favour of himself or herself,

(b) property disposed of by a spouse but over which the spouse has, alone or in conjunction with another person, a power to revoke the disposition or a power to consume or dispose of the property, and

R.S.O. 1980, c. 373

(c) in the case of a spouse's rights under a pension plan that have vested, the spouse's interest in the plan

↑ 166

Mr. Payne says unvested is Property for Act

including contributions made by other persons.
[S.O. 1986, c. 35, s. 1(1)]

"valuation date" "valuation date" means the earliest of the following dates:

1. The date the spouses separate and there is no reasonable prospect that they will resume cohabitation.
2. The date a divorce is granted.
3. The date the marriage is declared a nullity.
4. The date one of the spouses commences an application based on subsection 5(3) (improvident depletion) that is subsequently granted.
5. The date before the date on which one of the spouses dies leaving the other spouse surviving.

Excluded property (2) The value of the following property that a spouse owns on the valuation date does not form part of the spouse's net family property:

1. Property, other than a matrimonial home, that was acquired by gift or inheritance from a third person after the date of the marriage.
2. Income from property referred to in paragraph 1, if the donor or testator has expressly stated that it is to be excluded from the spouse's net family property.
3. Damages or a right to damages for personal injuries, nervous shock, mental distress or loss of guidance, care and companionship, or the part of a settlement that represents those damages.

R.S.O. 1980, c. 218
4. Proceeds or a right to proceeds of a policy of life insurance, as defined in the *Insurance Act*, that are payable on the death of the life insured. [S.O. 1986, c. 35, s. 1(2)]
5. Property, other than a matrimonial home, into which property referred to in paragraphs 1 to 4 can be traced.
6. Property that the spouses have agreed by a domestic contract is not to be included in the spouse's net family property.

Onus of proof re deductions and exclusions (3) The onus of proving a deduction under the definition of "net family property" or an exclusion under subsection (2) is on the person claiming it.

Close of business (4) When this section requires that a value be calculated as

167

of a given date, it shall be calculated as of close of business on that date.

Net family property not to be less than zero

(5) If a spouse's "net family property" as calculated under subsections (1), (2) and (4) is less than zero, it shall be deemed to be equal to zero.

Equalization of net family properties

without "trigg event" no s.5 equal scheme

subj to s.7(3) limit period

5.—(1) When a divorce is granted or a marriage is declared a nullity, or when the spouses are separated and there is no reasonable prospect that they will resume cohabitation, the spouse whose net family property is the lesser of the two net family properties is entitled to one-half the difference between them.

"trigg events" required for s.5 equal

Idem

only if nfp of deceased spouse is greater than surviving spouse

(2) When a spouse dies, if the net family property of the deceased spouse exceeds the net family property of the surviving spouse, the surviving spouse is entitled to one-half the difference between them.

negligent / intentional / inadvertent — if any occ its covered under s.3(3)

Improvident depletion of spouse's net family property

one shot at s.5(3). So try "Guardianship" first. If you blow s.5(3) no s.5 equal allowed.

(3) When spouses are cohabiting, if there is a serious danger that one spouse may improvidently deplete his or her net family property, the other spouse may on an application under section 7 have the difference between the net family properties divided as if the spouses were separated and there were no reasonable prospect that they would resume cohabitation.

+ s.1 re stu fault deple

No further division

if improvident depletion order made, can't divide under s.5 again

(4) After the court has made an order for division based on subsection (3), neither spouse may make a further application under section 7 in respect of their marriage.

Idem

(5) Subsection (4) applies even though the spouses continue to cohabit, unless a domestic contract between the spouses provides otherwise. *Ct doesn't have to deviate from equal / some "discretion" if 1) unconscionable to eq 2) plus factors (a)-(h)*

Variation of share

Unequal Division

(6) The court may award a spouse an amount that is more or less than half the difference between the net family properties if the court is of the opinion that equalizing the net family properties would be unconscionable, having regard to,

beyon equal / unfair / unconscionable must shock / 1) std must satisf

(a) a spouse's failure to disclose to the other spouse debts or other liabilities existing at the date of the marriage;

(b) the fact that debts or other liabilities claimed in reduction of a spouse's net family property were incurred recklessly or in bad faith; *negligent mismanagemt not enough - but try (6)*

inter-spousal gifts

(c) the part of a spouse's net family property that consists of gifts made by the other spouse; *inter-spousal gif*

(d) a spouse's <u>intentional</u> or <u>reckless depletion</u> of his or her net family property;

(e) the fact that the amount a <u>spouse</u> would otherwise receive under subsection (1), (2) or (3) is dispropor- tionately large in relation to a period of cohabitation that is <u>less than five years</u>;

(f) the fact that one spouse has <u>incurred a dispropor-</u> tionately <u>larger amount of debts</u> or other liabilities than the other spouse for the <u>support of the family</u>;

(g) a written agreement between the spouses that is not a domestic contract; or

(h) <u>any other circumstance</u> relating to the acquisition, disposition, preservation, maintenance or improve- ment of property.

Purpose   (7) The purpose of this section is to recognize that <u>child care, household management and financial provision</u> are the <u>joint responsibilities of the spouses</u> and that inherent in the marital relationship there is <u>equal contribution</u>, whether financial or otherwise, by the spouses to the assumption of these responsibilities, entitling each spouse to the equalization of the net family properties, <u>subject only to the equitable considerations set out in subsection (6)</u>.

Election: spouse's will   **6.**—(1) When a spouse dies leaving a will, the surviving spouse shall <u>elect</u> to take under the will or to receive the entitlement under <u>section 5</u>.

Idem: spouse's intestacy R.S.O. 1980, c. 488   (2) When a spouse dies <u>intestate</u>, the surviving spouse shall elect to receive the entitlement under <u>Part II of the *Succession Law Reform Act* or</u> to receive the entitlement under <u>section 5</u>.

Idem: spouse's partial intestacy   (3) When a spouse dies testate as to some property and intestate as to other property, the surviving spouse shall elect to take under the will and to receive the entitlement under Part II of the *Succession Law Reform Act*, or to receive the entitlement under <u>section 5</u>.

Property out- side estate   (4) A surviving spouse who elects to take under the will or to receive the entitlement under Part II of the *Succession Law Reform Act*, or both in the case of a partial intestacy, shall also receive the other property to which he or she is entitled because of the first spouse's death.

Gifts by will   (5) The surviving spouse shall receive the gifts made to him or her in the deceased spouse's will in addition to the entitlement under section 5 if the will expressly provides for that result.

Insurance, etc. (6) Where a surviving spouse,

    (a) is the beneficiary,

        (i) of a policy of life insurance, as defined in the *Insurance Act*, that was taken out on the life of the deceased spouse and owned by the deceased spouse or was taken out on the lives of a group of which he or she was a member, or

        (ii) of a lump sum payment provided under a pension or similar plan on the death of the deceased spouse; and

    (b) elects or has elected to receive the entitlement under section 5,

the payment under the policy or plan shall be credited against the surviving spouse's entitlement under section 5, unless a written designation by the deceased spouse provides that the surviving spouse shall receive payment under the policy or plan in addition to the entitlement under section 5. [S.O. 1986, c. 35, s. 2(1)]

Idem (6a) If a surviving spouse,

    (a) elects or has elected to receive the entitlement under section 5; and

    (b) receives payment under a life insurance policy or a lump sum payment provided under a pension or similar plan that is in excess of the entitlement under section 5,

and there is no written designation by the deceased spouse described in subsection (6), the deceased spouse's personal representative may recover the excess amount from the surviving spouse. [S.O. 1986, c. 35, s. 2(1)]*

Effect of election to receive entitlement under section 5 (7) When a surviving spouse elects to receive the entitlement under section 5, the gifts made to him or her in the deceased spouse's will are revoked and the will shall be interpreted as if the surviving spouse had died before the other, unless the will expressly provides that the gifts are in addition to the entitlement under section 5.

Idem (8) When a surviving spouse elects to receive the entitlement under section 5, the spouse shall be deemed to have disclaimed,

    (a) the entitlement under Part II of the *Succession Law Reform Act*; and

    (b) [Repealed by S.O. 1986, c. 35, s. 2(2)]

R.S.O. 1980, c. 488

*S.O. 1986, c. 35, s. 3 provides as follows:

    3. Subsections 6(6) and (6a) of the said Act, as set out in subsection 2(1) of this Act, apply with respect to deaths that occurred before or occur after the coming into force of this Act.

[Handwritten marginal notes:]
If equalization claim taken — no 1) life Insurance under will 2) pension s. 6 benefit you keep, credited against equaliz claim. unless spouse said you got both.
If you took no life Insurance under will. Like (as Pension Benefit.
see s. 1(2)(4) →
→ survivorship benefits
(6) applies to spouse who pursues an equaliz claim
unless deceeased spouse says surv spouse gets both.
If s. 5 equalization under section 5 chosen 6(7) see s. 6(5) no-gifts via will Unless will says so
If s. 5 equalization chosen then Part II is disclaimed

[handwritten: elect within 6 months]

Manner of making election

(9) The surviving spouse's election shall be in the form prescribed by the regulations made under this Act and be filed in the office of the Surrogate Clerk for Ontario within six months after the first spouse's death.
[S.O. 1986, c. 35, s. 2(3)]

Deemed election

R.S.O. 1980, c. 488

(10) If the surviving spouse does not file the election within that time, he or she shall be deemed to have elected to take under the will or to receive the entitlement under the *Succession Law Reform Act,* or both, as the case may be, unless the court, on application, orders otherwise.

[handwritten: if you don't elect w/in 6 months you get SLRA entitlement or will]

Priority of spouse's entitlement

(11) The spouse's entitlement under section 5 has priority over,

[handwritten: 1) gifts in will 2) Part II SLRA 3) Part V SLRA]

R.S.O. 1980, c. 488

(a) the gifts made in the deceased spouse's will, if any, subject to subsection (12);

(b) a person's right to a share of the estate under Part II (Intestate Succession) of the *Succession Law Reform Act;* *[handwritten: s. 46]*

(c) an order made against the estate under Part V (Support of Dependants) of the *Succession Law Reform Act,* except an order in favour of a child of the deceased spouse.

[handwritten: except]

[handwritten: Part V dependants claim; except in favour of a child]

Exception

(12) The spouse's entitlement under section 5 does not have priority over a gift by will made in accordance with a contract that the deceased spouse entered into in good faith and for valuable consideration, except to the extent that the value of the gift, in the court's opinion, exceeds the consideration.

Distribution within six months of death restricted

(13) No distribution shall be made in the administration of a deceased spouse's estate within six months of the spouse's death, unless,

[handwritten: freeze on estate dist. for 6 months]

[handwritten: reasonable advances to dependants excepted in (16)]

(a) the surviving spouse gives written consent to the distribution; or

(b) the court authorizes the distribution.

Idem, notice of application

(14) No distribution shall be made in the administration of a deceased spouse's death after the personal representative has received notice of an application under this Part, unless,

[handwritten: P. s.67 SLRA]

(a) the applicant gives written consent to the distribution; or

(b) the court authorizes the distribution.

Extension of limitation period

[handwritten: s. 2(8) if no "prej"]

(15) If the court extends the time for a spouse's application based on subsection 5(2), any property of the deceased spouse that is distributed before the date of the order and without

notice of the application shall not be brought into the calculation of the deceased spouse's net family property.

Exception (16) Subsections (13) and (14) do not prohibit reasonable advances to dependants of the deceased spouse for their support. → *but. s.6 (11) s.5 gets "priority" over* ⌐(c) *Dependants (except child)*

Definition R.S.O. 1980, c. 488 (17) In subsection (16), "dependant" has the same meaning as in Part V of the *Succession Law Reform Act.*

Liability of personal representative (18) If the personal representative makes a distribution that contravenes subsection (13) or (14), the court makes an order against the estate under this Part and the undistributed portion of the estate is not sufficient to satisfy the order, the personal representative is personally liable to the applicant for the amount that was distributed or the amount that is required to satisfy the order, whichever is less.

Order suspending administration (19) On motion by the surviving spouse, the court may make an order suspending the administration of the deceased spouse's estate for the time and to the extent that the court decides.

← procedural section + s.8 Fin's req'd form 70 for s.5

Application to court **7.**—(1) The court may, on the application of a spouse, former spouse or deceased spouse's personal representative, determine any matter respecting the spouses' entitlement under section 5.

Personal action: estates (2) Entitlement under subsections 5(1), (2) and (3) is personal as between the spouses but,

(a) an application based on subsection 5(1) or (3) and commenced before a spouse's death may be continued by or against the deceased spouse's estate; and

(b) an application based on subsection 5(2) may be made by or against a deceased spouse's estate.

Limitation (3) An application based on subsection 5(1) or (2) shall not be brought after the earliest of, / *Limit # period depends on "type" of trigg even / its earliest of:*

Limitation period s. 5(1) r 5(2) can't be brought
- *2 years after divorce*
- *6 years after separate*
- *6 months after death.*

if "bar" by limit period try s. 2(8) extension of time

(a) two years after the day the marriage is terminated by divorce or judgment of nullity;

(b) six years after the day the spouses separate and there is no reasonable prospect that they will resume cohabitation;

(c) six months after the first spouse's death.

Statement of property **8.** In an application under section 7, each party shall serve on the other and file with the court, in the manner and form prescribed by the rules of the court, a statement verified by

(or)

C-T constructive trust Pethus " *1) unj. enrich of one Pethus will be looked 2) depriv of another contrib substant to 3) absence of judic reason, will the ...*

[handwritten: Fin statements form 70K prescribed ↙]

[handwritten top right: Menage v. Hodges — Burden of justifying value is on party who owns the property]

oath or statutory declaration disclosing particulars of,

    (a) the party's property and debts and other liabilities,

        (i) as of the date of the marriage,

        (ii) as of the valuation date, and

        (iii) as of the date of the statement;

    (b) the deductions that the party claims under the definition of "net family property";

    (c) the exclusions that the party claims under subsection 4(2); and

    (d) all property that the party disposed of during the two years immediately preceding the making of the statement, or during the marriage, whichever period is shorter.

[handwritten: can't be used for s. 10 payouts]   *[handwritten: → s.5 equal claim]*

Powers of court

9.—(1) In an application under section 7, the court may order, *[handwritten: discretionary]*

[handwritten: $ Money →]   (a) that one spouse pay to the other spouse the amount *[handwritten: (a) lump sum payment of s.5 amount]* to which the court finds that spouse to be entitled under this Part; *[handwritten: equalization amount]*

[handwritten: mortgage vary or discharge security order s.13]   (b) that security, including a charge on property, be given for the performance of an obligation imposed by the order; *[handwritten: use security for deferred or install payments — lump sum payment]* *[handwritten: mashaan said 10 year rule doesn't apply to pension out (trust) under if pension authorized formula]*

[handwritten: Installments →]   (c) that, if necessary to avoid hardship, an amount referred to in clause (a) be paid in instalments during a period not exceeding ten years or that payment of all or part of the amount be delayed for a period not exceeding ten years; and *[handwritten: 10 year maximum — may vary instal order — s.9(4)] [handwritten: {s.9(4) 10 year "can't be extended, etc(s)} deferred orders — 10 year rule only applies to payouts]*

[handwritten: trust — judicial powers are "discret" →]   (d) that, if appropriate to satisfy an obligation imposed by the order, *[handwritten: 10 year pay out rule not — s.9(d) Mashaan invoked. H) made "trustee" for "if + when" pension payable 10 year rule won't apply to "trust" only to payouts]*

[handwritten: transfer →]   (i) property be transferred to or in trust for or vested in a spouse, whether absolutely, for life or for a term of years, or *[handwritten: (to trust)]*

        (ii) any property be partitioned or sold.

Financial information, inspections

(2) The court may, at the time of making an order for instalment or delayed payments or on motion at a later time, order that the spouse who has the obligations to make payments shall, *[handwritten: s.9(1)(c)]* *[handwritten: ct can only order financial disclosure if deferred or installment payments ordered per s. 9(1)(c)]*

    (a) furnish the other spouse with specified financial information, which may include periodic financial statements; and *[handwritten: limited to orders under s. 9(1)(c)]*

(b) permit inspections of specified property of the spouse by or on behalf of the other spouse, as the court directs.

(3) If the court is satisfied that there has been a "material change" in the circumstances of the spouse who has the obligation to make instalment or delayed payments, the court may, on motion, vary the order, but shall not vary the amount to which the court found the spouse to be entitled under this Part.

(4) Subsections (3) and 2(8) (extension of times) do not permit the postponement of payment beyond the ten year period mentioned in clause (1)(c).

Determination of questions of title between spouses 10.—(1) A person may apply to the court for the determination of a question between that person and his or her spouse or former spouse as to the ownership or right to possession of particular property, other than a question arising out of an equalization of net family properties under section 5, and the court may,

(a) declare the ownership or right to possession;

(b) if the property has been disposed of, order payment in compensation for the interest of either party;

(c) order that the property be partitioned or sold for the purpose of realizing the interests in it; and

(d) order that either or both spouses give security, including a charge on property, for the performance of an obligation imposed by the order,

and may make ancillary orders or give ancillary directions.

Estates (2) An application based on subsection (1) may be made by or continued against the estate of a deceased spouse.

Operating business or farm 11.—(1) An order made under section 9 or 10 shall not be made so as to require or result in the sale of an operating business or farm or so as to seriously impair its operation, unless there is no reasonable alternative method of satisfying the award.

Idem (2) To comply with subsection (1), the court may,

(a) order that one spouse pay to the other a share of the profits from the business or farm; and

(b) if the business or farm is incorporated, order that one spouse transfer or have the corporation issue to the other shares in the corporation.

174

[handwritten: Use for improvident depletion of net family property]

[handwritten: s. 12 "preventive" in nature can't set aside transaction already completed.]

Orders for preservation **12.** In an application under section 7 or 10, if the court considers it necessary for the protection of the other spouse's interests under this Part, the court may make an interim or final order,

[handwritten: interim / final]

    (a) restraining the depletion of a spouse's property; and

    (b) for the possession, delivering up, safekeeping and preservation of the property.

[handwritten: interim restraining order on Property]

Variation and realization of security **13.** If the court has ordered security or charged a property with security for the performance of an obligation under this Part, the court may, on motion,

[handwritten: 9 (1) (b) — "security" ordered; 10 (1) (a)]

    (a) vary or discharge the order; or

    (b) on notice to all persons having an interest in the property, direct its sale for the purpose of realizing the security or charge.

[handwritten: rebuttable [title section,]

Presumptions **14.** The rule of law applying a presumption of a resulting trust shall be applied in questions of the ownership of property between husband and wife, as if they were not married, except that,

    (a) the fact that property is held in the name of spouses as joint tenants is *prima facie* proof that the spouses are intended to own the property as joint tenants; and

    (b) money on deposit in the name of both spouses shall be deemed to be in the name of the spouses as joint tenants for the purposes of clause (a).

Conflict of laws **15.** The property rights of spouses arising out of the marital relationship are governed by the internal law of the place where both spouses had their last common habitual residence or, if there is no place where the spouses had a common habitual residence, by the law of Ontario.

Application of Part **16.**—(1) This Part applies to property owned by spouses,

[handwritten: Part I applies to pre-FLRA marriage property]

    (a) whether they were married before or after this Act comes into force; and

    (b) whether the property was acquired before or after this Act comes into force.

Application of s. 14 (2) Section 14 applies whether the event giving rise to the presumption occurred before or after this Act comes into force.

[handwritten: s. 14 applies to property acquired prior to the F.L.A. ← retroactive.]

175

PART II
MATRIMONIAL HOME

Definitions   **17.** In this Part,

"court"   "court" means a court as defined in subsection 1(1) but does not include the Provincial Court (Family Division);

"property"   "property" means real or personal property. *[handwritten: applies to real or personal property boats, etc.]*

[handwritten: 2 repts for s. (8²⁴ — → ①]

Matrimonial home   **18.**—(1) Every property in which a person has an interest and that is or, if the spouses have separated, was at the time of separation ordinarily occupied by the person and his or her spouse as their family residence is their matrimonial home. *[handwritten: family residence is a matrimonial home]*

Ownership of shares   (2) The ownership of a share or shares, or of an interest in a share or shares, of a corporation entitling the owner to occupy a housing unit owned by the corporation shall be deemed to be an interest in the unit for the purposes of subsection (1).

Residence on farmland, etc.   (3) If property that includes a matrimonial home is normally used for a purpose other than residential, the matrimonial home is only the part of the property that may reasonably be regarded as necessary to the use and enjoyment of the residence.

Possession of matrimonial home   **19.**—(1) Both spouses have an equal right to possession of a matrimonial home.

Idem   (2) When only one of the spouses has an interest in a matrimonial home, the other spouse's right of possession,

     (a) is personal as against the first spouse; and

     (b) ends when they cease to be spouses, unless a separation agreement or court order provides otherwise.

Designation of matrimonial home   **20.**—(1) One or both spouses may designate property owned by one or both of them as a matrimonial home, in the form prescribed by the regulations made under this Act.

Contiguous property   (2) The designation may include property that is described in the designation and is contiguous to the matrimonial home.

Registration   (3) The designation may be registered in the proper land registry office.

Effect of designation by both spouses   (4) On the registration of a designation made by both spouses, any other property that is a matrimonial home under section 18 but is not designated by both spouses ceases to be a matrimonial home.

Effect of designation by one spouse

(5) On the registration of a designation made by one spouse only, any other property that is a matrimonial home under section 18 remains a matrimonial home.

Cancellation of designation

(6) The designation of a matrimonial home is cancelled, and the property ceases to be a matrimonial home, on the registration or deposit of,

    (a) a cancellation, executed by the person or persons who made the original designation, in the form prescribed by the regulations made under this Act;

    (b) a decree absolute of divorce or judgment of nullity;

    (c) an order under clause 23(e) cancelling the designation; or

    (d) proof of death of one of the spouses.

Revival of other matrimonial homes

(7) When a designation of a matrimonial home made by both spouses is cancelled, section 18 applies again in respect of other property that is a matrimonial home.

Alienation of matrimonial home

21.—(1) No spouse shall dispose of or encumber an interest in a matrimonial home unless,

    (a) the other spouse joins in the instrument or consents to the transaction;

    (b) the other spouse has released all rights under this Part by a separation agreement;

    (c) a court order has authorized the transaction or has released the property from the application of this Part; or

    (d) the property is not designated by both spouses as a matrimonial home and a designation of another property as a matrimonial home, made by both spouses, is registered and not cancelled.

Setting aside transaction

(2) If a spouse disposes of or encumbers an interest in a matrimonial home in contravention of subsection (1), the transaction may be set aside on an application under section 23, unless the person holding the interest or encumbrance at the time of the application acquired it for value, in good faith and without notice, at the time of acquiring it or making an agreement to acquire it, that the property was a matrimonial home.

Proof that property not a matrimonial home

(3) For the purpose of subsection (2), a statement by the person making the disposition or encumbrance,

(a) verifying that he or she is not, or was not, a spouse at the time of the disposition or encumbrance;

(b) verifying that the person is a spouse who is not separated from his or her spouse and that the property is not ordinarily occupied by the spouses as their family residence;

(c) verifying that the person is a spouse who is separated from his or her spouse and that the property was not ordinarily occupied by the spouses, at the time of their separation, as their family residence;

(d) where the property is not designated by both spouses as a matrimonial home, verifying that a designation of another property as a matrimonial home, made by both spouses, is registered and not cancelled; or

(c) verifying that the other spouse has released all rights under this Part by a separation agreement,

shall, unless the person to whom the disposition or encumbrance is made had notice to the contrary, be deemed to be sufficient proof that the property is not a matrimonial home.

Idem, attorney's personal knowledge (4) The statement shall be deemed to be sufficient proof that the property is not a matrimonial home if it is made by the attorney of the person making the disposition or encumbrance, on the basis of the attorney's personal knowledge.

Liens arising by operation of law R.S.O. 1980, c. 234 (5) This section does not apply to the acquisition of an interest in property by operation of law or to the acquisition of a lien under section 18 of the *Legal Aid Act*.

Right of redemption and to notice 22.—(1) When a person proceeds to realize upon a lien, encumbrance or execution or exercises a forfeiture against property that is a matrimonial home, the spouse who has a right of possession under section 19 has the same right of redemption or relief against forfeiture as the other spouse and is entitled to the same notice respecting the claim and its enforcement or realization.

Service of notice (2) A notice to which a spouse is entitled under subsection (1) shall be deemed to be sufficiently given if served or given personally or by registered mail addressed to the spouse at his or her usual or last known address or, if none, the address of the matrimonial home, and, if notice is served or given by mail, the service shall be deemed to have been made on the fifth day after the day of mailing.

Idem: power (3) When a person exercises a power of sale against

178

of sale
R.S.O. 1980,
c. 296
property that is a matrimonial home, sections 32 and 33 of the *Mortgages Act* apply and subsection (2) does not apply.

Payments by spouse
(4) If a spouse makes a payment in exercise of the right conferred by subsection (1), the payment shall be applied in satisfaction of the claim giving rise to the lien, encumbrance, execution or forfeiture.

Realization may continue in spouse's absence

R.S.O. 1980, c. 296
(5) Despite any other Act, when a person who proceeds to realize upon a lien, encumbrance or execution or exercises a forfeiture does not have sufficient particulars of a spouse for the purpose and there is no response to a notice given under subsection (2) or under section 32 of the *Mortgages Act,* the realization or exercise of forfeiture may continue in the absence and without regard to the interest of the spouse and the spouse's rights under this section end on the completion of the realization or forfeiture.

Powers of court respecting alienation
23. The court may, on the application of a spouse or person having an interest in property, by order,

   (a) determine whether or not the property is a matrimonial home and, if so, its extent;

   (b) authorize the disposition or encumbrance of the matrimonial home if the court finds that the spouse whose consent is required,

      (i) cannot be found or is not available,

      (ii) is not capable of giving or withholding consent, or

      (iii) is unreasonably withholding consent,

   subject to any conditions, including provision of other comparable accommodation or payment in place of it, that the court considers appropriate;

   (c) dispense with a notice required to be given under section 22;

   (d) direct the setting aside of a transaction disposing of or encumbering an interest in the matrimonial home contrary to subsection 21(1) and the revesting of the interest or any part of it on the conditions that the court considers appropriate; and

   (e) cancel a designation made under section 20 if the property is not a matrimonial home.

Order for possession of matrimonial home
24.—(1) Regardless of the ownership of a matrimonial home and its contents, and despite section 19 (spouse's right of possession), the court may on application, by order,

(a) provide for the delivering up, safekeeping and preservation of the matrimonial home and its contents;

(b) direct that one spouse be given exclusive possession of the matrimonial home or part of it for the period that the court directs and release other property that is a matrimonial home from the application of this Part;

(c) direct a spouse to whom exclusive possession of the matrimonial home is given to make periodic payments to the other spouse;

(d) direct that the contents of the matrimonial home, or any part of them,

    (i) remain in the home for the use of the spouse given possession, or

    (ii) be removed from the home for the use of a spouse or child;

(e) order a spouse to pay for all or part of the repair and maintenance of the matrimonial home and of other liabilities arising in respect of it, or to make periodic payments to the other spouse for those purposes;

(f) authorize the disposition or encumbrance of a spouse's interest in the matrimonial home, subject to the other spouse's right of exclusive possession as ordered; and

(g) where a false statement is made under subsection 21(3), direct,

    (i) the person who made the false statement, or

    (ii) a person who knew at the time he or she acquired an interest in the property that the statement was false and afterwards conveyed the interest,

to substitute other real property for the matrimonial home, or direct the person to set aside money or security to stand in place of it, subject to any conditions that the court considers appropriate.

Temporary or interim order (2) The court may, on motion, make a temporary or interim order under clause (1)(a), (b), (c), (d) or (e).

Order for exclusive possession: criteria (3) In determining whether to make an order for exclusive possession, the court shall consider,

(a) the best interests of the children affected;

(b) any existing orders under Part I (Family Property) and any existing support orders;

(c) the financial position of both spouses;

180

[handwritten: ✓ not a sep'n agreement]

    (d) any written agreement between the parties;

    (e) the availability of other suitable and affordable accommodation; and *[handwritten: "psychological" violence]*

    (f) any violence committed by a spouse against the other spouse or the children.

Best interests of child   (4) In determining the best interests of a child, the court shall consider,

    (a) the possible disruptive effects on the child of a move to other accommodation; and

    (b) the child's views and preferences, if they can reasonably be ascertained.

Offence   (5) A person who contravenes an order for exclusive possession is guilty of an offence and upon conviction is liable,

    (a) in the case of a first offence, to a fine of not more than $1,000 or to imprisonment for a term of not more than three months, or to both; and

    (b) in the case of a second or subsequent offence, to a fine of not more than $10,000 or to imprisonment for a term of not more than two years, or to both.

Arrest without warrant   (6) A police officer may arrest without warrant a person the police officer believes on reasonable and probable grounds to have contravened an order for exclusive possession.

Existing orders   (7) Subsections (5) and (6) also apply in respect of contraventions, committed after this Act comes into force, of orders for exclusive possession made under Part III of the *Family Law Reform Act.*

R.S.O. 1980, c. 152

Variation of possessory order   **25.**—(1) On the application of a person named in an order made under clause 24(1)(a), (b), (c), (d) or (e) or his or her personal representative, if the court is satisfied that there has been a material change in circumstances, the court may discharge, vary or suspend the order.

Variation of conditions of sale   (2) On the motion of a person who is subject to conditions imposed in an order made under clause 23(b) or (d) or 24(1)(g), or his or her personal representative, if the court is satisfied that the conditions are no longer appropriate, the court may discharge, vary or suspend them.

Existing orders   (3) Subsections (1) and (2) also apply to orders made under the corresponding provisions of Part III of the *Family Law Reform Act.*

R.S.O. 1980, c. 152

26.—(1) If a spouse dies owning an interest in a matrimonial home as a joint tenant with a third person and not with the other spouse, the joint tenancy shall be deemed to have been severed immediately before the time of death. *∴ tenants in common*

Joint tenancy in matrimonial home

(2) Despite clauses 19(2)(a) and (b) (termination of spouse's right of possession), a spouse who has no interest in a matrimonial home but is occupying it at the time of the other spouse's death, whether under an order for exclusive possession or otherwise, is entitled to retain possession against the spouse's estate, rent free, for sixty days after the spouse's death. *→ 60 days rent free on death*

Sixty day period after spouse's death

27. Orders made under this Part or under Part III of the *Family Law Reform Act* are registrable against land under the *Registry Act* and the *Land Titles Act*.

Registration of order
R.S.O. 1980, cc. 152, 445, 230

28.—(1) This Part applies to matrimonial homes that are situated in Ontario.

Application of Part

Form 70K fin starts filed

(2) This Part applies,

Idem

SCOE enforced
s. 20(3) enforced

① FLA is needs-based ability to pay

(a) whether the spouses were married before or after this Act comes into force; and

(b) whether the matrimonial home was acquired before or after this Act comes into force.

② need must be causally-connected to marriage

FLA support is needs based

④ FLA support claim can be made at any time

⑤ Fixed term promotes self-sufficiency

PART III
SUPPORT OBLIGATIONS

s.37 Variation support order

⑥ shift from means & needs test to econ self-sufficiency w/ FLA & D.A.S.

29. In this Part,

Definitions

to get su need - ability to pay

"dependant" means a person to whom another has an obligation to provide support under this Part;

"dependant"

"spouse" means a spouse as defined in subsection 1(1), and in addition includes either of a man and woman who are not married to each other and have cohabited,

"spouse"

Common law spouse

(a) continuously for a period of not less than three years, or

(b) in a relationship of some permanence, if they are the natural or adoptive parents of a child.

entitlement to support

30. Every spouse has an obligation to provide support for himself or herself and for the other spouse, in accordance with need, to the extent that he or she is capable of doing so.

Obligation of spouses for support

- need + means section →
- c→ connection between need and marriage

182

Obligation of parent to support child   **31.**—(1) Every parent has an obligation to provide support, in accordance with need, for his or her unmarried child who is a minor or is enrolled in a full time program of education, to the extent that the parent is capable of doing so.

Idem   (2) The obligation under subsection (1) does not extend to a child who is sixteen years of age or older and has withdrawn from parental control.

Obligation of child to support parent   **32.** Every child who is not a minor has an obligation to provide support, in accordance with need, for his or her parent who has cared for or provided support for the child, to the extent that the child is capable of doing so.

Order for support   **33.**—(1) A court may, on application, order a person to provide support for his or her dependants and determine the amount of support.

Applicants   (2) An application for an order for the support of a dependant may be made by the dependant or the dependant's parent.

Idem   (3) An application for an order for the support of a dependant who is the respondent's spouse or child may also be made by one of the following agencies:

> (a) the Ministry of Community and Social Services in the name of the Minister;
>
> (b) a municipal corporation, including a metropolitan, district or regional municipality, but not including an area municipality;

R.S.O. 1980, c. 122

> (c) a district welfare administration board under the *District Welfare Administration Boards Act*; or

R.S.O. 1980, c. 188

> (d) a band approved under section 15 of the *General Welfare Assistance Act*,

R.S.O. 1980, cc. 151, 188   if the agency is providing or has provided a benefit under the *Family Benefits Act* or assistance under the *General Welfare Assistance Act* in respect of the dependant's support, or if an application for such a benefit or assistance has been made to the agency by or on behalf of the dependant.

Setting aside domestic contract   (4) The court may set aside a provision for support or a waiver of the right to support in a domestic contract or paternity agreement and may determine and order support in an application under subsection (1) although the contract or agreement contains an express provision excluding the application of this section,

> (a) if the provision for support or the waiver of the right

183

to support results in unconscionable circumstances;

(b) if the provision for support is in favour of or the waiver is by or on behalf of a dependant who qualifies for an allowance for support out of public money; or   ↳ ie · welfare, UIC

(c) if there is default in the payment of support under the contract or agreement at the time the application is made.

Adding party (5) In an application the court may, on a respondent's motion, add as a party another person who may have an obligation to provide support to the same dependant.

Idem (6) In an action in the Supreme Court or District Court, the defendant may add as a third party another person who may have an obligation to provide support to the same dependant.

Purposes of order for support of child (7) An order for the support of a child should,

objectives

(a) recognize that each parent has an obligation to provide support for the child;

(b) recognize that the obligation of a natural or adoptive parent outweighs the obligation of a parent who is not a natural or adoptive parent; and

(c) apportion the obligation according to the capacities of the parents to provide support.

Purposes of order for support of spouse (8) An order for the support of a spouse should,

(a) recognize the spouse's contribution to the relationship and the economic consequences of the relationship for the spouse;

(b) share the economic burden of child support equitably;

Compensatory support

(c) make fair provision to assist the spouse to become able to contribute to his or her own support; and

Amount and duration of support

(d) relieve financial hardship, if this has not been done by orders under Parts I (Family Property) and II (Matrimonial Home). (supp) needs based under FLA

Determination of amount (9) In determining the amount and duration, if any, of support in relation to need, the court shall consider all the circumstances of the parties, including,

FLA is needs based s. 30

(a) the dependant's and respondent's current assets and means;

(b) the assets and means that the dependant and respondent are likely to have in the future;

Statement of Claim
Notice of Application

(c) the dependant's capacity to contribute to his or her own support;

1) Prov. Ct (Family Div)
2) UFCt
3) UC or SC do support

184

(d) the respondent's capacity to provide support;

(e) the dependant's and respondent's age and physical and mental health;

(f) the dependant's needs, in determining which the court shall have regard to the accustomed standard of living while the parties resided together;

(g) the measures available for the dependant to become able to provide for his or her own support and the length of time and cost involved to enable the dependant to take those measures;

(h) any legal obligation of the respondent or dependant to provide support for another person;

(i) the desirability of the dependant or respondent remaining at home to care for a child;

(j) a contribution by the dependant to the realization of the respondent's career potential;

Keast
Compensatory
support

(k) if the dependant is a child,

    (i) the child's aptitude for and reasonable prospects of obtaining an education, and

    (ii) the child's need for a stable environment;

(l) if the dependant is a spouse,

    (i) the length of time the dependant and respondent cohabited,

Corless

    (ii) the effect on the spouse's earning capacity of the responsibilities assumed during cohabitation,

    (iii) whether the spouse has undertaken the care of a child who is of the age of eighteen years or over and unable by reason of illness, disability or other cause to withdraw from the charge of his or her parents,

    (iv) whether the spouse has undertaken to assist in the continuation of a program of education for a child eighteen years of age or over who is unable for that reason to withdraw from the charge of his or her parents,

    (v) any housekeeping, child care or other domestic service performed by the spouse for the family, as if the spouse were devoting the time spent in performing that service in remunerative employment and were contributing the earnings to the family's support,

    (vi) the effect on the spouse's earnings and career development of the responsibility of caring for a child; and

185

(m) any other legal right of the dependant to support, other than out of public money.

Conduct   (10) The obligation to provide support for a spouse exists without regard to the conduct of either spouse, but the court may in determining the amount of support have regard to a course of conduct that is so unconscionable as to constitute an obvious and gross repudiation of the relationship.

Powers of court   **34.**—(1) In an application under section 33, the court may make an interim or final order,

(a) requiring that an amount be paid periodically, whether annually or otherwise and whether for an indefinite or limited period, or until the happening of a specified event;

(b) requiring that a lump sum be paid or held in trust;

(c) requiring that property be transferred to or in trust for or vested in the dependant, whether absolutely, for life or for a term of years;

(d) respecting any matter authorized to be ordered under clause 24(1)(a), (b), (c), (d) or (e) (matrimonial home);

(e) requiring that some or all of the money payable under the order be paid into court or to another appropriate person or agency for the dependant's benefit;

(f) requiring that support be paid in respect of any period before the date of the order;

(g) requiring payment to an agency referred to in subsection 33(3) of an amount in reimbursement for a benefit or assistance referred to in that subsection, including a benefit or assistance provided before the date of the order;

(h) requiring payment of expenses in respect of a child's prenatal care and birth;

R.S.O. 1980, c. 218   (i) requiring that a spouse who has a policy of life insurance as defined in the *Insurance Act* designate the other spouse or a child as the beneficiary irrevocably;

(j) requiring that a spouse who has an interest in a pension plan or other benefit plan designate the other spouse or a child as beneficiary under the plan and not change that designation; and

(k) requiring the securing of payment under the order, by a charge on property or otherwise.

186

Limitation on family court's jurisdiction
(2) The Provincial Court (Family Division) shall not make an order under clause (1)(b), (c), (i), (j) or (k) except for the provision of necessities or to prevent the dependant from becoming or continuing to be a public charge, and shall not make an order under clause (d).

Assignment of support
(3) An order for support may be assigned to an agency referred to in subsection 33(3).

Support order binds estate
(4) An order for support binds the estate of the person having the support obligation unless the order provides otherwise.

Indexing of support payments
(5) In an order made under clause (1)(a), the court may provide that the amount payable shall be increased annually on the order's anniversary date by the indexing factor, as defined in subsection (6), for November of the previous year.

Definition
(6) The indexing factor for a given month is the percentage change in the Consumer Price Index for Canada for prices of all items since the same month of the previous year, as published by Statistics Canada.

Domestic contract, etc., may be filed with court
35.—(1) A person who is a party to a domestic contract or paternity agreement may file the contract or agreement with the clerk of the Provincial Court (Family Division) or of the Unified Family Court together with the person's affidavit stating that the contract or agreement is in effect and has not been set aside or varied by a court or agreement.

Effect of filing
(2) A provision for support or maintenance contained in a contract or agreement that is filed in this manner,

 (a) may be enforced; and

 (b) may be varied under section 37 and increased under section 38,

as if it were an order of the court where it is filed.

Setting aside available
(3) Subsection 33(4) (setting aside in unconscionable circumstances, etc.) applies to a contract or agreement that is filed in this manner.

Filing and enforcement available despite waiver
(4) Subsection (1) and clause (2)(a) apply despite an agreement to the contrary.

Existing contracts, etc.
(5) Subsections (1) and (2) also apply to contracts and agreements made before this Act comes into force.

Existing arrears
(6) Clause (2)(a) also applies to arrears accrued before this Act comes into force.

Effect of divorce proceeding R.S.C. 1970, c. D-8

36.—(1) When a divorce proceeding is commenced under the *Divorce Act* (Canada), an application for support under this Part that has not been adjudicated is stayed, unless the court orders otherwise.

Arrears may be included in order under R.S.C. 1970, c. D-8

(2) The court that deals with a divorce proceeding under the *Divorce Act* (Canada) may determine the amount of arrears owing under an order for support made under this Part and make an order respecting that amount at the same time as it makes an order under the *Divorce Act* (Canada).

Idem

(3) If a marriage is terminated by divorce or judgment of nullity and the question of support is not adjudicated in the divorce or nullity proceedings, an order for support made under this Part continues in force according to its terms.

Application for variation

37.—(1) A dependant or respondent named in an order made or confirmed under this Part, the respondent's personal representative, or an agency referred to in subsection 33(3), may apply to the court for variation of the order.

Powers of court

(2) If the court is satisfied that there has been a material change in the dependant's or respondent's circumstances or that evidence not available on the previous hearing has become available, the court may discharge, vary or suspend a term of the order, prospectively or retroactively, relieve the respondent from the payment of part or all of the arrears or any interest due on them and make any other order under section 34 that the court considers appropriate in the circumstances referred to in section 33.

Limitation on applications for variation

(3) No application for variation shall be made within six months after the making of the order for support or the disposition of another application for variation in respect of the same order, except by leave of the court.

Application to have existing order indexed

38.—(1) If an order made or confirmed under this Part is not indexed under subsection 34(5), the dependant, or an agency referred to in subsection 33(3), may apply to the court to have the order indexed in accordance with subsection 34(5).

Power of court

(2) The court shall, unless the respondent shows that his or her income, assets and means have not increased sufficiently to permit the increase, order that the amount payable be increased by the "indexing" factor, as defined in subsection 34(6), for November of the year before the year in which the application is made and be increased in the same way

188

annually thereafter on the anniversary date of the order under this section.

Existing orders **39.** Sections 36 to 38 also apply to orders for maintenance or alimony made before the 31st day of March, 1978 or in proceedings commenced before the 31st day of March, 1978 R.S.O. 1980, and to orders for support made under Part II of the *Family* c. 152 *Law Reform Act.*

Restraining orders **40.** The court may, on application, make an interim or final order restraining the depletion of a spouse's property that would impair or defeat a claim under this Part.

Financial statement **41.** In an application under section 33 or 37, each party shall serve on the other and file with the court a financial statement verified by oath or statutory declaration in the manner and form prescribed by the rules of the court.

Order for return by employer **42.**—(1) In an application under section 33 or 37, the court may order the employer of a party to the application to make a written return to the court showing the party's wages or other remuneration during the preceding twelve months.

Return as evidence (2) A return purporting to be signed by the employer may be received in evidence as *prima facie* proof of its contents.

Order for access to information (3) The court may, on motion, make an order under subsection (4) if it appears to the court that, in order to make an application under section 33 or 37, the moving party needs to learn or confirm the proposed respondent's whereabouts.

Idem (4) The order shall require the person or public body to whom it is directed to provide the court or the moving party with any information that is shown on a record in the person's or public body's possession or control and that indicates the proposed respondent's place of employment, address or location.

Crown bound (5) This section binds the Crown in right of Ontario.

Arrest of absconding debtor **43.**—(1) If an application is made under section 33 or 37 and the court is satisfied that the respondent is about to leave Ontario and that there are reasonable grounds for believing that the respondent intends to evade his or her responsibilities under this Act, the court may issue a warrant for the respondent's arrest for the purpose of bringing him or her before the court.

Bail
R.S.O. 1980,
c. 400

(2) Section 134 (interim release by justice of the peace) of the *Provincial Offences Act* applies, with necessary modifications, to an arrest under the warrant.

Provisional orders

44.—(1) In an application under section 33 or 37 in the Provincial Court (Family Division) or the Unified Family Court, the court shall proceed under this section, whether or not the respondent in the application files a financial statement, if,

(a) the respondent fails to appear;

(b) it appears to the court that the respondent resides in a locality in Ontario that is more than 150 kilometres away from the place where the court sits; and

(c) the court is of the opinion, in the circumstances of the case, that the issues can be adequately determined by proceeding under this section.

Idem

(2) If the court determines that it would be proper to make a final order, were it not for the respondent's failure to appear, the court shall make an order for support that is provisional only and has no effect until it is confirmed by the Provincial Court (Family Division) or the Unified Family Court sitting nearest the place where the respondent resides.

Transmission for hearing

(3) The court that makes a provisional order shall send to the court in the locality in which the respondent resides copies of such documents and records, certified in such manner, as are prescribed by the rules of the court.

Show cause

(4) The court to which the documents and records are sent shall cause them to be served upon the respondent, together with a notice to file with the court the financial statement required by section 41, and to appear and show cause why the provisional order should not be confirmed.

Confirmation of order

(5) At the hearing, the respondent may raise any defence that might have been raised in the original proceeding, but if the respondent fails to satisfy the court that the order ought not to be confirmed, the court may confirm the order without variation or with the variation that the court considers proper having regard to all the evidence.

Adjournment for further evidence

(6) If the respondent appears before the court and satisfies the court that for the purpose of a defence or for the taking of further evidence or otherwise it is necessary to remit the case to the court where the applicant resides, the court may remit the case and adjourn the proceeding for that purpose.

Where order not confirmed (7) If the respondent appears before the court and the court, having regard to all the evidence, is of the opinion that the order ought not to be confirmed, the court shall remit the case to the court sitting where the order was made with a statement of the reasons for doing so, and the court sitting where the order was made shall dispose of the application in accordance with the statement.

Certificates as evidence (8) A certificate certifying copies of documents or records for the purpose of this section and purporting to be signed by the clerk of the court is, without proof of the clerk's office or signature, admissible in evidence in a court to which it is transmitted under this section as *prima facie* proof of the copy's authenticity.

Right of appeal (9) No appeal lies from a provisional order made under this section, but a person bound by an order confirmed under this section has the same right of appeal as he or she would have had if the order had been made under section 34.

Pledging credit for necessities **45.**—(1) During cohabitation, a spouse has authority to render himself or herself and his or her spouse jointly and severally liable to a third party for necessities of life, unless the spouse has notified the third party that he or she has withdrawn the authority.

Liability for necessities of minor (2) If a person is entitled to recover against a minor in respect of the provision of necessities for the minor, every parent who has an obligation to support the minor is liable for them jointly and severally with the minor.

Recovery between persons jointly liable (3) If persons are jointly and severally liable under this section, their liability to each other shall be determined in accordance with their obligation to provide support.

Common law supplanted (4) This section applies in place of the rules of common law by which a wife may pledge her husband's credit.

Order restraining harassment **46.**—(1) On application, a court may make an interim or final order restraining the applicant's spouse or former spouse from molesting, annoying or harassing the applicant or children in the applicant's lawful custody, or from communicating with the applicant or children, except as the order provides, and may require the applicant's spouse or former spouse to enter into the recognizance that the court considers appropriate.

Offence (2) A person who contravenes a restraining order is guilty

191

of an offence and upon conviction is liable,

(a) in the case of a first offence, to a fine of not more than $1,000 or to imprisonment for a term of not more than three months, or to both; and

(b) in the case of a second or subsequent offence, to a fine of not more than $10,000 or to imprisonment for a term of not more than two years, or to both.

Arrest without warrant   (3) A police officer may arrest without warrant a person the police officer believes on reasonable and probable grounds to have contravened a restraining order.

Existing orders   (4) Subsections (2) and (3) also apply in respect of R.S.O. 1980, c. 152   contraventions, committed after this Act comes into force, of restraining orders made under Part II of the *Family Law Reform Act.*

Application for custody   **47.** The court may direct that an application for support R.S.O. 1980, c. 68   stand over until an application for custody under the *Children's Law Reform Act* has been determined.

Appeal from Provincial Court (Family Division)   **48.** An appeal lies from an order of the Provincial Court (Family Division) under this Part to the District Court.

Contempt of orders of Provincial Court (Family Division)   **49.**—(1) In addition to its powers in respect of contempt, the Provincial Court (Family Division) may punish by fine or imprisonment, or by both, any wilful contempt of or resistance to its process, rules or orders under this Act, but the fine shall not exceed $1,000 nor shall the imprisonment exceed ninety days.

Conditions of imprisonment   (2) An order for imprisonment under subsection (1) may be conditional upon default in the performance of a condition set out in the order and may provide for the imprisonment to be served intermittently.

Limitation   **50.**—(1) No action or application for an order for the support of a spouse shall be brought under this Part after two years from the day the spouses separate.

Idem   (2) If the spouses provided for support on separation in a domestic contract, subsection (1) does not apply and no action or application for an order for the support of a spouse shall be brought after default under the contract has subsisted for two years.

192

PART IV
DOMESTIC CONTRACTS

Definitions   **51.** In this Part,

"cohabitation agreement"   "cohabitation agreement" means an agreement entered into under section 53;

"domestic contract"   "domestic contract" means a marriage contract, separation agreement or cohabitation agreement;

"marriage contract"   "marriage contract" means an agreement entered into under section 52;

"paternity agreement"   "paternity agreement" means an agreement entered into under section 59;

"separation agreement"   "separation agreement" means an agreement entered into under section 54.

Marriage contracts   **52.**—(1) A man and a woman who are married to each other or intend to marry may enter into an agreement in which they agree on their respective rights and obligations under the marriage or on separation, on the annulment or dissolution of the marriage or on death, including,

    (a) ownership in or division of property;

    (b) support obligations;

    (c) the right to direct the education and moral training of their children, but not the right to custody of or access to their children; and

    (d) any other matter in the settlement of their affairs.

Rights re matrimonial home excepted   (2) A provision in a marriage contract purporting to limit a spouse's rights under Part II (Matrimonial Home) is unenforceable.

Cohabitation agreements   **53.**—(1) A man and a woman who are cohabiting or intend to cohabit and who are not married to each other may enter into an agreement in which they agree on their respective rights and obligations during cohabitation, or on ceasing to cohabit or on death, including,

    (a) ownership in or division of property;

    (b) support obligations;

    (c) the right to direct the education and moral training of their children, but not the right to custody of or access to their children; and

    (d) any other matter in the settlement of their affairs.

Effect of mar-   (2) If the parties to a cohabitation agreement marry each

<table>
<tr><td>riage on a-greement</td><td>other, the agreement shall be deemed to be a marriage contract.</td></tr>
</table>

Separation a-greements

54. A man and a woman who cohabited and are living separate and apart may enter into an agreement in which they agree on their respective rights and obligations, including,

    (a) ownership in or division of property;

    (b) support obligations;

    (c) the right to direct the education and moral training of their children;

    (d) the right to custody of and access to their children; and

    (e) any other matter in the settlement of their affairs.

Form of contract

55. —(1) A domestic contract and an agreement to amend or rescind a domestic contract are unenforceable unless made in writing, signed by the parties and witnessed.

Capacity of minor

(2) A minor has capacity to enter into a domestic contract, subject to the approval of the court, which may be given before or after the minor enters into the contract.

Agreement on behalf of mentally incompetent person

(3) If a person is mentally incompetent,

    (a) the person's committee, if any, unless the person's spouse is the committee;

    (b) in all other cases, the Public Trustee,

may enter into a domestic contract or give any waiver or consent under this Act on the mentally incompetent person's behalf, subject to the prior approval of the court.

Contracts subject to best interests of child

56.—(1) In the determination of a matter respecting the support, education, moral training or custody of or access to a child, the court may disregard any provision of a domestic contract pertaining to the matter where, in the opinion of the court, to do so is in the best interests of the child.

Dum casta clauses

(2) A provision in a domestic contract to take effect on separation whereby any right of a party is dependent upon remaining chaste is unenforceable, but this subsection shall not be construed to affect a contingency upon marriage or cohabitation with another.

Idem

(3) A provision in a domestic contract made before this section comes into force whereby any right of a party is dependent upon remaining chaste shall be given effect as a contingency upon marriage or cohabitation with another.

Appendices

Setting aside domestic contract

(4) A court may, on application, set aside a domestic contract or a provision in it,

    (a) if a party failed to disclose to the other significant assets, or significant debts or other liabilities, existing when the domestic contract was made;

    (b) if a party did not understand the nature or consequences of the domestic contract; or

    (c) otherwise in accordance with the law of contract.

Barriers to re-marriage

(5) The court may, on application, set aside all or part of a separation agreement or settlement, if the court is satisfied that the removal by one spouse of barriers that would prevent the other spouse's remarriage within that spouse's faith was a consideration in the making of the agreement or settlement.

Idem

(6) Subsection (5) also applies to consent orders, releases, notices of discontinuance and abandonment and other written or oral arrangements.

Application of subss. (4, 5, 6)

(7) Subsections (4), (5) and (6) apply despite any agreement to the contrary.

Rights of donors of gifts

57. If a domestic contract provides that specific gifts made to one or both parties may not be disposed of or encumbered without the consent of the donor, the donor shall be deemed to be a party to the contract for the purpose of enforcement or amendment of the provision.

Contracts made outside Ontario

58. The manner and formalities of making a domestic contract and its essential validity and effect are governed by the proper law of the contract, except that,

    (a) a contract of which the proper law is that of a jurisdiction other than Ontario is also valid and enforceable in Ontario if entered into in accordance with Ontario's internal law;

    (b) subsection 33(4) (setting aside provision for support or waiver) and section 56 apply in Ontario to contracts for which the proper law is that of a jurisdiction other than Ontario; and

    (c) a provision in a marriage contract or cohabitation agreement respecting the right to custody of or access to children is not enforceable in Ontario.

Paternity agreements

59.—(1) If a man and a woman who are not spouses enter into an agreement for,

195

(a) the payment of the expenses of a child's prenatal care and birth;

(b) support of a child; or

(c) funeral expenses of the child or mother,

on the application of a party, or a children's aid society, to the Provincial Court (Family Division) or the Unified Family Court, the court may incorporate the agreement in an order, and Part III (Support Obligations) applies to the order in the same manner as if it were an order made under that Part.

Absconding respondent

(2) If an application is made under subsection (1) and a judge of the court is satisfied that the respondent is about to leave Ontario and that there are reasonable grounds to believe that the respondent intends to evade his or her responsibilities under the agreement, the judge may issue a warrant in the form prescribed by the rules of the court for the respondent's arrest.

Bail
R.S.O. 1980, c. 400

(3) Section 134 (interim release by justice of the peace) of the *Provincial Offences Act* applies, with necessary modifications, to an arrest under the warrant.

Capacity of minor

(4) A minor has capacity to enter into an agreement under subsection (1) that is approved by the court, whether the approval is given before or after the minor enters into the agreement.

Application to existing agreements

(5) This section applies to paternity agreements that were made before the day this Act comes into force.

Application of Act to existing contracts

60.—(1) A domestic contract validly made before the day this Act comes into force shall be deemed to be a domestic contract for the purposes of this Act.

Contracts entered into before coming into force of Act

(2) If a domestic contract was entered into before the day this Act comes into force and the contract or any part would have been valid if entered into on or after that day, the contract or part is not invalid for the reason only that it was entered into before that day.

Idem

(3) If property is transferred, under an agreement or understanding reached before the 31st day of March, 1978, between spouses who are living separate and apart, the transfer is effective as if made under a domestic contract.

PART V
DEPENDANTS' CLAIM FOR DAMAGES

Right of dependants to sue in tort **61.**—(1) If a person is injured or killed by the fault or neglect of another under circumstances where the person is entitled to recover damages, or would have been entitled if not killed, the spouse, as defined in Part III (Support Obligations), children, grandchildren, parents, grandparents, brothers and sisters of the person are entitled to recover their pecuniary loss resulting from the injury or death from the person from whom the person injured or killed is entitled to recover or would have been entitled if not killed, and to maintain an action for the purpose in a court of competent jurisdiction.

Damages in case of injury (2) The damages recoverable in a claim under subsection (1) may include,

    (a) actual expenses reasonably incurred for the benefit of the person injured or killed;

    (b) actual funeral expenses reasonably incurred;

    (c) a reasonable allowance for travel expenses actually incurred in visiting the person during his or her treatment or recovery;

    (d) where, as a result of the injury, the claimant provides nursing, housekeeping or other services for the person, a reasonable allowance for loss of income or the value of the services; and

    (e) an amount to compensate for the loss of guidance, care and companionship that the claimant might reasonably have expected to receive from the person if the injury or death had not occurred.

Contributory negligence (3) In an action under subsection (1), the right to damages is subject to any apportionment of damages due to contributory fault or neglect of the person who was injured or killed.

Limitations of actions (4) No action shall be brought under subsection (1) after the expiration of two years from the time the cause of action arose.

Offer to settle for global sum **62.**—(1) The defendant may make an offer to settle for one sum of money as compensation for his or her fault or neglect to all plaintiffs, without specifying the shares into which it is to be divided.

Apportionment (2) If the offer is accepted and the compensation has not been otherwise apportioned, the court may, on motion, apportion it among the plaintiffs.

Payment before apportionment   (3) The court may direct payment from the fund before apportionment.

Payment may be postponed   (4) The court may postpone the distribution of money to which minors are entitled.

Assessment of damages, insurance   **63.** In assessing damages in an action brought under this Part, the court shall not take into account any sum paid or payable as a result of the death or injury under a contract of insurance.

PART VI
AMENDMENTS TO THE COMMON LAW

Unity of legal personality absolished   **64.**—(1) For all purposes of the law of Ontario, a married person has a legal personality that is independent, separate and distinct from that of his or her spouse.

Capacity of married person   (2) A married person has and shall be accorded legal capacity for all purposes and in all respects as if he or she were an unmarried person and, in particular, has the same right of action in tort against his or her spouse as if they were not married.

Purpose of subss. (1, 2)   (3) The purpose of subsections (1) and (2) is to make the same law apply, and apply equally, to married men and married women and to remove any difference in it resulting from any common law rule or doctrine.

Actions between parent and child   **65.** No person is disentitled from bringing an action or other proceeding against another for the reason only that they are parent and child.

Recovery for prenatal injuries   **66.** No person is disentitled from recovering damages in respect of injuries for the reason only that the injuries were incurred before his or her birth.

Domicile of minor   **67.** The domicile of a person who is a minor is,
   (a) if the minor habitually resides with both parents and the parents have a common domicile, that domicile;
   (b) if the minor habitually resides with one parent only, that parent's domicile;
   (c) if the minor resides with another person who has

lawful custody of him or her, that person's domicile; or

    (d) if the minor's domicile can not be determined under clause (a), (b) or (c), the jurisdiction with which the minor has the closest connection.

Parental liability for torts of child: onus of proof   **68.** In an action against a parent for damage to property or for personal injury or death caused by the fault or neglect of a child who is a minor, the onus of establishing that the parent exercised reasonable supervision and control over the child rests with the parent.

GENERAL

Regulations   **69.** The Lieutenant Governor in Council may make regulations respecting any matter referred to as prescribed by the regulations.

Application of ss. 5-8 R.S.O. 1980, c. 152   **70.**—(1) Sections 5 to 8 apply unless,

    (a) an application under section 4 of the *Family Law Reform Act* was adjudicated or settled before the 4th day of June, 1985; or

    (b) the first spouse's death occurs before the day this Act comes into force.

Extension of limitation period   (2) The limitation period set out in clause 7(3)(b) does not expire until six months after this Act comes into force.

Application of Part II   (3) Part II (Matrimonial Home) applies unless a proceeding under Part III of the *Family Law Reform Act* to determine the rights between spouses in respect of the property concerned was adjudicated or settled before the 4th day of June, 1985.

Interpretation of existing contracts   (4) A separation agreement or marriage contract that is validly made before the day this Act comes into force and that excludes a spouse's property from the application of sections 4 and 8 of the *Family Law Reform Act*,

    (a) shall be deemed to exclude that property from the application of section 5 of this Act; and

    (b) shall be read with necessary modifications.

    71.—(1) **The *Family Law Reform Act*, being chapter 152 of the Revised Statutes of Ontario, 1980, except the title, subsection 27(1) and sections 69, 70 and 71, is repealed.**

(2) Subsection 27(1) of the *Family Law Reform Act* is repealed.

(3) Section 3 of the *Children's Law Reform Amendment Act, 1982*, being chapter 20, section 179 of the *Courts of Justice Act, 1984*, being chapter 11 and section 18 of the *Land Registration Reform Act, 1984*, being chapter 32, are repealed.

(4) The title to the *Family Law Reform Act* is repealed and the following substituted therefor:

DOWER AND MISCELLANEOUS ABOLITION ACT

72. Subsection 12(2) of the *Ontario Municipal Employees Retirement System Act*, being chapter 348 of the Revised Statutes of Ontario, 1980, is repealed and the following substituted therefor:

Application of subs. (1) (2) Notwithstanding subsection (1), payment to a person out of the Fund is subject to execution, seizure or attachment in satisfaction of an order for support or maintenance enforceable in Ontario.

73. Subsection 27(3) of the *Pension Benefits Act*, being chapter 373 of the Revised Statutes of Ontario, 1980, as enacted by the Statutes of Ontario, 1983, chapter 2, section 5, is repealed.

74. Subsection 34(4) of the *Public Service Superannuation Act*, being chapter 419 of the Revised Statutes of Ontario, 1980, as enacted by the Statutes of Ontario, 1984, chapter 22, section 15, is repealed.

75. Subsection 43(3) of the *Teachers' Superannuation Act, 1983*, being chapter 84, is repealed.

Commencement **76.** This Act comes into force on a day to be named by proclamation of the Lieutenant Governor.

Short title **77.** The short title of this Act is the *Family Law Act, 1986.*

APPENDIX B

BANKRUPTCY ACT

(R.S.C. 1970, c. B-3, as amended by S.C. 1985, c. 26, s. 81, proclaimed in force October 15, 1985, and S.C. 1986, c. 4, s. 28, effective June 1, 1986)

147. Fraudulent settlements.—In either of the following cases, that is to say:

    (*a*) in the case of a settlement made before and in consideration of marriage where the settlor is not at the time of making the settlement able to pay all his debts without the aid of the property comprised in the settlement; or

    (*b*) in the case of any covenant or contract made in consideration of marriage for the future settlement on or for the settlor's spouse or children of any property wherein the settlor had not at the date of marriage any estate or interest, not being property of or in right of his or her spouse;

if the settlor becomes bankrupt, and it appears to the court that such settlement, covenant or contract was made in order to defeat or delay his creditors, or was unjustifiable having regard to the state of the settlor's affairs at the time when it was made, the court may refuse or suspend an order of discharge or grant an order subject to conditions in like manner as in cases where the bankrupt has been guilty of fraud.
[S.C. 1985, c. 26, s. 81]

148. Debts not released by order of discharge.—(1) An order of discharge does not release the bankrupt from

    (*a*) any fine or penalty imposed by a court or any debt arising out of a recognizance or bail bond;

    (*b*) any debt or liability for alimony;

    (*c*) any debt or liability under a support, maintenance or affiliation order or under an agreement for maintenance and support of a spouse or child living apart from the bankrupt;
[S.C. 1986, c. 4, s. 28]

* * *

(2) *Claims released.*—An order of discharge releases the bankrupt from all other claims provable in bankruptcy.

APPENDIX C

PENSION BENEFITS STANDARDS ACT, 1985
(S.C. 1986, c. 40, section 25)

Distribution of Pension Benefits and Pension Benefit
Credits on Divorce, Annulment or Separation

Definitions   **25.** (1) In this section,

"provincial property law"   "provincial property law" means the law of a province relating to the distribution, pursuant to court order or agreement between the spouses, of the property of the spouses on divorce, annulment or separation;

"spouse"   "spouse" has

(a) in the definition "provincial property law" in this subsection, the same meaning that it has in the applicable provincial property law, regardless of whether the provincial property law uses the word "spouse" or uses another expression, and

(b) in subsections (2) to (8),

(i) in relation to a court order, the same meaning that it has in the applicable provincial property law, regardless of whether the provincial property law uses the word "spouse" or uses another expression, or

(ii) in relation to an assignment or agreement referred to in this section, the same meaning as in the definition "spouse" in subsection 2(1).

Application of provincial property law   (2) Subject to this section, pension benefits, pension benefit credits and any other benefits under a pension plan shall, on divorce, annulment or separation, be subject to the applicable provincial property law.

Non-application of this Act   (3) A pension benefit, pension benefit credit or other benefit under a pension plan that is subject to provincial property law pursuant to this section is not subject to the provisions of this Act relating to the valuation or distribution of pension benefits, pension benefit credits or other benefits under a pension plan, as the case may be.

Power to assign to spouse   (4) Notwithstanding anything in this section or in provincial property law, a member or former member of a pension plan may assign all or part of that person's pension benefit, pension benefit credit or other benefit under the plan to that person's spouse, effective as of divorce, annulment or separation, and in the event of such an assignment the spouse shall, in respect of the assigned portion of the pension benefit, pension benefit credit or other benefit, be deemed for the purpose of this Act, except subsections 21(2) to (6),

> (*a*) to have been a member of that pension plan, and
>
> (*b*) to have ceased to be a member of that pension plan as of the effective date of the assignment,

but a subsequent spouse of that spouse is not entitled to any pension benefit, pension benefit credit or other benefit under the pension plan in respect of that assigned portion.

Duty of administrator

(5) Where, pursuant to this section, all or part of a pension benefit, pension benefit credit or other benefit under a pension plan of a member or former member is required to be distributed to that person's spouse under a court order or an agreement between the spouses, the administrator, on receipt of

> (*a*) a written request from either the member or former member or that person's spouse that all or part of the pension benefit, pension benefit credit or other benefit, as the case may be, be distributed in accordance with the court order or the agreement, and
>
> (*b*) a copy of the court order or agreement,

shall determine and henceforth administer the pension benefit, pension benefit credit or other benefit, as the case may be, in prescribed manner, in accordance with the court order or the agreement; however, in the case of a court order, the administrator shall not administer the pension benefit, pension benefit credit or other benefit in accordance with the court order until all appeals therefrom have been finally determined or the time for appealing has expired.

Other spouse to be notified

(6) On receipt of a request referred to in subsection (5), the administrator shall notify the non-requesting spouse of the request and shall provide that spouse with a copy of the court order or agreement submitted in support of the request, but this requirement does not apply in respect of a request or an agreement received by the administrator in a form or manner that indicates that it was jointly submitted by the two spouses.

Splitting of joint and survivor pension benefit

(7) A pension plan may provide that, where, pursuant to this section, all or part of a pension benefit of a member or former member is required to be distributed to that person's spouse under a court order or an agreement between the spouses, a joint and survivor pension benefit may be adjusted

204

so that it becomes payable as two separate pensions, one to the member or former member and the other to that person's spouse, if the aggregate of the actuarial present values of the two pensions is not less than the actuarial present value of the joint and survivor pension benefit.

Limitation   (8) Notwithstanding subsection (2), the aggregate of

    (*a*) the actuarial present value of the pension benefit or other benefit paid to the member or former member, and

    (*b*) the actuarial present value of the pension benefit or other benefit paid to the spouse of the member or former member

pursuant to this section shall be not greater than the actuarial present value of the pension benefit or other benefit, as the case may be, that would have been payable to the member or former member had the divorce, annulment or separation not occurred.

As to application of this Act, see *ibid*, section 4.

Note

See also *An Act to Amend the Canada Pension Plan and the Federal Court Act*, S.C. 1986, c. 38, especially sections 23 and 33.

APPENDIX D

RULES OF CIVIL PROCEDURE
(O. Reg. 560/84)

Note: O. Reg. 560/84, filed August 27/84, gazetted September 22/84, effective January 1/85. These Rules repealed and replaced the Matrimonial Causes Rules, R.R.O. 1980, Reg. 540. Only those sections which pertain to family law are reproduced.

Amendments: O. Reg. 786/84, filed December 11/84, gazetted December 29/84, effective January 1/85; O. Reg. 478/85, gazetted October 5/85, in force October 1/85; O. Reg. 221/86, filed April 25/86, gazetted May 10/86, effective May 5/86 except s. 1, paras. 8, 9, 13, 15 and 17; s. 1, paras. 8, 9, 13, 15 and 17 in force June 1/86; O. Reg. 323/86, filed June 2/86, gazetted June 21/86, effective June 1/86; O. Reg. 484/86, ss. 5, 6.

* * *

RULE 70

DIVORCE ACTIONS

Financial Statements
70.14. Where Required—(1) Where a petition contains a claim for support or division of property, the petitioner shall file and serve a financial statement (Form 70K) with the petition and the respondent spouse shall deliver a financial statement with the answer.

(2) Where no claim for support or division of property is made in the petition, but such a claim is made in the counterpetition, the respondent spouse shall deliver a financial statement with the answer and counterpetition and the petitioner shall deliver a financial statement with the answer to counterpetition.

(3) *Waiver of Financial Statements.*—Subrules (1) and (2) do not apply in respect of a claim for support under the Act if both spouses have filed a waiver of financial statements (Form 70L), but the spouses may not waive the obligation to deliver financial statements in respect of a claim under the *Family Law Act, 1986.*

(4) *Registrar to Refuse Documents Unless Accompanied by Financial Statements.*—Where a financial statement is required to be filed or delivered with a petition or counterpetition, or an answer to it, the registrar shall not accept the petition, counterpetition or answer for issuing or filing without the financial statement.

(5) *Respondent must File Even When Not Defending.*—A respondent

206

spouse who does not intend to defend a claim for support or division of property shall nevertheless deliver a financial statement within the time prescribed for delivery of an answer or answer to counterpetition, but the failure of the respondent spouse to do so does not prevent the petitioner from setting the action down for trial or moving for judgment.

(6) *Order to Require Delivery.*—Where a respondent spouse fails to deliver a financial statement within the time prescribed for delivery of the answer or answer to counterpetition, the court may, on motion without notice, make an order requiring the delivery of a financial statement within a specified time.

(7) If a claim is made in the action for custody of a child, the court may order the parties to deliver financial statements (short form) (Form 70M) within a specified time.

(8) *Particulars of Financial Statement.*—Where a financial statement lacks particularity, a spouse may demand particulars and if the other spouse fails to supply them within seven days the court may, on such terms as are just,

    (*a*) order particulars to be delivered within a specified time; or

    (*b*) strike out the financial statement and order that a new financial statement be delivered within a specified time.

(9) *Sanctions for Failure to Deliver Financial Statement or to Give Particulars.*—Where a spouse fails to comply with an order to deliver a financial statement, a new financial statement or particulars,

    (*a*) the court may dismiss the spouse's action or strike out his or her answer; and

    (*b*) a judge may make a contempt order against the spouse.

(10) *Cross-examination on Financial Statement.*—A spouse may cross-examine the other spouse on his or her financial statement.

(11) A cross-examination on a financial statement may be used,

    (*a*) on a motion for interim relief; and

    (*b*) at trial, in the same manner as an examination for discovery.

(12) A spouse who has set the action down for trial or who has consented to the action being placed on a trial list may not cross-examine before trial on the other spouse's financial statement without leave of the court, but is not relieved of the obligation imposed by subrules (13) to (15).

(13) *Duty to Correct Financial Statement and Answers on Cross-examination.*—A spouse who has delivered a financial statement and subsequently discovers,

    (*a*) that any information in the financial statement or answer or cross-examination on it was incorrect or incomplete when made; or

(b) that there has been a material change in any information contained in it,

shall forthwith provide information concerning the change or correction in writing to the other spouse, and subrules 31.09(2) and (3) (correcting answers and sanctions for failure to correct) apply, with necessary modifications.

(14) A spouse who has delivered a financial statement shall deliver a fresh financial statement at least seven days before the commencement of the trial of the action, but may not be cross-examined before trial on the fresh financial statement except with leave of the court.

(15) *Net Family Property Statement.*—In an action in which a claim is made for a division of property, each spouse shall deliver a net family property statement (Form 70N) at least seven days before each of the following:
1. A pre-trial conference.
2. A motion for judgment.
3. The trial.

[O. Reg. 323/86, s. 1, para. 10]

Interim Relief

70.15. Notice of Motion.—(1) A notice of motion for interim relief shall set out the precise relief sought, including the amount of support claimed for each dependant.

(2) *Pre-motion Conference.*—At the hearing of the motion, the court may direct a pre-motion conference to consider the possibility of settling any or all the issues raised by the motion or the action.

(3) The costs of a pre-motion conference shall be assessed as part of the costs of the action, unless a judge or master who conducts the conference orders otherwise.

(4) A judge or officer who conducts a pre-motion conference under subrule (2) shall not preside at a motion for interim relief, the trial, a reference in the action or a motion for judgment, except that where the pre-trial conference has resolved all the issues in the action, a judge who conducted it may preside at a motion for judgment on consent of the parties.

(5) *Written Proposal for Settlement and Costs of Interim Motion.*—In exercising his or her discretion concerning costs, the judge or officer who hears a motion for interim relief shall take into account any written

proposal for settlement of the motion or the failure to make such a proposal.

(6) *Failure to Comply with Interim Order.*—Where a party fails to comply with an order for interim relief and the court is satisfied that the party is able to comply with the order, the court may postpone the trial of the action or strike out any pleading or affidavit of the party in default.

[O. Reg. 323/86, s. 1, para. 10]

Reference to a Family Law Commissioner

70.21. (1) A judge sitting at Toronto or Ottawa may, on consent of the parties, refer any question or issue arising in the action relating to custody, support or access to a family law commissioner for inquiry and report.

(2) Where a reference is directed under subrule (1), the commissioner shall inquire into the question or issue referred and shall make a report.

(3) The report may be confirmed only on a motion to,
   (*a*) a High Court judge, where a High Court judge directed the reference;
   (*b*) a local judge, where a local judge directed the reference; or
   (*c*) the referring judge, where the order of reference so directs,
and the judge may require the commissioner to give reasons for his or her findings or conclusions and may confirm the report in whole or in part or make such other order as is just.

[O. Reg. 786/84, s. 1, para. 19; O. Reg. 323/86, s. 1, para. 10]

RULE 71

FAMILY LAW PROCEEDINGS

Application of the Rule

71.01.—Rules 71.02 to 71.13 apply to proceedings under Parts I, II and III of the *Family Law Act, 1986* and Part III of the *Children's Law Reform Act.*

[O. Reg. 221/86, s. 1, para. 18]

Definitions

71.02. In rules 71.03 to 71.13,
   (*a*) "applicant" includes a plaintiff;

(*b*) "respondent" includes a defendant; and

(*c*) "responding document" means a statement of defence, defence to counterclaim or affidavit in opposition to an application.

Originating Process

71.03. Claim for Relief.—(1) An originating process that contains a claim for support or division of property shall set out the nature and amount of relief claimed and, if support is claimed, the amount for each dependant.

(2) *Application by Government Agency.*—Where the Ministry of Community Social Services, a municipality, a district welfare administration board or a band is an applicant for an order for the support of a dependant under subsection 33(3) of the *Family Law Act, 1986,* it shall serve the originating process on the dependant.

[O. Reg. 221/86, s. 1, para. 19; 323/86, s. 2.1, para. 11]

Financial Statements

71.04. Applicant's Financial Statement.—(1) Where an order is sought under section 7 (division of property), 33 (support) or 37 (variation of support) of the *Family Law Act, 1986,* a financial statement (Form 70K) shall be filed and served with the originating process, together with a notice to file financial statement (Form 70V).

(2) Where the originating process is a notice of action, the financial statement shall be delivered with the statement of claim.

(3) *Respondent's Financial Statement.*—A respondent served with the applicant's financial statement shall deliver a financial statement with his or her responding document.

(4) A respondent who does not intend to defend the proceeding shall nevertheless deliver a financial statement within the time prescribed for the delivery of his or her responding document, but a respondent's failure to do so does not prevent the applicant from bringing the proceeding on for hearing or moving for judgment.

(5) *Registrar to Refuse Documents Unless Accompanied by Financial Statement.*—Where a financial statement is required to be filed or delivered with an originating process, statement of claim or responding document, the registrar shall not accept the originating process, statement of claim or responding document for issuing or filing without the financial statement.

(6) *Order for Delivery.*—Where a respondent fails to comply with a notice to file financial statement, the applicant may move without notice

for an order requiring the delivery of a financial statement within a specified time.

(7) In a proceeding in which a claim is made for custody of a child, the court may order the parties to deliver financial statements (short form) (Form 70M) within a specified time.

(8) *Subrule 70.14(8) to (14) Apply.*—Subrules 70.14(8) to (14) (particulars, failure to deliver, cross-examination, duty to correct) apply, with necessary modifications, to financial statements referred to in subrules (1) to (7).

(9) *Net Family Property Statement.*—In a proceeding in which a claim is made for a division of property, each spouse shall deliver a net family property statement (Form 70N) at least seven days before each of the following.

1. A pre-trial conference.
2. A motion for judgment.
3. The hearing.

(10) *Divorce Action.*—Where a claim under the *Family Law Act, 1986* or the *Children's Law Reform Act* is made in a divorce action, the obligations of the spouses respecting financial statements are governed by rule 70.14.

[O. Reg. 221/86, s. 1, para. 20; O. Reg. 323/86, s. 1, para. 11]

Place of Hearing

71.05. (1) An applicant who makes a claim for custody of or access to a child who ordinarily resides in Ontario shall name in the originating process as the place of hearing a place where the court normally sits in the county in which the child ordinarily resides.

(2) Where a claim referred to in subrule (1) is made in a divorce action, the place of trial is governed by rule 70.17.

(3) The hearing shall be held at the place named in the originating process unless an order is made under rule 46.03 to change the place of hearing, and for the purpose of changing the place of hearing an application shall be treated as an action.

[O. Reg. 323/86, s. 1, para. 11]

Reference to a Family Law Commissioner

71.06.—Rule 70.21 (reference to family law commissioner) applies, with necessary modifications, to any question or issue arising under the *Family Law Act, 1986* or the *Children's Law Reform Act.*

[O. Reg. 221/86, s. 1, para. 18; O. Reg. 484/86, s. 5]

Interim Relief

71.07.—Rule 70.15 (interim relief) applies, with necessary modifications, to a motion for interim relief in a proceeding under the *Family Law Act, 1986* or the *Children's Law Reform Act.*

[O. Reg. 221/86, s. 1, para. 18; O. Reg. 484/86, s. 6]

Proceeding transferred from Provincial Court (Family Division)

71.08.—(1) Where a proceeding is transferred from the Provincial Court (Family Division) to the District Court or the Supreme Court under subsection 2(2) of the *Family Law Act, 1986* or section 67 of the *Children's Law Reform Act,* the proceeding shall continue without duplication of any steps taken before the transfer unless the court to which the proceeding is transferred directs otherwise.

(2) The court to which a proceeding is transferred may, on motion, give directions for the conduct of the proceeding.

[O. Reg. 221/86, s. 1, para. 18]

Appeal from Provincial Court (Family Division)

71.09. (1) *Commencement of Appeal.*—An appeal from the Provincial Court (Family Division) to the District Court under section 48 of the *Family Law Act, 1986* or section 76 of the *Children's Law Reform Act* shall be commenced by serving a notice of appeal (Form 71B) on all parties whose interests are affected by the appeal, within thirty days after the date of the order appealed from.

(2) *Filing Notice of Appeal.*—The notice of appeal, with proof of service, shall be filed in the office of the local registrar of the District Court within five days after service.

(3) *Grounds to be Stated.*—The notice of appeal (Form 71B) shall state the relief sought and shall set out the grounds of appeal, and no other grounds may be argued except by leave of the court.

(4) *Appeal Record.*—The appellant shall, at least ten days before the hearing of the appeal, file with the local registrar of the District Court and serve on each respondent an appeal record containing, in the following order,
>   (*a*) a table of contents describing each document, including each exhibit, by its nature and date and, in the case of an exhibit, by exhibit number or letter;
>   (*b*) a copy of the notice of appeal;
>   (*c*) a copy of the order appealed from, as signed, and the reasons, if any;

(*d*) a transcript of the evidence; and

(*e*) such other material that was before the court appealed from as is necessary for the hearing of the appeal,

and a factum of a concise statement, without argument, of the facts and law relied on by the appellant.

(5) Each respondent shall, at least three days before the hearing of the appeal, file with the local registrar and serve on every other party,

(*a*) any further material that was before the court appealed from and is necessary for the hearing of the appeal; and

(*b*) a factum consisting of a concise statement, without argument, of the facts and law relied on by the respondent.

(6) *Dispensing with Compliance.*—A judge of the District Court may, before or at the hearing of the Appeal, dispense with compliance with subrule (4) or (5) in whole or in part.

[O. Reg. 221/86, s. 1, paras. 18, 21]

Warrant for Arrest

71.10.—A warrant for the arrest of a debtor or respondent referred to in section 43 of the *Family Law Act, 1986* or section 13 of the *Support and Custody Orders Enforcement Act, 1985* shall be in Form 71C.

[O. Reg. 221/86, s. 1, para. 22]

Recognizance

71.11.—A recognizance required by an order made under subsection 46(1) of the *Family Law Act, 1986* or section 36 of the *Children's Law Reform Act* shall be in Form 71D and shall be entered into before the registrar or such other officer as a judge directs.

[O. Reg. 221/86, s. 1, paras. 18, 23]

Reciprocal Enforcement of Maintenance Orders

71.12.—On receipt by the registrar of a written request under subsection 2(3) of the *Reciprocal Enforcement of Maintenance Orders Act, 1982,* the registrar shall deem a final order of the court within the meaning of clause 1(*f*) of that Act that is referred to in the request to be a registered order under subsection 2(3) of that Act and shall issue a certificate accordingly.

Request by Extra-provincial Tribunal for Evidence in Custody Cases

71.13. (1) *Issuing Summons to Give Evidence.*—Where the Attorney

General refers a request of an extra-provincial tribunal to the court under section 34 of the *Children's Law Reform Act,* the registrar shall issue a summons in Form 71E requiring the person named in the request to produce or give evidence in accordance with the request.

(2) *Service of Summons.*—The summons and a copy of the request of the extra-provincial tribunal and any supporting material that accompanied the request shall be served on the person named in the request, personally and not by an alternative to personal service, at least five days before he or she is required to produce or give evidence.

(3) Where the person named in the request is not a party to the proceeding before the extra-provincial tribunal and the summons requires the person to give oral evidence, attendance money calculated in accordance with Tariff A shall be paid or tendered to the person when the summons is served.

(4) A copy of the summons shall be served on the Attorney General within the time prescribed by subrule (2).

(5) *Affidavit Evidence.*—Where the summons does not require the person to give oral evidence, the person may file with the registrar the evidence required, verified by the person's affidavit.

(6) *Oral Evidence.*—Where the summons requires the person to give oral evidence, the person shall attend before a judge or officer of the court, as set out in the summons, to be examined in accordance with the summons.

(7) *Evidence to be Sent to Extra-Provincial Tribunal.*—The registrar shall send to the extra-provincial tribunal a certified copy of evidence produced or given under this rule.

(8) *Sanctions for Disobeying Summons.*—Subrules 53.04(7) and (8) apply, with necessary modifications, to a person who after having been served in accordance with subrules (2) and (3) fails to comply with the summons.

FORMS

SUPREME AND DISTRICT COURT
(Rules of Civil Procedure, O. Reg. 560/84
[am. O. Regs. 786/84, 478/85, 221/86, 323/86, 484/86])

FORM 70K
FINANCIAL STATEMENT

(General heading)

FINANCIAL STATEMENT

I, _____
(Full name of deponent)

of the _____ of _____ in the
(City, Town, etc.)

_____ of _____ MAKE OATH AND SAY (or AFFIRM)
(County, Regional Municipality, etc.)

    1. Particulars of my financial situation and of all my property are accurately set out below, to the best of my knowledge, information and belief.

ALL INCOME AND MONEY RECEIVED

(Include all income and other money received from all sources, whether taxable or not. Show gross amount here and show deductions on pages 2, 3, 4 & 5. Give current actual amount where known or ascertainable. Where amount cannot be ascertained, give your best estimate. Use weekly, monthly or yearly column as appropriate.)

Category	Weekly	Monthly	Yearly
1. Salary or wages			
2. Bonuses			
3. Fees			
4. Commissions			
5. Family allowance			
6. Unemployment insurance			
7. Workers' compensation			
8. Public assistance			
9. Pension			
10. Dividends			
11. Interest			
12. Rental income			
13. Allowances and support from others			
14. Other (Specify)			
TOTAL	$	(A)$	$

Weekly total $_____ × 4.33 = (B)$_____ monthly

Yearly total $_____ ÷ 12 = (C)$_____ monthly

GROSS MONTHLY INCOME (A) + (B) + (C) = (D)$_____

OTHER BENEFITS

(Show all non-monetary benefits from all sources, such as use of a vehicle or room and board, and include such items as insurance or dental plans or other expenses paid on your behalf. Give your best estimate where you cannot ascertain the actual value.)

Item	Particulars	Monthly Market Value

TOTAL (E) $_____

GROSS MONTHLY INCOME AND BENEFITS (D) + (E) = $_____

ACTUAL AND PROPOSED BUDGETS

	ACTUAL BUDGET for twelve month period from _____ 19___ to _____ 19___ Show actual expenses, or your best estimate where you cannot ascertain actual amount.			PROPOSED BUDGET Show your proposed budget, giving your best estimate where you cannot ascertain actual amount.		
CATEGORY	Weekly	Monthly	Yearly	Weekly	Monthly	Yearly
Housing						
1. Rent				1		
2. Real property taxes				2		
3. Mortgage				3		
4. Common expense charges				4		
5 Water				5		
6. Electricity				6		
7 Natural gas				7		
8. Fuel oil				8		
9 Telephone				9		
10 Cable T.V.				10		
11. Home insurance				11		
12. Repairs and maintenance				12		
13. Gardening and snow removal				13		
14. Other (Specify)				14		
Food, Toiletries and Sundries						
15. Groceries				15		
16. Meals outside home				16		
17. Toiletries and sundries				17		
18. Grooming				18		

Form 70K, p. 3

CATEGORY	ACTUAL BUDGET			PROPOSED BUDGET		
Food Toiletries and Sundries—cont'd.	Weekly	Monthly	Yearly	Weekly	Monthly	Yearly
19. General household supplies				19		
20. Laundry, dry cleaning				20		
21. Other (Specify)				21		
Clothing						
22. Children				22		
23. Self				23		
Transportation						
24. Public transit				24		
25. Taxis, car pools				25		
26. Car insurance				26		
27. Licence				27		
28. Car maintenance				28		
29. Gasoline, oil				29		
30. Parking				30		
31. Other (Specify)				31		
Health and Medical						
32. Doctors, chiropractors				32		
33. Dentist (regular care)				33		
34. Orthodontist or special dental care				34		
35. Insurance premiums				35		
36. Drugs				36		
37. Other (Specify)				37		
Deductions from Income						
38. Income tax				38		
39. Canada Pension Plan				39		
40. Unemployment insurance				40		
41. Employer pension				41		
42. Union or other dues				42		

219

Form 70K, p. 4

CATEGORY	ACTUAL BUDGET			PROPOSED BUDGET		
Deductions from income—cont'd.	Weekly	Monthly	Yearly	Weekly	Monthly	Yearly
43. Group insurance				43		
44. Credit union loan				44		
45. Credit union savings				45		
46. Other (Specify)				46		
Miscellaneous						
47. Life insurance premiums				47		
48. Tuition fees, books, etc.				48		
49. Entertainment				49		
50. Recreation				50		
51. Vacation				51		
52. Gifts				52		
53. Babysitting, day care				53		
54. Children's allowances				54		
55. Children's activities				55		
56. Support payments				56		
57. Newspapers, periodicals				57		
58. Alcohol, tobacco				58		
59. Charities				59		
60. Income tax (not deducted at source)				60		
61. Other (Specify)				61		
Loan Payments						
62. Banks				62		
63. Finance companies				63		
64. Credit unions				64		
65. Department stores				65		
66. Other (Specify)				66		

Form 70K, p. 5

CATEGORY	ACTUAL BUDGET			PROPOSED BUDGET		
	Weekly	Monthly	Yearly	Weekly	Monthly	Yearly
Savings						
67. R.R.S.P.				67		
68. Other (Specify)				68		
	$	$	$	$	$	$

TOTALS OF ACTUAL BUDGET

Monthly Total $_____

Weekly Total $_____ × 4.33 = $_____

Yearly Total $_____ ÷ 12 = $_____

MONTHLY ACTUAL BUDGET   (F) $_____

TOTALS OF PROPOSED BUDGET

Monthly Total $_____

Weekly Total $_____ × 4.33 = $_____

Yearly Total $_____ ÷ 12 = $_____

MONTHLY PROPOSED BUDGET   (G) $_____

SUMMARY OF INCOME AND EXPENSES

Actual

Gross monthly income
(Amount D from page 1) $_____

Subtract Monthly actual budget
(Amount F from page 5)   − $_____

ACTUAL MONTHLY SURPLUS / DEFICIT $_____

Proposed

Gross monthly income
(Amount D from page 1) $_____

Subtract Proposed monthly budget
(Amount G from page 5)   − $_____

PROPOSED MONTHLY SURPLUS / DEFICIT $_____

Form 70K, p. 6

LAND

(Include any interest in land owned on the valuation date, including leasehold interests and mortgages, whether or not you are registered as owner. Include claims to an interest in land, but do not include claims that you are making against your spouse in this or a related proceeding Show estimated market value of your interest without deducting encumbrances or costs of disposition, and show encumbrances and costs of disposition under Debts and Other Liabilities on page 9.)

Nature and Type of Ownership State percentage interest where relevant.	Nature and Address of Property	Estimated Market Value of Your Interest as of: See instructions above		
		Date of Marriage	Valuation Date	Date of Statement
	TOTAL $		(H)	

GENERAL HOUSEHOLD ITEMS AND VEHICLES

(Show estimated market value, not cost of replacement for these items owned on the valuation date. Do not deduct encumbrances here, but show encumbrances under Debts and Other Liabilities on page 9.)

Item	Particulars	Estimated Market Value of Your Interest as of: See instructions above.		
		Date of Marriage	Valuation Date	Date of Statement
General household contents excluding special items (a) at matrimonial home(s)				
(b) elsewhere				
Jewellery				
Works of art				
Vehicles and boats				
Other special items				
	TOTAL $		(I)	

SAVINGS AND SAVINGS PLANS

Form 70K, p. 7

(Show items owned on the valuation date by category. Include cash, accounts in financial institutions, registered retirement or other savings plans, deposit receipts, pensions and any other savings.)

Category	Institution	Account Number	Amount as of:		
			Date of Marriage	Valuation Date	Date of Statement
		TOTAL $		(J)	

SECURITIES

(Show items owned on the valuation date by category. Include shares, bonds, warrants, options, debentures, notes and any other securities. Give your best estimate of market value if the items were to be sold on an open market.)

Category	Number	Description	Estimated Market Value as of:		
			Date of Marriage	Valuation Date	Date of Statement
		TOTAL $		(K)	

LIFE AND DISABILITY INSURANCE

(List all policies owned on the valuation date.)

Company and Policy No.	Kind of Policy	Owner	Beneficiary	Face Amount	Cash Surrender Value as of:		
					Date of Marriage	Valuation Date	Date of Statement
				TOTAL $		(L)	

223

Form 70K, p. 8

ACCOUNTS RECEIVABLE

(Give particulars of all debts owing to you on the valuation date, whether arising from business or from personal dealings.)

Particulars	Amount as of:		
	Date of Marriage	Valuation Date	Date of Statement
TOTAL $		(M)	

BUSINESS INTERESTS

(Show any interest in an unincorporated business owned on the valuation date. A controlling interest in an incorporated business may be shown here or under Securities on page 7. Give your best estimate of market value if the business were to be sold on an open market.)

Name of Firm or Company	Interest	Estimated Market Value as of:		
		Date of Marriage	Valuation Date	Date of Statement
TOTAL $			(N)	

OTHER PROPERTY

(Show other property owned on the valuation date by categories. Include property of any kind not shown above. Give your best estimate of market value.)

Category	Particulars	Estimated Market Value as of:		
		Date of Marriage	Valuation Date	Date of Statement
TOTAL $			(O)	

Form 70K, p. 9

DEBTS AND OTHER LIABILITIES

(Show your debts and other liabilities on the valuation date, whether arising from personal or business dealings, by category such as mortgages, charges, liens, notes, credit cards and accounts payable. Include contingent liabilities such as guarantees and indicate that they are contingent.)

Category	Particulars	Date of Marriage	Valuation Date	Date of Statement
	TOTAL $		(P)	

PROPERTY, DEBTS AND OTHER LIABILITIES ON DATE OF MARRIAGE

(Show by category the value of your property and your debts and other liabilities calculated as of the date of your marriage. Do not includ the value of a matrimonial home that you owned at the date of marriage.)

Category	Particulars	Assets	Liabilities
	TOTAL $	(Q) $	(R) $

NET VALUE OF PROPERTY OWNED ON DATE OF MARRIAGE (Amount Q Subtract Amount R) = (S) $_____

Form 70K, p. 1?

EXCLUDED PROPERTY

(Show the value by category of property owned on the valuation date that is excluded from the definition of "net family property".)

Category	Particulars	Value on Valuation Date
	TOTAL	(T) $

DISPOSAL OF PROPERTY

(Show the value by category of all property that you disposed of during the two years immediately preceding the making of thi statement, or during the marriage, whichever period is shorter.)

Category	Particulars	Value
	TOTAL	(U) $

Form 70K, p. 11

CALCULATION OF NET FAMILY PROPERTY

Value of all property owned on valuation date (Amounts H,I,J,K,L,M,N and O
from pages 6 to 8) $_____

Subtract value of all deductions (Amounts P and S from page 9)   — $_____

Subtract value of all excluded property (Amount T from page 10)   — $_____

                                  NET FAMILY PROPERTY $_____

2. The name(s) and address(es) of my employer(s) are:

3. Attached to this affidavit are a copy of my income tax return filed with the Department of National
Revenue for the last taxation year, together with all material filed with it, and a copy of any notice of assessment or reassessment that I have received from the Department for that year.

4. I do not anticipate any material changes in the information set out above.

*(Delete inapplicable
paragraph 4)*

4. I anticipate the following material changes in the information set out above:

    Sworn, etc.

                                       _____

                                       Signature of deponent

FORM 70L

WAIVER OF FINANCIAL STATEMENTS

(General heading)

WAIVER OF FINANCIAL STATEMENTS

        The husband and the wife waive financial statements in respect of claims made in this action for support under the *Divorce Act*.

(Date)	*(Signature of wife's solicitor or wife)*	*(Date)*	*(Signature of husband's solicitor or husband)*
	(Name, address and telephone number)		*(Name, address and telephone number)*

(Note: Financial statements may not be waived in respect of a claim under the Family Law Act. *)*

FORM 70M

FINANCIAL STATEMENT (SHORT FORM)

70.

(General heading)

FINANCIAL STATEMENT (SHORT FORM)

I,

(Full name of deponent)

of the _____ of _____ in the

(City Town etc)

_____ of _____ MAKE OATH AND SAY (or AFFIRM

(County Regional Municipality etc)

1. Particulars of my financial situation and of all my property are accurately set out below, to the best of my knowledge, information and belief.

ALL INCOME AND MONEY RECEIVED

(Include all income and other money received from all sources, whether taxable or not. Show gross amount here and show deductions on pages 2, 3, 4 & 5. Give current actual amount where known or ascertainable. Where amount cannot be ascertained, give your best estimate. Use weekly, monthly or yearly column as appropriate.)

Category	Weekly	Monthly	Yearly
1. Salary or wages			
2. Bonuses			
3. Fees			
4. Commissions			
5. Family allowance			
6. Unemployment insurance			
7. Workers' compensation			
8. Public assistance			
9. Pension			
10. Dividends			
11. Interest			
12. Rental income			
13. Allowances and support from others			
14. Other (Specify)			
TOTAL	$	(A)$	$

Weekly total $ _____ × 4.33 = (B)$ _____ monthly

Yearly total $ _____ ÷ 12 = (C)$ _____ monthly

GROSS MONTHLY INCOME (A) + (B) + (C) = (D)$ _____

OTHER BENEFITS

Form 70M,

(Show all non-monetary benefits from all sources, such as use of a vehicle or room and board, and include such items as insurance or dental plans or other expenses paid on your behalf. Give your best estimate where you cannot ascertain the actual value.)

Item	Particulars	Monthly Market Value

TOTAL (E) $_____

GROSS MONTHLY INCOME AND BENEFITS (D) + (E)=$_____

(The respondent may omit the budgets unless the court orders otherwise.)

ACTUAL AND PROPOSED BUDGETS

	ACTUAL BUDGET for twelve month period from _____ 19____ to _____ 19____ Show actual expenses, or your best estimate where you cannot ascertain actual amount.			PROPOSED BUDGET Show your proposed budget, giving your best estimate where you cannot ascertain actual amount.		
CATEGORY	Weekly	Monthly	Yearly	Weekly	Monthly	Yearly
Housing						
1. Rent				1		
2. Real property taxes				2		
3. Mortgage				3		
4. Common expense charges				4		
5. Water				5		
6. Electricity				6		
7. Natural gas				7		
8. Fuel oil				8		
9. Telephone				9		
10. Cable T.V.				10		
11. Home insurance				11		
12. Repairs and maintenance				12		
13. Gardening and snow removal				13		
14. Other (Specify)				14		
Food, Toiletries and Sundries						
15. Groceries				15		
16. Meals outside home				16		
17. Toiletries and sundries				17		
18. Grooming				18		

Form 70M, p. 3

CATEGORY	ACTUAL BUDGET			PROPOSED BUDGET		
Food Toiletries and Sundries—cont'd.	Weekly	Monthly	Yearly	Weekly	Monthly	Yearly
19 General household supplies				19		
20 Laundry, dry cleaning				20		
21 Other (Specify)				21		
Clothing						
22 Children				22		
23 Self				23		
Transportation						
24 Public transit				24		
25 Taxis, car pools				25		
26 Car insurance				26		
27 Licence				27		
28 Car maintenance				28		
29 Gasoline, oil				29		
30 Parking				30		
31 Other (Specify)				31		
Health and Medical						
32 Doctors; chiropractors				32		
33 Dentist (regular care)				33		
34 Orthodontist or special dental care				34		
35 Insurance premiums				35		
36 Drugs				36		
37 Other (Specify)				37		
Deductions from Income						
38 Income tax				38		
39 Canada Pension Plan				39		
40 Unemployment insurance				40		
41 Employer pension				41		
42 Union or other dues				42		

Form 70M, p. 4

CATEGORY	ACTUAL BUDGET			PROPOSED BUDGET		
Deductions from income–cont'd.	Weekly	Monthly	Yearly	Weekly	Monthly	Yearly
43. Group insurance				43		
44. Credit union loan				44		
45. Credit union savings				45		
46. Other (Specify)				46		
Miscellaneous						
47. Life insurance premiums				47		
48. Tuition fees, books, etc				48		
49. Entertainment				49		
50. Recreation				50		
51. Vacation				51		
52. Gifts				52		
53. Babysitting, day care				53		
54. Children's allowances				54		
55. Children's activities				55		
56. Support payments				56		
57. Newspapers, periodicals				57		
58. Alcohol, tobacco				58		
59. Charities				59		
60. Income tax (not deducted at source)				60		
61. Other (Specify)				61		
Loan Payments						
62. Banks				62		
63. Finance companies				63		
64. Credit unions				64		
65. Department stores				65		
66. Other (Specify)				66		

Form 70M, p. 5

CATEGORY	ACTUAL BUDGET			PROPOSED BUDGET		
	Weekly	Monthly	Yearly	Weekly	Monthly	Yearly
Savings 67 R R S P				67		
68 Other (Specify)				68		
	$	$	$	$	$	$

TOTALS OF ACTUAL BUDGET

Monthly Total $_____

Weekly Total $_____ × 4 33 = $_____

Yearly Total $_____ – 12 = $_____

MONTHLY ACTUAL BUDGET (F) $_____

TOTALS OF PROPOSED BUDGET

Monthly Total $_____

Weekly Total $_____ × 4 33 = $_____

Yearly Total $_____ – 12 = $_____

MONTHLY PROPOSED BUDGET (G) $_____

SUMMARY OF INCOME AND EXPENSES

Actual

Gross monthly income
(Amount D from page 1) $_____

Subtract Monthly actual budget
(Amount F from page 5) – $_____

ACTUAL MONTHLY SURPLUS / DEFICIT $_____

Proposed

Gross monthly income
(Amount D from page 1) $_____

Subtract Proposed monthly budget
(Amount G from page 5) – $_____

PROPOSED MONTHLY SURPLUS / DEFICIT $_____

Form 70M, p. 6

LAND

(Include any interest in land, including leasehold interests and mortgages, whether or not you are registered as owner. Show estimated market value of your interest without deducting encumbrances, and show encumbrances under Debts and Other Liabilities on page 9.)

Nature and Type of Ownership State percentage interest where relevant.	Nature and Address of Property	Estimated Market Value of Your Interest See instructions above.
	TOTAL	

GENERAL HOUSEHOLD ITEMS AND VEHICLES

(Show estimated market value, net cost of replacement, and do not deduct encumbrance here. Show encumbrances under Debts and Other Liabilities on page 9.)

Item	Particulars	Estimated Market Value of Your Interest See instructions above.
General household contents excluding special items (a) at matrimonial home(s)		
(b) elsewhere		
Jewellery		
Works of art		
Vehicles and boats		
Other special items		
	TOTAL	

234

Form 70M, p. 7

SAVINGS AND PLANS

(Show items by category. Include cash, accounts in financial institutions, registered retirement or other savings plans, deposit receipts, pensions and any other savings.)

Category	Institution	Account Number	Amount
			TOTAL

SECURITIES

(Show items by category. Include shares, bonds, warrants, options, debentures, notes and any other securities. Give your best estimate of market value if the items were to be sold on an open market.)

Category	Number	Description	Estimated Market Value
			TOTAL

LIFE AND DISABILITY INSURANCE

Company and Policy Number	Kind of Policy	Owner	Beneficiary	Face Amount	Present Cash Surrender Value
				TOTALS $	

235

ACCOUNTS RECEIVABLE   Form 70M, p. 8

(Give particulars of all debts owing to you whether arising from business or from personal dealings.)

Particulars	Amount
	$
TOTAL	(S) $

BUSINESS INTERESTS

(Show any interest in an unincorporated business. A controlling interest in an incorporated business may be shown here or under Securities on page 7. Give your best estimate of market value if the business were to be sold on an open market.)

Name of Firm or Company	Interest	Estimated Market Value
		$
	TOTAL	(T) $

OTHER PROPERTY

(Show other property by categories. Include property of any kind not shown above. Give your best estimate of market value.)

Category	Particulars	Estimated Market Value
		$
	TOTAL	(U) $

Appendices

DEBTS AND OTHER LIABILITIES   Form 70M, p. 9

(Show your debts and other liabilities, whether arising from personal or business dealings, by category such as mortgages, charges, liens, notes, credit cards and accounts payable. Include contingent liabilities such as guarantees and indicate that they are contingent.)

Category	Particulars	Amount
	TOTAL	

SUMMARY OF ASSETS AND DEBTS Form 70M, p. 10

Total assets $_____

Total debts   − $_____

NET WORTH $_____

2. The name(s) and address(es) of my employer(s) are:

3. Attached to this affidavit are a copy of my income tax return filed with the Department of National Revenue for the last taxation year, together with all material filed with it, and a copy of any notice of assessment or reassessment that I have received from the Department for that year.

4. I do not anticipate any material changes in the information set out above.

(Delete inapplicable paragraph 4.)

4. I anticipate the following material changes in the information set out above:

Sworn, etc.

_____
Signature of deponent

237

FORM 70N

NET FAMILY PROPERTY STATEMENT

(General heading)

WIFE'S *(or* HUSBAND'S *)* NET FAMILY PROPERTY STATEMENT

Valuation date _____ Statement date _____

(Complete columns for both husband and wife, showing your assets, debts, etc. and those of your spouse.)

ITEM	HUSBAND	WIFE
1. Value of assets owned on valuation date *(by category with reference to the financial statements)*		
TOTAL 1.		
2. Value of debts and other liabilities on valuation date *(by category with reference to the financial statements)*		
TOTAL 2.		

ITEM	HUSBAND	WIFE
3. Net value of property, other than a matrimonial home, owned on date of marriage *(by category with reference to the financial statements)*		
TOTAL 3.		
4. Value of property excluded under subs. 4(2) of the <u>Family Law Act</u> *(by category with reference to the financial statements)*		
TOTAL 4.		
5. Net family property *(Total 1 minus Totals 2, 3 and 4)*		

(Name, address and telephone number of solicitor or party)

FORM 70V

NOTICE TO FILE FINANCIAL STATEMENT

(The body of this form may be incorporated in an originating process.)

(General Heading)

NOTICE TO FILE FINANCIAL STATEMENT

TO *(name of respondent or defendant)*

In this proceeding a claim has been made against you for custody *(or* support, variation of support *or* division of property*)*.

YOU ARE REQUIRED, WHETHER OR NOT YOU DEFEND THIS PRO-CEEDING, to serve and file a financial statement in Form 70M prescribed by the Rules of Civil Procedure. Your financial statement must accompany your responding document if you defend this proceeding and must be served and filed in any event within the time for delivering your responding document after the originating process in this proceeding was served on you.

If you fail to serve and file a financial statement as required, an order may be made, without further notice, to compel you to file a financial statement.

(Date)   *(Name, address and telephone number of solicitor or party serving notice)*

TO   *(Name and Address of solicitor or party receiving notice)*

[en. O. Reg. 32386, s.13]

APPENDIX E

ONTARIO REGULATION 95/86

FAMILY LAW ACT, 1986

Designation of Matrimonial
Home — Forms.
Made — February 19th, 1986.
Filed — February 21st, 1986.

REGULATION MADE UNDER THE FAMILY LAW ACT, 1986

DESIGNATION OF MATRIMONIAL HOME — FORMS

1. A designation of a matrimonial home under subsection 20(1) of the Act shall be in Form 1.

2. A cancellation of a designation of a matrimonial home under clause 20(6)(*a*) of the Act shall be in Form 2.

3. Regulation 319 of Revised Regulations of Ontario, 1980 is revoked.

4. This Regulation comes into force on the 1st day of March, 1986.

Form 1

Family Law Act, 1986

DESIGNATION OF MATRIMONIAL HOME

Province of Ontario

Document General
Form 4 — Land Registration Reform Act, 1984

D

(1) Registry ☐ Land Titles ☐	(2) Page 1 of pages

(3) Property Identifier(s)   Block   Property   Additional See Schedule ☐

(4) Nature of Document
Designation of matrimonial home
(Family Law Act, s. 20)

(5) Consideration
Not applicable ——————— Dollars $

(6) Description

FOR OFFICE USE ONLY

New Property Identifiers   Additional See Schedule ☐

Executions   Additional See Schedule ☐

(7) This Document Contains: (a) Redescription New Easement Plan/Sketch ☐   (b) Schedule for: Description ☐ Additional Parties ☐ Other ☐

(8) This Document provides as follows:

(Check appropriate box and strike out inapplicable paragraph)

☐ The parties signing in box 10, who are spouses of each other, designate the property described in box 6 as a matrimonial home.

☐ The party signing in box 10, who is the spouse of _____ ,
                                                (name)

designates the property described in box 6 as a matrimonial home.

Continued on Schedule ☐

(9) This Document relates to instrument number(s)
Not applicable ———————

(10) Party(ies) (Set out Status or Interest)

Name(s)	Signature(s)	Date of Signature Y M D

(11) Address for Service

(12) Party(ies) (Set out Status or Interest)

Name(s)	Signature(s)	Date of Signature Y M D
Not applicable ———————		

(13) Address for Service   Not applicable ———————

(14) Municipal Address of Property | (15) Document Prepared by: | Fees and Tax

Registration Fee

FOR OFFICE USE ONLY

Total

Appendices

Form 2
Family Law Act, 1986
CANCELLATION OF DESIGNATION OF MATRIMONIAL HOME

Document General

Form 4 — Land Registration Reform Act, 1984

D

| Province of Ontario |

(1) Registry ☐   Land Titles ☐   (2) Page 1 of   pages

(3) Property Identifier(s)   Block   Property   Additional See Schedule ☐

(4) Nature of Document

Cancellation of designation of matrimonial home
(Family Law Act, s. 20)

(5) Consideration

Not applicable ——————— Dollars $

(6) Description

New Property Identifiers   Additional See Schedule ☐

Executions   Additional See Schedule ☐

(7) This Document Contains: (a) Redescription New Easement Plan/Sketch ☐   (b) Schedule for: Description ☐ Additional Parties ☐ Other ☐

(8) This Document provides as follows:
(Check appropriate box and strike out inapplicable paragraph)

☐ The parties signing in box 10, who are spouses of each other, cancel the designation by them of the property described in box 6 as a matrimonial home in the instrument referred to in box 9.

☐ The party signing in box 10, who is the spouse of _____,
                                          (name)

cancels the designation by him/her of the property described in box 6 as a matrimonial home in the instrument referred to in box 9.

Continued on Schedule ☐

(9) This Document relates to instrument number(s)

(10) Party(ies) (Set out Status or Interest)
Name(s)   Signature(s)   Date of Signature Y M D

(11) Address for Service

(12) Party(ies) (Set out Status or Interest)
Name(s)   Signature(s)   Date of Signature Y M D

Not applicable

(13) Address for Service   Not applicable

(14) Municipal Address of Property   (15) Document Prepared by:

Fees and Tax
Registration Fee

Total

243

APPENDIX F

REGULATION MADE UNDER THE FAMILY LAW ACT, 1986

ELECTION OF SURVIVING SPOUSE

1. An election made under section 6 of the Act shall be in Form 1. O. Reg. 606/86, s 1.

Form 1

Election Under The Family Law Act, 1986

Court File No.

_____

This election is filed by (solicitors)

_____

Name of deceased   Surname   Given name(s)

_____

Last address of deceased   Street or postal address   City, town, etc.

_____

Date of death   Day, month, year

_____

Surviving spouse   Surname   Given name(s)

_____

Address of spouse   Street or postal address City, town, etc. Postal Code

I, : _____ the surviving spouse, elect:
     (Please print)

- to receive the entitlement under section 5 of the *Family Law Act, 1986;*
  OR (check one box only)

- to receive the entitlement under the will, or under Part II of the *Succession Law Reform Act,* if there is an intestacy, or both, if there is a partial intestacy.

_____   _____

Signature of surviving spouse   Date

NOTE: THIS ELECTION HAS IMPORTANT EFFECTS ON YOUR RIGHTS.
YOU SHOULD HAVE LEGAL ADVICE BEFORE SIGNING IT.

SELECTED BIBLIOGRAPHY

Books

Adamson, M.S. *The Valuation of Company Shares and Business* (Law Book Company, Australia, 1986).

Bissett-Johnson, A. and W. Holland, *Matrimonial Property Law in Canada* (Carswell, 1987).

Goldberg, B. *Valuation of Divorce Assets* (West Publishing Company, 1984).

Hainsworth, T.W. *The Ontario Family Law Act Manual* (Canada Law Book, 1986).

Kronby, M. and J. Wilson, *Family Law Reform Reporter* (F.L.R. Publications, 1986-).

The Law Society of Upper Canada, *Bar Admission Course Materials*, 1986-1987, *Family Law* (3 volumes).

MacDonald, J.C., K. Weiler, R. Mesbur, C. Perkins and A. Wilton, *Law and Practice under the Family Law Act of Ontario* (Carswell, 1986).

Payne, J.D. and M. Payne, *Payne's Divorce and Family Law Digest* (Richard De Boo Publishers, 1986-).

Stark, H.G. and K.J. MacLise, *Domestic Contracts* (Carswell, 1987).

Touche Ross & Co., *Valuing a Business and the Family Law Act, 1986.*

Reports

Institute of Law Research and Reform, Alberta, *Matrimonial Property: Division of Pension Benefits upon Marriage Breakdown*, Report No. 48, June, 1986.

Law Reform Commission of British Columbia, Working Paper No. 51, *Spousal Agreements,* 1985.

Law Reform Commission of British Columbia, *Study Paper on Family Property,* 1985.

Law Reform Commission of Saskatchewan, *Tentative Proposals for Reform of Matrimonial Property Act,* September 1984.

Law Reform Commission of Saskatchewan, *Proposals Relating to Matrimonial Property Legislation,* October, 1985.

Newsletters

Richard De Boo Publishers, *Money and Family Law,* September 1986-

Symposia

A.B.A., Dividing The Pie: A Special Issue on Valuation, *Family Advocate*, Summer, 1979, Vol. 2, No. 1.

A.B.A., Special Issue on Deferred Compensation, *Family Advocate*, 1983, Vol. 5, No. 4.

A.B.A., Valuation: Businesses, Practices, Licences and Degrees, *Family Advocate*, 1984, Vol. 7, No. 1.

A.B.A., Pension Plans and Divorce, *Family Advocate*, 1985, Vol. 8, No. 2.

A.B.A., *O'Brien v. O'Brien, Family Advocate,* 1986, Vol. 9, No. 2.

Canadian Bar Association — Ontario and The Law Society of Upper Canada, *The New Family Law Act and The New Divorce Act,* January 25, 1986.

Canadian Bar Association — Ontario, *Family Law for the Specialist; Precedents and Principles, A Comprehensive Review of Domestic Contracts,* February 7, 1986.

Insight Educational Services Limited, *Property Division After the New Family Law Act,* March 7, 1986.

The Law Society of Upper Canada, *The New Family Law Act — For Solicitors,* March 4, 1986.

The Law Society of Upper Canada, *Valuing Family Property,* May 14, 1986.

The Law Society of Upper Canada, *Valuation of Family Property and the Family Law Act — A Series* (7 sets of materials), 1986-1987.

The Law Society of Upper Canada, *Marriage Contracts and Separation Agreements,* November 15, 1986.

Richard De Boo Publishers, *Family Law Act, 1986 — One Year Later,* February 20, 1987.

Articles

Bell, P. "The Evolution of the Community-Out-First Presumption: A Matter of Trust" (1983), 24 S. Tex. L.J. 191.

Black, V. "Quebec Marriage Contracts in Common Law Courts: Room for Improvement" (1985), 45 R.F.L. (2d) 93.

Blumberg, G.G. "Marital Property Treatment of Pensions, Disability Pay, Workers' Compensation and Other Wage Substitutes" (1986), 33 U.C.L.A. Law Rev. 1250.

Cachia, E. "The True Value of Accountants", Canadian Lawyer, June 1987, p. 16.

Cole, S.R. "Family Law Valuation Concepts", Canadian Bar Association — Ontario and Law Society of Upper Canada, *The New Family Law Act and the New Divorce Act,* January 24 and 25, 1986.

Corbin, B.S. "Income Tax Implications of Ontario's Family Law Act" (1986), 34 Can. Tax J. 320, 3 R.F.L. (3d) 228 (including addendum).

Corbin, B.S. "The Impact of Ontario's Family Law Act, 1986 on Estate Administration" (1986), 7 Estates Qtly 208.

Cullity, M.C. "The Family Law Act 1986: Estates and Estate Planning", The Law Society of Upper Canada Continuing Education Program, *The New Family Law Act — For Solicitors,* March 4, 1986.

Dart, R.J. and D.W. Smith, "Estate Planning: A New Era" (1986), 34 Can. Tax J. 1.

Gach, L. "The Mix-Hicks Mix: Tracing Troubles under California's Community Property System" (1978-79), 26 U.C.L.A. Law Rev. 1231.

Goodman, W.D. "Depletion of Net Family Property and Defeating a Spouse's Claim to an Equalizing Payment at Death" (1986), 7 Estates Qtly 289.

Holder, K.P. "In Sickness and in Health? Disability Benefits as Marital Property" (1985-86), 24 J. Fam. Law 657.

Hovius, B. "The Matrimonial Home: Part III of the Family Law Reform Act, 1978", published in *Payne's Digest on Divorce in Canada*, 1968-80, at 224.

Hovius, B. "Domestic Contracts: Part IV of the Family Law Reform Act, 1978", published in *Payne's Digest on Divorce in Canada,* 1968-80, at 233.

Hull, R. "The Effect of the *Family Law Act, 1986* on Estates" (1986), 1 Can. Fam. Law Qtly 1.

Hull, R. "The Effect of the New *Family Law Act* on Surviving Spouses and the Estates of Deceased Spouses" (1986), 50 R.F.L. (2d) 47.

Krishna, V. "Determining the Value of Company Shares" (1987) The Company Lawyer, Vol. 8, No. 2, p. 66.

Kroft, E. "The Private Corporation as a Family Asset — Breaking Up is Hard to Do — Some Tax Issues" (1985), 45 R.F.L. (2d) 68.

Kronby, M. "Cost of Disposition: Deductibility of Debts and Other Liabilities in the Calculation of Net Family Property" (1987), 9 Fam. Law Reform Reptr, February, 1987, Issue No. 8.

Leon, J.S. and I.J.T. Cross, "Valuing Pension Benefits under the *Family Law Act, 1986*" (1986), 1 Can. Fam. Law Qtly 139.

Lyon, J.S. and K.J. Higginson, "The Developing Concept of Net Family Property" (1986), 1 Can. Fam. L. Qtly 249.

Marmer, J. "Computation of Net Family Property under the *Family Law Act, 1986*" (1986), 1 Can. Fam. Law Qtly 27.

McBean, J. "The Treatment of Pensions under the Alberta Property Act: Some Unresolved Issues", *Payne's Divorce and Family Law Digest*, 1986, Essays tab, E-25.

Melville, A.J. "Educational Degrees At Divorce: Toward an Educated Dissolution" (1986), 59 Southern California L. Rev. 1351.

Mendes da Costa, D. "Conveyance by One Joint Tenant to Self" (1984), 18 L.S.U.C. Gazette 213.

Parkman, A. "The Treatment of Professional Goodwill in Divorce Proceedings" (1984-85), 18 Fam. L.Q. 213.

Patterson, J.B. "Determining a Realistically High Value of the Spouse's Interest in the Employee's Pension" (1987), 1 Can. Fam. Law Qtly 345.

Patterson, J.B. "Determining a Realistically Low Value for Employee's Pension (in Spite of Unrealistically Large Claims being made by the Spouse)" (1987), 1 Can. Fam. Law Qtly 365.

Payne, J.D. "Selected Annotations of Cases on the Division and

Valuation of Pensions in Matrimonial Causes", *Payne's Divorce and Family Law Digest*, Essays tab, at E-43.

Roche, E.M. "Treatment of Pensions Upon Marriage Breakdown in Canada: A Comparative Study" (1986), 1 Can. Fam. L. Qtly 189.

Shultz, C.G. "Income Tax Law and Policy Applicable to Periodic Maintenance and Division of Matrimonial Property" (1987), 1 Can. Fam. Law Qtly 293.

Shiff, D. and P. Waters, "Bankruptcy and Family Law: First Come, First Served" (1985), 8 Univ. New South Wales L.J. 40.

Short, D.A. "Pensions and Family Law" (1986), 1 Can. Fam. Law Qtly 73.

Ziff, B. "Recent Developments in Canadian Law: Marriage and Divorce" (1986), 18 Ottawa L. Rev. 121.